Catholic Social Teaching and United States Welfare Reform

Thomas Massaro, S.J.

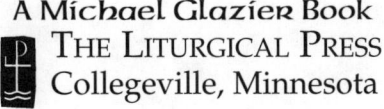

A Michael Glazier Book
THE LITURGICAL PRESS
Collegeville, Minnesota

A Michael Glazier Book published by The Liturgical Press

Cover design by David Manahan, O.S.B.

© 1998 by The Order of St. Benedict, Inc., Collegeville, Minnesota. All rights reserved. No part of this book may be reproduced in any form or by any means, electronic or mechanical, including photocopying, recording, taping, or any retrieval system without the written permission of The Liturgical Press, Collegeville, Minnesota 56321. Printed in the United States of America.

1	2	3	4	5	6	7	8

Library of Congress Cataloging-in-Publication Data

Massaro, Thomas, 1961–
    Catholic social teaching and United States welfare reform / Thomas Massaro.
      p. cm.
    "A Michael Glazier book."
    Includes bibliographical references and index.
    ISBN 0-8146-5927-6 (alk. paper)
    1. Public welfare—Religious aspects—Catholic Church.
2. Sociology, Christian (Catholic)—United States. 3. Public welfare—United States. 4. United States—Social policy.
5. Catholic Church—Doctrines. I. Title.
BX1795.P794M37   1998
261.8'32582'08822—dc21   97–49882
                                                                                     CIP

Contents

List of Abbreviations   vii

Abbreviations and Sources of Documents of the Catholic Church   viii

Preface   ix

Part One

    Catholic Social Teaching: Its Offer of Guidance to Social Policy   1

    Chapter 1

        Selected Goods and Positions Within Catholic Social Teaching   3

            Three Goods   6

                1. Human dignity   6
                2. Solidarity   8
                3. The common good   10

            Positions on Three Topics Germane to Social Policy   13

                1. The transcendent character of human personhood   13
                2. Private property   17
                3. The role of the state   21

    Chapter 2

        Three General Principles for Social Policy   37

                1. Social membership must be universal   40
                2. No person is to be considered a surplus person   45
                3. Preferential option for the poor   51

        Catholic Social Teaching in the American Context   55

Part Two

    Welfare Reform in the 1990s: Context, Measures, and Rationales   59

Chapter 3

The Historical Context of U.S. Welfare Policy   61

The Roots of American Social Policy   62

The New Deal and Its Legacy   67

The "Permanent Crisis" of AFDC   71

The Role of Charitable Organizations in Welfare Reform   77

1. Private compassion and public assistance, past and present   78
2. Does government "crowd out" private charitable activities?   82

Chapter 4

The Welfare Law of 1996   87

1. The block-granting of welfare   88
2. Time limitation of benefits   95
3. Work requirements   101
4. Anti-illegitimacy measures   106
5. Other new conditions on benefits   110
6. Other provisions of the new law   116
7. Probable effects of the new law   119
8. What is missing in the new welfare law   124

Part Three

The Bishops' Contribution to the Welfare Reform Debate   131

Chapter 5

A "Public Church" Addresses Welfare Reform   133

The "New Welfare Consensus" of the 1980s and the Bishops' Demurral   134

Documents of the U.S. Catholic Church, 1994–1996   144

Chapter 6

Five Guidelines for Social Policy   151

1. Focus on the struggle against poverty itself, not merely against welfare dependency   152
2. Acknowledge insuperable barriers to employment where they exist   154

3. Respect some absolute moral
   prohibitions for policy   158
4. Recognize "carrots and sticks" without
   subscribing to a reductionistic view
   of the human person   161
5. Avoid fostering the demonization or
   marginalization of recipients of public assistance   164

Part Four

Toward an Overlapping Consensus   169

Chapter 7

Four Arguments About Practical Issues   171

1. Social policy cannot be successful in
   ushering people to self-sufficiency
   unless it commits adequate resources
   to empowering low-income citizens to
   move into work on reasonable terms   172
2. Social policy which invests in improving
   the lives of recipients will yield
   cost savings in the long run   178
3. The well-being of family life deserves
   special policy attention because
   children represent the future of a nation   184
4. There is no practical substitute for
   the role of the federal government in
   serving as the primary conduit of social
   assistance to low-income families   187

Chapter 8

Toward a Shared Vision of Fairness:
The Contributions of John Rawls and John Courtney Murray   189

Rawls: An "Overlapping Consensus" Based
Upon a "Political Conception of Justice"   190

Murray: The "Public Consensus" Based
Upon Natural Reason   196

Participating in a Public Dialogue
About Economic Fairness   203

Chapter 9

Building a Consensus for a Humanized Economy:
The Role of Middle Axioms   209

    1. Recognizing human dependency   211
    2. Fulfilling social obligations   213
    3. Extending the practice of decommodification   216
    4. Advancing the health of family life   218
    5. Preserving a social safety net through public action   219

Part Five

Guidelines and Prospects for the Postindustrial Era   225

Chapter 10

Postindustrial Social Policy   227

    The Postindustrial Challenge   230

    Toward a New Logic of Distribution   236

    Prospects for the Future: Political
    Culture, Religious Values and
    Social Learning   245

Epilogue   225
Bibliography   259
Index   273

List of Abbreviations

ADC	Aid to Dependent Children
AFDC	Aid to Families with Dependent Children
CBO	Congressional Budget Office
CDF	Children's Defense Fund
EITC	Earned Income Tax Credit
FSA	Family Support Act of 1988
GAI	Guaranteed Annual Income
HHS	Department of Health and Human Services
JOBS	Job Opportunities and Basic Skills Training
NCCB	National Conference of Catholic Bishops
SSI	Supplemental Security Income
TANF	Temporary Assistance to Needy Families
USCC	United States Catholic Conference
WIC	Women, Infants and Children Nutrition Program

Abbreviations and Sources of Documents of the Catholic Church

RN   *Rerum novarum* (Pope Leo XIII, 1891)

QA   *Quadragesimo anno* (Pope Pius XI, 1931)

MM   *Mater et Magistra* (Pope John XXIII, 1961)

PT   *Pacem in terris* (Pope John XXIII, 1963)

GS   *Gaudium et spes* (Second Vatican Council, 1965)

PP   *Populorum progressio* (Pope Paul VI, 1967)

OA   *Octogesima adveniens* (Pope Paul VI, 1971)

JW   Justice in the World (Synod of Bishops, 1971)

LE   *Laborem exercens* (Pope John Paul II, 1981)

EJA   Economic Justice for All (U.S. Bishops, 1986)

SRS   *Sollicitudo rei socialis* (Pope John Paul II, 1987)

CA   *Centesimus annus* (Pope John Paul II, 1991)

TWS   Transforming the Welfare System (Catholic Charities USA, 1994)

MPP   Moral Principles and Policy Priorities for Welfare Reform (U.S. Bishops, 1995)

Preface

On 22 August 1996 President Clinton signed into law PL 104-193, also known as The Personal Responsibility and Work Opportunity Act. This bill, the final product of years of debate over welfare reform, ended the federal government's sixty-one-year commitment to providing income to poor children and their resident parents, mostly single mothers. The Aid to Families with Dependent Children (AFDC) program, which heretofore provided the means-tested benefits which most Americans call "welfare," was abolished and replaced by a system of capped block grants to the states. The new welfare law continues to allocate substantial federal moneys intended for low-income families. However, the reconfigured funding has changed not only in name (now called Temporary Assistance to Needy Families, or TANF), but in nature: from an open-ended guaranteed income entitlement for all eligible low-income mothers and children to a highly conditional benefit that may be withdrawn for any number of reasons.

The fifty states previously had shared the cost of this form of poor relief with Washington on a matching fund basis that included many regulations to protect the entitlement nature of the program. The terms of the new law give states wide discretion to restrict eligibility and benefits. In fact, the law mandates a set of new conditions which the new state programs must place on cash assistance: a work requirement, time limitation and categorical restrictions against giving some types of assistance to immigrant families, unwed teenage mothers, felons, drug abusers and those not cooperating with program rules such as the establishment of paternity and participation in work preparation. The new law would save the federal government $54.1 billion over six years, although most of the savings come not from the ending of AFDC, but rather from other provisions of the welfare bill (namely, cuts in the food stamp program and social services to legal immigrants) which the Republican-dominated Congress sent to President Clinton as a package.

Months earlier, a *Washington Post* columnist aptly summarized the endgame of welfare reform maneuvering by claiming: "Few subjects have so tried the soul of Bill Clinton as welfare reform."[1] As a man of compassion, Clinton did not want to sign a punitive bill that would relegate millions of children to poverty, depriving them of the benefits of the safety net which AFDC provided to previous generations of needy families. Yet as a "New Democrat" who had campaigned in 1992 on the promise to "end welfare as we know it," Clinton felt immense political pressure to distance himself from the liberal wing of the Democratic Party which was perceived as defending an unpopular status quo in social policy. After vetoing two previous versions of the welfare bill, Clinton was in danger of handing the Republicans a prime campaign issue in the coming (1996) election season. All eyes were on Clinton when, three weeks before the signing, he made the dramatic announcement of his intention to sign the newly passed version of the welfare bill. At that press conference on the afternoon of 31 July 1996, the President acknowledged that the legislation is "far from perfect . . . but on balance, this bill is a real step forward for our country, our values, and for people who are on welfare."[2]

For those seeking to conduct a moral analysis of this change in U.S. social policy, this last sentence lies at the heart of the matter. Amidst the sometimes acrimonious claims and counter-claims which comprised the welfare reform debate during the 103rd and 104th Congresses (1992-6), all sides sought to justify their positions based on this triad: what is good for the nation, its values, and the poor themselves. I propose at the outset, as a procedural guideline for this study, that we take all parties to the debate at their word. While it is surely possible to question the sincerity of the claims of some would-be welfare reformers, our moral analysis will be most illuminating if it prescinds from accusing any public actors of cynical or hidden motivation. Questioning the good faith of one's political adversaries is all too frequently the currency of American politics, as witnessed in editorial columns, television and radio public affairs broadcasts and even in congressional proceedings. Liberals accuse conservatives of giving mere lip-service to concern for the poor, since the true zeal of many on the right often seems to be for budget-cutting and smaller government. Conservatives accuse liberals of either naivete or cynicism in defending a status quo of bloated programs and dependent populations in which they seem to have a political stake. Moderates are accused of opportunism and a lack of conviction. In the end, all sides plug their ears, turn up the rhetoric and forego opportunities to work together.

1. Mary McGrory, "Welfare Checkmate," *Washington Post*, 23 May 1996, A2.
2. "Text of President Clinton's Announcement on Welfare Legislation," *New York Times*, 1 August 1996, A24.

The most constructive moral analysis of public policy, and the one most appropriate for academic inquiries into religious social ethics, proceeds quite differently. In the interest of civility and the search for greater common ground, a proper starting point is to assume that those who contribute to the debate are sincere in their pursuit of the most commonly professed goals: fostering an economic prosperity which may be enjoyed by all, expanding opportunity for the most vulnerable members of our society, promoting family stability and protecting children from the mistakes of their parents. Everyone claims to want poor children to thrive and disadvantaged American families to advance into the social mainstream. We do well to take all sides at their word. This does not, of course, necessitate ignoring the substantial differences which exist among American observers concerning: (1) priorities among social goals which often conflict (by reason of logical incompatibility or budgetary constraint); and (2) preferred policy strategies for attaining these shared goals.

In fact, the moral analysis of the following chapters is intended to serve precisely as an exploration of the terms by which certain religiously grounded principles support one set of strategies and priorities and rule out others. At stake is nothing less than the moral justification of public policy directions. In the case of the new welfare law, a central facet of the public debate is whether U.S. social policy should adopt a novel and nearly unmitigated reliance on a work-based solution to the income needs of poor families, and whether it is wise and just to eliminate the safeguards of the social safety net. As we shall see, greater agreement exists on the "ends" (namely, that poor families should be better off in the future) than on the "means" by which public policy fosters those ends. Our goal will be to come to a deeper understanding of the terms of this disagreement, all the while assuming the good faith of policy contributors across the political spectrum. Ultimately, we hope to use the insights of Catholic social teaching to evaluate which strategies for realizing mutual gains are most morally desirable on terms upon which most Americans can agree.

A brief sketch of the politics of the most recent round of welfare reform is a necessary prelude to the moral argument to follow. In the recent welfare reform debates, the starting point was, understandably, the status quo in social policy. All sides expressed a desire to make significant changes in what was universally perceived as a "failed welfare system." However, predictably, visions soon diverged. Conservative Republicans, riding the wave of the 1994 election that gave them a congressional majority for the first time in decades, sought the most sweeping reforms. They worked to enact the welfare plank (labelled the "Personal Responsibility

Act") of their "Contract with America." Its stated goal is to reduce illegitimacy, require work, save taxpayer money and replace the welfare state with what Newt Gingrich calls "the opportunity society," fostering a culture of productivity rather than a culture of entitlement and redistribution.[3]

Even the most moderate Republicans embraced the belief that such changes in social policy would be effective in improving the actual condition of low-income Americans. Moderate Republican Senators William V. Roth, Jr. of Delaware and Pete V. Domenici of New Mexico expressed similar opinions in the final days of deliberation before the final bill's passage. The former declared: "The safety net has become a snare." The latter looked forward to "start[ing] over with a new system that has a chance of giving people an opportunity instead of a handout."[4] I propose that we consider Gingrich to be sincere when he says about the newly passed legislation: "I believe this bill will dramatically help young Americans to have a chance to rise and to do better."[5]

If the Republicans who won the day focused on what was wrong with the welfare status quo, then the liberal Democrats who were ultimately out-voted desired to preserve what was, in their opinion, right about AFDC. Despite the program's flaws, the principle of guaranteeing a floor of income for poor families was deemed still to be desirable. To discontinue this policy seemed to them too risky to recommend. Incremental reforms building on the present structure of AFDC seemed preferable to radical reforms such as workfare and block granting, especially since most versions of proposed legislation omitted significant new funding for the job training and day care that would move single mothers from welfare to work.

Senator Daniel Patrick Moynihan of New York, a veteran of several national welfare policy battles, summarized his opposition to this form of welfare reform by claiming: "The premise of this legislation is that the behavior of certain adults can be changed by making the lives of their children as wretched as possible. This is a fearsome assumption."[6] Yet this is an assumption that exactly one-half of the Democrats in the House

---

3. Ed Gillespie and Bob Schellhas, eds., *Contract With America: The Bold Plan by Rep. Newt Gingrich, Rep. Dick Armey and the House Republicans to Change the Nation* (N.Y.: Times Books of Random House, Inc., 1994) 65–77.

4. "More Voices on Welfare," *Congressional Quarterly Weekly Report*, 27 July 1996: 2118.

5. "Remarks by Gingrich and Other G.O.P. Supporters," *New York Times*, 1 August 1996, A25.

6. R. W. Apple, Jr., "His Battle Now Lost, Moynihan Still Cries Out," *New York Times*, 2 August 1996, A16.

of Representatives and the Senate ultimately accepted.[7] Ostensibly because they were convinced by the cogency of new arguments about the causes of dependency and illegitimacy (but perhaps also because they were intimidated by the prospect of another electoral defeat), half the congressional Democrats voted to revoke one of the planks of the New Deal on which their party had stood for decades: the principle of an income entitlement for poor children.

One of the major buzzwords of the welfare reform debate has been "compassion." Since both the triumphant conservatives and the retreating liberals marshaled sophisticated arguments that theirs was the more compassionate policy, there seemed to be no obvious way to adjudicate their rival claims. Even assuming that both were sincerely interested in improving the lives of the poor in America, there was a seeming dearth of commonly held principles or criteria by which to analyze the moral significance of the case for either radical change or incremental adjustment in welfare policy. In this regard, a comment Senator Moynihan made at the very moment the welfare bill passed Congress is quite revealing. When asked about the intense lobbying done by the nation's Roman Catholic bishops in opposition to the welfare bill, the Senator reflected that the bishops "admittedly have an easier task with matters of this sort. When principles are at stake, they simply look them up. Too many liberals, alas, simply make them up."[8]

Moynihan's comments require a heavy dose of nuance. Much more needs to be said about how Catholic bishops (or any other religious group for that matter) derive and make use of faith-based moral principles in public policy analysis. Nevertheless, what the Senator suggests about the potential and distinctive contribution of religiously grounded principles merits much attention. Because religious traditions have deep roots in theological and philosophical thought, revered texts and rich social practices and attitudes, they offer a voice that frequently would improve the quality of public policy debates. While politics has a tendency to produce standoffs between rival material or ideological interests, religious voices may indeed play a needed and constructive role in supplying a principle-based perspective beyond the power relationships that characterize the interest-group pluralism of modern liberal democratic society.

---

7. The final House vote on the welfare reform bill on 31 July 1996 was 328–101, with Republicans supporting the conference committee report 230–2 and Democrats split 98–98. The Senate vote the next day was 78–21, with Democrats splitting 25–21 in favor, joining the unanimous Republicans majority of 53.

8. Apple, "Moynihan," A16.

In some policy areas (welfare policy emerges as a prime candidate), religiously grounded principles may reveal convincing arguments about the possibilities for mutual gains and common interests—arguments which hold the potential to win acceptance among nearly all members of society. At the very least, such principles serve as a reminder of values and priorities which may become overlooked in the rough and tumble of the policy process. By consulting the moral principles articulated within religious traditions, any policy observers may enrich the set of intellectual resources at their disposal, and this enrichment may lead some observers to judge certain policy options to be incompatible with what reasonable people would, upon serious reflection, desire for the public life of their society.

The above claims cannot be reduced to an uncritical call for a more active or effective religious lobby. The task of "speaking truth to power" should not be so narrowly construed. The role of religion in public life is a multiform one which includes diverse types of witness, persuasion, conscience formation and private discernment as well as public moral deliberation. Ultimately, when religion enters the political arena as "public church," it seeks to foster the making of sound judgments by citizens and public officials—judgments to change or reaffirm the existing public order so that the best of our shared convictions can be brought to bear on social issues.[9] The hope behind such public involvement is that public policy be guided not just by what seems popular or feasible at a specific moment, but also by what is morally desirable and defensible in light of established traditions of ethical reflection.

Even if politics will always remain "the art of the possible," the prudent contribution of religious social ethics may be able to expand our notion of what is possible. This allows us to exercise an option much preferable to the lamentable but frequent abandonment of politics by those who judge it to be a sphere of inevitable immorality. At their best, the efforts of religious voices to subject public policy to moral scrutiny contribute constructively to public life by advancing the dialogue between faith and culture—a dialogue especially important in nations (such as the United States) with vital religious communities.

The goal of this study is to explore the dynamics and implications of one episode when one faith tradition attempted the task of serving as a "public church." In the U.S. welfare reform debate of the 1990s, the Catholic Church attempted to make a constructive contribution to public

---

9. Religious influence on public life is a phenomenon about which many observers are, justifiably, deeply ambivalent. Actors pursuing religiously inspired visions of public life may frequently overstep the bounds of prudence and even constitutional law.

policymaking. In the course of writing documents, lobbying in Washington, offering congressional testimony and otherwise speaking out about how Catholic social teaching sheds light on issues of equity in welfare policy, Catholic leaders served as spokespersons of a particular vision of social justice. The central message of this study is not that all Americans should adopt as their own all the recommendations of Catholic social teaching, but rather that all may benefit by attending to the process and possibilities of social learning that may be achieved under the tutelage of traditions of religious ethics, as illustrated by the bishops' recent contributions. In articulating a set of ethical principles and policy priorities, these religious voices engaged in activities that constitute a case study in the constructive interplay of distinctiveness and potential convergence, confessionalism and possible consensus. The lessons we might draw from this episode in the development of "public church" may be attributed to two complementary aspects of Catholic social teaching.

First, Catholic social thought offers a distinctive enough perspective on social issues facing the U.S. that its contribution deserves careful attention. Because it draws from richer imaginative resources than the dominant strands of the American political culture of market liberalism, its more corporatist and organic perspective can serve as a helpful check on the dominant brands of individualism. As we shall see, Catholic social teaching offers a distinctive basis for balancing such concerns as individual freedom and social responsibility, as property rights and common good. It draws from a distinctive set of anthropological assumptions in developing such themes as human dignity and universal solidarity, which in turn entail particular stands on social priorities. Neither of the major camps in American politics, liberals nor conservatives, invokes quite the same style of rationality (in the sense of "reason-giving") to justify policy on a moral basis. In applying Catholic social thought to the context of American economic life, bishops and theologians suggest a number of policy principles which constitute potential criteria for making clear judgments about the moral adequacy of various welfare reform strategies.

Second, in its frequent re-articulation by popes and bishops, modern Catholic social thought increasingly holds the potential to build bridges to other religious traditions and to those who identify with no religious tradition at all. Because of the propensity of Catholic social teaching to advance policy recommendations in the form of "middle axioms" which may be supported on nontheological bases, it is possible realistically to hope for growth toward what has been called "an overlapping consensus" on the meaning of distributive justice. By building upon preexisting agreement on practical and philosophical points rather than relying primarily on its distinctive theological beliefs, Catholic social thought is well positioned to serve as a catalyst for forging increasingly broad social agreement on matters of public policy.

The tension between these two realities—the distinctiveness of Catholic social thought, on the one hand, and its potential to coalesce other strands of thought into a new consensus on wise welfare policy, on the other—will constitute a leitmotif in the chapters that follow. Each of the five parts of this study contributes in its own way to a moral evaluation of the competing views about American social welfare policy. Part One will examine Catholic social teaching as an ethical tradition which proposes a distinctive normative view of such realities as the dignity of the human person, the common good, the role of the state and private property. After investigating the moral methodology employed in the documents of this tradition and by those who use them, Part One identifies three moral principles of the most general kind which are proposed in Catholic social thought and which address the proper role and features of social welfare policies. Later, Part Three examines how the U.S. Catholic bishops applied and articulated these general principles in their contribution to the recent welfare reform debate. The bishops did so by proposing a number (we shall identify five) of more specific guidelines for the formation of social policy. Part Two serves as a necessary interlude between our initial survey of Catholic social thought and our investigation of its application to the context of American social policy. Part Two describes the context in which the bishops spoke by sketching the recent development of U.S. welfare policy, especially the major features of, and moral assumptions behind, the newest welfare legislation.

With Part Four we move from the "distinctiveness" pole to the "commonality" pole of our argument. Here we explore how Catholic social teaching lends itself to building an overlapping consensus on issues of distributive justice. Part Four first considers four arguments about practical issues—items on which the bishops' advice is seconded by criteria (such as long-term cost savings and policy effectiveness) on which serious objections are unlikely. In the search for even more substantial welfare agreement, Part Four next considers some key contributions from the writings of John Rawls and John Courtney Murray. Here we discover several concepts which suggest how Catholic social teaching may be used as a point of departure to forge a new and overlapping consensus on what constitutes an ethically sound social welfare policy for our times. Key here will be the role played by "middle axioms" such as the three general principles identified in Part One and the five more specific policy guidelines identified in Part Three.

Part Five broadens the scope of the previous analysis by considering how this same dynamic of a new, growing consensus on issues of distributive justice might apply to those wider economic developments that are increasingly described as features of the dawning "postindustrial" age. Economic forces already at work within the context of the global economy are threatening to render a larger sector of the U.S. population "surplus people" who will find themselves marginalized as their potential contribution is increasingly de-valued in labor markets. The same moral principles that justify social provision for poor families today may be applied to a coming era of increasing joblessness and economic insecurity—a situation in which income maintenance may be recognized as a good which justifies a thoroughly new logic of distribution, one based on need rather than work contribution alone. The final section of Part Five concludes this study by charting the course and evaluating the prospects for the "social learning" necessitated by the economic and social challenges the United States will encounter in the coming years.

The issues treated in this study—the immediate concerns of welfare policy as well as the more long-term trends associated with postindustrial society—are enormously complex and admit of no quick and simple solutions. Emblematic of this complexity is the realization that the problems of poor families cannot be measured merely in terms of low income. Any attempt to assist those in need, whether undertaken by public policy or organized charities or even on an informal one-on-one basis, is subject to failure on a practical level and criticism on a moral level. Even those values upon which most Americans agree because of a broadly shared political culture (including a high regard for work, two-parent families and a compassionate regard for the less fortunate) often operate at cross-purposes and force agonizing trade-offs. When something goes wrong—domestic abuse, job loss, divorce, drug abuse in a family—value conflicts are exacerbated.

Often the simplest solutions, such as taking children away from parents who seem unfit because of low earnings or flagrant irresponsibility, are unpalatable for reasons deeply embedded in our culture. Further, it has proven impossible to help poor children (universally deemed the "deserving poor") without helping their parents, who all too often offend some of our shared moral sensibilities through nonwork or other violations that render them, in the eyes of most observers, the "undeserving poor." The welfare system, which has provided a safety net allowing families to remain intact despite such problems, has been America's uneasy compromise. Now that AFDC has been eliminated and the U.S. has revoked the principle of income entitlement for poor families, it is necessary to reexamine the regulative norms which govern the way we collectively think about and act toward the poor. Since these norms are never derived merely from technical criteria but invoke justifications which have quasi-theological status, we naturally turn to theological traditions to enlighten our public policies which affect the lives of low-income families. How this has been done in one episode in recent months, and how it could constructively be done amidst new challenges in the coming years, is the focus of this study.

I wish to thank three groups of people without whose assistance this book would not be possible. First, I am grateful to my colleagues at Emory University and Weston Jesuit School of Theology for serving as thoughtful dialogue partners and gracious fellow learners. Second, I owe a great debt of gratitude to my brother Jesuits, especially my superiors in the New England Province of the Society of Jesus. Third, I cannot express enough appreciation for the greatest gift I have ever received—the ceaseless love of my family. This study of theology and public policy in support of families would not be complete without my expression of heartfelt thanks to the people who have bestowed upon me such a joyous family life: my parents, sisters and entire extended family. If everyone enjoyed the privileges with which they have graced me, there would be no need to study the problems associated with the persistence of poverty in an affluent society.

I dedicate this book to all who work directly for the cause of social justice. For every theologian, researcher or policy analyst who spends time primarily with books and data, there is need for ten thousand others to work in ministries, professions and voluntary activities of direct service to the needy. Progress in the struggle against the many faces of injustice depends upon their efforts, to which academic research, Church leadership and policy advocacy may serve as ancillary resources. It is my hope that this volume will advance in some small way the ecumenical contribution of religious social ethics to the achievement of racial, gender and distributive justice in America.

Part One

Catholic Social Teaching: Its Offer of Guidance to Social Policy

Chapter 1

Selected Goods and Positions Within Catholic Social Teaching

Christian social ethics in every era is a product of dialogue between Church and world, gospel and culture. It cannot be otherwise, for the preaching of Jesus reveals no detailed program of social reform, nor has Christian witness displayed a uniform social philosophy. As Ernst Troeltsch famously proclaimed: "Nowhere does there exist an absolute Christian ethic, which only awaits discovery."[1]

Nevertheless, in its mission to evangelize culture, the Church does consistently address issues of economic and political order. Since at least the time of Augustine, Christians have described themselves as residents simultaneously of two cities, the earthly and heavenly. As such, they feel the call to take history seriously, although not overly seriously. To strike the proper balance of finding some, but not all of their hope within history, Christians have sought to tame but not to sanctify secular institutions such as governments, economic markets and social structures. We should not be surprised that, whenever the Church directs its attention to social issues in the secular sphere, its analysis is "composed of a complicated mass of ideas borrowed from various directions and also of actual historical facts by which it was conditioned."[2]

An important attempt to advance the Church-world dialogue takes place within the tradition of modern Catholic social teaching. Since the publication in 1891 by Pope Leo XIII of the encyclical letter *Rerum novarum*, the Catholic Church has developed an evolving body of teaching on political, economic, social and cultural matters. Although the meaning of the phrase "Catholic social teaching" may be extended to include the writings of theologians and others on a local level, it usually refers to a

---

1. Ernst Troeltsch, *The Social Teaching of the Christian Churches*, trans. Olive Wyon (Louisville, Ky.: Westminster/John Knox Press, 1992 [1931]), 2:1013.
2. Ibid., 284.

specific set of documents authored in recent decades by popes, the Second Vatican Council and synods of bishops. It is from a dozen of these documents (those which contain the most sustained, developed and exclusive focus on economic and political matters) that we shall focus.[3] National conferences of Catholic bishops have also published numerous pastoral letters and other statements on social and economic issues; we will have occasion to consider some of the arguments about social policy raised in several statements from the United States bishops.

It is important to clarify at the outset the genre of these documents. While some categories of authoritative pronouncements within the Catholic Church are intended primarily to define and clarify doctrines which bind the consciences of Catholics, the purpose of the documents in question is the more fluid task of providing moral wisdom to assist in the formation of conscience. Decisions about economic and political matters are, at most, matters of "applied theology." This is why the phrase "Catholic social teaching" is usually preferable to "Catholic social doctrine." In fact, since 1963 when Pope John XXIII addressed *Pacem in terris* to "all men[4] of good will," the documents have consciously directed their moral guidance beyond the confines of a Catholic audience. Since the topics addressed in these documents are so far from the inner core of theological dogma, they are best understood as dealing with matters situated in the arena of prudential judgments, where some measure of disagreement even among people of good will is to be expected. With the possible exception of Pope Pius XI's 1931 encyclical *Quadragesimo anno*, these documents eschew the pretense of containing doctrinally grounded blueprints for social life. Rather, they seek to offer a more modest blend of moral exhortation and social analysis highlighting central principles and ethical values for life in complex modern societies.

At the beginning of his 1971 *Octogesima adveniens*, Pope Paul VI links the necessary modesty of the claims contained within the docu-

3. The official English texts of these dozen (as well as two pastoral letters from the U.S. bishops) are found in David J. O'Brien and Thomas A. Shannon, eds., *Catholic Social Teaching: The Documentary Heritage* (Maryknoll, N.Y.: Orbis Books, 1992). In making citations, I will follow the convention of using the Latin names for documents originating in Rome, as well as the standard paragraph or section numbers.

4. For the sake of accuracy, I will cite the official English translations of Vatican documents, most of which are derived from Latin originals. My discomfort with the gender-exclusive language of these texts is only partially mitigated by the knowledge that behind masculinist renderings in English frequently lie gender-inclusive Latin terms such as "homo" for human person. The use of noninclusive pronouns which appear in original texts is maintained only in order to avoid an anachronistic concealment of the approach of these documents.

ments of Catholic social teaching to his understanding of the mission of the Church:

> In the face of such widely varying situations it is difficult for us to utter a unified message and to put forward a solution which has universal validity. Such is not our ambition, nor is it our mission. It is up to the Christian communities to analyze with objectivity the situation which is proper to their own country, to shed on it the light of the Gospel's unalterable words and to draw principles of reflection, norms of judgment and directives for action from the social teachings of the church.[5]

In this and other similar texts,[6] Catholic social teaching has staked out a middle ground between two extreme positions it has sought to avoid. On the one hand, if its recommendations become too specific, entering the realm of detailed policy prescription, Catholic social teaching runs the danger of politicizing the faith. It would stray from the area of competence it claims (in matters that are theological or moral in nature) into the domain of technical solutions to temporal problems. In espousing a policy agenda that is too partisan in nature, any religious voice risks sacrificing its focus on the transcendent in order to pursue immanent concerns.

On the other hand, Catholic social teaching cannot be satisfied with the quietism of a privatized faith. Neutrality or indifference in public matters is too high a price to pay for the good of prophetic integrity. Although there are subgroups (such as monastic orders) within Catholicism which follow the counsels of sectarian idealism, the Church as a whole pursues a mission which includes public witness and socially responsible engagement with worldly affairs. Even if the task of Catholic social teaching is not to espouse detailed recipes for action, it nevertheless articulates a number of ethical priorities which correspond to a broad constructive agenda of values such as peace, justice, freedom, responsible stewardship of resources, human dignity, universal solidarity, and the advancement of the common good.

This briefest of introductions to the contours of Catholic social teaching raises numerous important questions about moral methodology as well as developmental, ideological and ecclesiological issues within this body of thought. Some of these questions will be addressed in the course of our subsequent analysis. Our primary task, however, is to identify and investigate those elements in Catholic social teaching which shed the most light on social policy in the context of a modern economy and polity. First, we will examine three general *goods* (or ends or values)

5. OA 4.
6. See also CA 43; SRS 41; QA 41; and EJA 134.

treated by these documents: (1) human dignity; (2) solidarity; and (3) the common good. Second, we will draw on these general themes to formulate some more specific *positions* which Catholic social teaching stakes out on three topics with relevance to social policy: (1) the transcendent character of human personhood; (2) the institution of private property; and (3) the role of the state. Chapter two will extend this analysis by identifying three general moral *principles* to guide an ethical evaluation of welfare policy and related issues of distributive justice.

Three Goods

1. Human dignity

It may seem rather otiose to assert the "unique value" and "incomparable dignity" of human persons as Pope John Paul II does in his retrospective of themes developed in the course of a century of Catholic social teaching.[7] The notion that people have great worth is hardly a novel or controversial claim. Nevertheless, an investigation of the warrants and implications of this claim as it is developed in these documents reveals some of the distinctive elements of Catholic theology as it is brought to bear on social issues.

One passage which reveals especially well the characteristic affirmations of Catholic theology on the origin, nature and destiny of human persons is found in *Sollicitudo rei socialis*:

> The church has confidence also in man, though she knows the evils of which he is capable. For she knows well that—in spite of the heritage of sin, and the sin that each one is capable of committing—there exist in the human person sufficient qualities and energies, a fundamental "goodness" (cf. Genesis 1:31), because he is the image of the Creator, placed under the redemptive influence of Christ, who united himself in some fashion with every man, and because the efficacious action of the Holy Spirit "fills the earth" (Wis 1:7).[8]

This is only one of many places in which the documents of Catholic social teaching refer to the creation narrative in Genesis as a warrant for human dignity. Each person is created as an *imago Dei*; collectively, we are deemed by our Creator to be good. Even the power of sin, original or actual, in no way cancels this bestowal of dignity. Our status as "children of God" sets humans apart from the rest of the created order (although

---

7. CA 10.
8. SRS 47.

this should not be interpreted as a rationale for denigrating the natural environment as lacking value except insofar as it can be exploited for human purposes).

Reverence for human persons is a reflection of the reverence due to God, just as "human nature" is a partial reflection of "divine nature." The Aristotelian-Thomistic tradition from which Catholic social teaching draws emphasizes the human rational faculty as the distinctive trademark of the human essence. What is owed to persons is the set of rights and duties consistent with their nature as rational animals. In recent decades, Catholic social teaching has tended to complement this mode of thought with other anthropological bases such as personalism and a more thoroughgoing scriptural grounding. Vatican II's *Gaudium et spes* reflects both of these when it frames the topic of human dignity in terms of the relationship between God and humans: "An outstanding cause of human dignity lies in man's call to communion with God. From the very circumstances of his origin, man is already invited to converse with God."[9]

We will address further aspects of human nature and destiny when, later in this chapter, we note how this distinctive moral anthropology leads Catholic social teaching to its rejection of various schools of thought (materialism, totalitarianism, atheistic socialism, the libertarianism of unfettered capitalism) which fail to recognize the totality of the human mystery. Even the few arguments already mentioned form a baseline from which extend numerous implications for moral behavior in social life, including public policy. To accord such a central place in a social philosophy to human dignity implies a number of commitments and priorities; by affirming human dignity as a desideratum, Catholic social teaching introduces normative elements into politics and economics. Of course, even universal agreement on the goal of promoting a particular view of human dignity does not settle all the practical matters of how public policy and private behavior may best serve these ends. Nevertheless, although many questions about policy strategies and trade-offs with other values remain unresolved, an initial commitment to promote human dignity in the social order does suggest certain courses of action.

If we wish to protect human dignity, we must also pursue an allocation of resources which allows people at least an opportunity to live in a manner commensurate with their innate worth.[10] Wherever possible and prudent, a decent minimum (the "absolute essentials"[11] of life) should be provided. Other goods beyond subsistence (participation, equity, some

9. GS 19.
10. MM 55.
11. GS 69.

measure of equality) may be identified as further and necessary implications of a commitment to human dignity. The promotion of human dignity becomes a key criterion for social development, allowing us to judge the intentions, strategies and outcomes of social processes in terms of the realization of conditions compatible with human dignity. While identifying these desirable conditions remains a legitimate source of much dispute, no one seeking to promote human dignity can for long avoid asking the question: amidst these social realities, what is happening to human persons?

2. Solidarity

Solidarity is an ethical ideal akin to the classical virtue of friendship and the religious notion of communion. The Catholic social teaching documents[12] which develop the theme of solidarity treat it as both a subjective, internal attitude and as an observable objective praxis. As such it constitutes a regulative norm by which we may judge institutions and policies, proposing such questions as: does a given practice foster cooperation and partnership, or does it increase social distance and diminish the achievement of the good of solidarity?

In giving a prominent place in its social ethic to the virtue of solidarity, Catholic social thought is advancing a particular, communal vision of human flourishing, one which supplements its construal of human dignity. It is possible to imagine individuals in isolation as the possessors of dignity, but to invoke the virtue of solidarity as a central value of ethical life is to call new attention to the relations among individuals. In order to be truly morally good, these relationships must be characterized by mutual concern for the well-being of others and by a willingness to make necessary sacrifices for the common good of the human community as a whole. Because the ties binding humans together are stronger and deeper than those envisioned by, for example, liberal theorists of classical economics, our expressions of other-regard must transcend the type of exchange characteristic of market relations, where mutual material benefit is the primary rationale for human interaction. Catholic social theory thus distances itself from the model of social benefit contained in strictly market theory, where any gains accruing to one person (or to the collectivity) from the economic activities of another are epiphenomenal, as in the notion of "trickle-down" benefits. In Catholic social teaching, human interdependence and social cooperation are not only empirical facts or salutary arrangements necessary for the maximization of quantifiable

---

12. See RN 21; MM 219; GS 32; SRS 38–40, 45; CA 10.

gains; rather, they constitute central normative values and inescapable features of our common human nature.

Catholic social teaching offers several theological warrants for its emphasis on community as the necessary locus where human dignity is recognized, realized and protected. Recent documents link solidarity in provocative ways to other components of Christian faith and praxis. They do so by invoking the communal aspects of: (1) events in the history of the people Israel and the life of Jesus;[13] (2) the Eucharistic meal shared as a sacrament;[14] and (3) the inner life of the Trinity of divine persons.[15] Even as early as 1891, *Rerum novarum* portrayed a theological vision of solidarity as the antidote to divisions along class lines:

> But, if Christian precepts prevail, the two classes will not only be united in the bonds of friendship, but also those of brotherly love. For they will understand and feel that all men are the children of the common Father, that is, of God; that all have the same end, which is God himself. . . ; that all and each are redeemed by Jesus Christ, and raised to the dignity of children of God, and are thus united in brotherly ties both with each other and with Jesus Christ . . .; that the blessings of nature and the gifts of grace belong in common to the whole human race . . . .[16]

Our sharing in gifts of a common nature, grace and destiny makes it possible to speak of "species solidarity," "sacramental solidarity," and "eschatological solidarity."[17] All three underline the necessity of "political solidarity" which demands the type of actions (e.g., restraint of selfishness and efforts for the attainment of justice) congruent with the bonds of identity all humans share.

Solidarity thus emerges as a regulative norm for judging the working of social institutions. By focusing on the theological warrants behind solidarity and the role it plays in Catholic social teaching, we revisit a recurring theme in Christian social ethics: the way in which the kingdom of God serves as the ultimate normative basis for judging social institutions in the temporal sphere.[18] If our institutions do not measure up to the

---

13. GS 32.
14. GS 38.
15. SRS 40.
16. RN 21.
17. Charles R. Strain introduces these labels in his essay "Beyond Madison and Marx: Civic Virtue, Solidarity and Justice in American Culture," in Charles R. Strain, ed., *Prophetic Visions and Economic Realities* (Grand Rapids, Mich.: William B. Eerdmans Publishing Company, 1989) 191–202.
18. This is, of course, done most famously and directly by figures in the "Social Gospel" movement. However, the kingdom serves as a regulative ideal throughout Chris-

vision of perfect communal harmony associated with the kingdom of God, then a certain burden of proof is placed upon the defenders of these institutions to explain why they do not. Additional insight into our mode of communal living is afforded by turning from the theological warrants that inform the virtue of solidarity to the more philosophical warrants that inform the notion of the common good as it is developed in Catholic social teaching.

3. The common good

The vision of human flourishing which makes reference to the kingdom of God is one which taps into Catholic theological doctrines concerning the supernatural order, where the ultimate good is a matter of what Thomas Aquinas calls *beatitudo*, or blessedness. However, the Catholic tradition also contains a parallel track of philosophical reflection which focuses on the natural good of *felicitas*, or earthly happiness. This good plays a major role in the development of Catholic political theory, a field which made a major advance when such scholastic theologians as Aquinas retrieved the corpus of the works of Aristotle in the thirteenth century.

Aristotle's anthropology begins with the claim that the human is by nature a social animal, a being of the polis.[19] Every person is a part of the polis, and the end of the polis is the common good. The purpose of law, therefore, is to govern the relation of a person to his or her true good, or genuine happiness. Aquinas borrows this notion when, in his "Treatise on Law," he asserts that "every law is ordained to the common good."[20] For Aquinas, as for Aristotle, the common good is not a morally neutral category, but is a normative notion, one commensurate with the claim put forth by both thinkers, that "the intention of every lawgiver is to make men good."[21] Further, the common good is a substantive notion; it is not merely the conglomeration of private interests or preferences, but an objective set of conditions which advance human flourishing.

Modern Catholic social teaching borrows from this inheritance in its definitions and treatment of the common good. Pope John XXIII in *Mater et Magistra* urges public authorities and "various intermediary bodies" to work together with a correct understanding of the common good which

---

tian social ethics. Even those (such as Reinhold Niebuhr) who argue against the immediate relevance of ethical ideals find themselves engaged in a dialectic in which kingdom-style love serves as the ultimate measure of justice.

19. Aristotle *Politics*, 1. 2.

20. St. Thomas Aquinas, *Summa Theologica* I-II, q. 90, a. 2. Translations are from the English Blackfriars edition, 60 vols. (N.Y.: McGraw-Hill Book Co., 1966).

21. Ibid., q. 92, a. 1, quoting Aristotle *Ethics* 2. 1. 1103b3.

"embraces the sum total of those conditions of social living whereby men are enabled more fully and more readily to achieve their own perfection."[22] Four years later, a document of the Second Vatican Council repeats this definition almost verbatim, adding the observation that the common good "today takes on an increasingly universal complexion and consequently involves rights and duties with respect to the whole human race."[23]

By itself, this "sum total of conditions" formulation is opaque, monolithic and unsatisfactory. For the notion of the common good to be constructive, some parsing and nuance are required. Helpful clarifications are provided in such later documents of official Catholic social teaching as *Sollicitudo rei socialis*, which in 1987 further defined common good as "the good of all and of each individual,"[24] thereby specifying that this package, when unbundled, includes the individual rights already enumerated in *Pacem in terris* and other Catholic documents. The common good thus becomes an umbrella term for describing patterns of human agency which allow for the protection of such values as freedom, equality, rights and justice—values which combine overlapping and sometimes competing concerns for both individuals and communities.

Other important clarifications of the meaning of common good are offered by twentieth-century theologians. Jacques Maritain's *The Person and the Common Good*[25] articulates the blend of individual and communal values which emanates from viewing common good as a notion analogous to the subsistent relations within the Trinity, an insight which typifies Maritain's brand of personalist communitarianism. The writings of Joseph Cardinal Bernardin[26] and David Hollenbach[27] explicate lists of partial goods (in both cases including peace, human rights and certain standards of justice) which comprise the wider common good.

Much more could be said about the vast subject of the common good as a traditional element of Catholic social ethics. For example, it is instructive to note how the biblical language of "covenant" (long influential in many circles of Protestant ethical reflection) has in recent decades come to be employed in Catholic writings (most prominently in the U.S.

22. MM 65.
23. GS 26.
24. SRS 38.
25. Trans. John T. Fitzgerald (N.Y.: Charles Scribner's Sons, 1947).
26. See Bernardin's addresses and essays contained in *A Consistent Ethic of Life*, ed. Thomas G. Fuechtmann (Kansas City, Mo.: Sheed and Ward, 1988), esp. 91.
27. *Justice, Peace and Human Rights: American Catholic Social Ethics in a Pluralistic Context* (N.Y.: The Crossroad Publishing Company, 1988).

bishops' *Economic Justice for All*) as a framework for understanding the common destiny and mutual obligations of people. Another development which must not be overlooked is the distinction drawn in recent decades between "common good" and "public order," two complementary ways of conceiving the relationship between state and society. While still recognizing that the good of each person is bound up with the good of the community, this distinction was introduced to accommodate the position of governments which, in modern pluralistic settings, face the challenge of restricting themselves to a more modest understanding of what constitutes "the sum total of conditions" for human flourishing. In the absence of broad social consensus (at least on the content of the supernatural *telos* of *beatitudo*, if not also on natural *felicitas*), goals more modest than the full realization of a robust sense of common good recommend themselves to modern political entities.[28]

In the context of an ongoing debate about the status of religious liberty, the American Jesuit theologian John Courtney Murray proposed, and the deliberators at Vatican II ultimately accepted,[29] the proposition that government rightly pursues the less ambitious goal of "public order." "The public order criterion sets limits on the use of coercive power of the state through its civil laws,"[30] but it still rests on the assumption that the state has positive moral responsibilities. It need not be construed so narrowly as to relinquish the Aristotelian-Thomistic claim that the purpose of the political sphere is to advance the common good. However, toward the goal of striking an appropriate balance between the state's authority and the role of individual rights and free conscience, the more maximal set of goods which previous definitions counted as elements of the common good are assigned to other social institutions besides the state. Here we rely on a society-state distinction which will be treated later in this chapter when we address how Catholic social teaching assumes its particular stance on the role of the state.

---

28. A general introduction to the historical development of this distinction is found in James L. Nash, "The Distinction Between Public Order and the Common Good in Roman Catholic Social Teaching" (unpublished paper given at the annual meeting of the Society of Christian Ethics, Savannah, Georgia, 7 January 1993).
29. See Vatican II's Declaration on Religious Freedom, nos. 2 and 7. The text as it appears in Walter Abbott, ed., *The Documents of Vatican II* (N.Y.: Guild Press, 1966) contains commentary by John Courtney Murray on the concept of "public order."
30. J. Bryan Hehir, "The Consistent Ethic: Public Policy Implications" in Fuechtmann, *A Consistent Ethic of Life*, 227.

Positions on Three Topics
Germane to Social Policy

Our survey of the above three themes reveals the existence of some tension between: (1) values associated with the individual (particularly freedom); and (2) values associated with the health of community life (social cooperation, unity). Every social theory has an implicit rationale for balancing these two concerns. Catholic social teaching draws on the theological and philosophical warrants explicated above in order to recommend to the consciences of its audience (whom the Church serves in the first instance as a pastor, and secondarily as a teacher) certain stances toward secular realities and institutions. Each of the three topics treated below calls for reflection on both the individual and communal nature of human existence.

1. The transcendent character of human personhood

The purpose of this section is to describe a small part of Catholic theology's vision of moral anthropology, restricting our focus to those positions most immediately relevant to the concerns of social policy. In one sense, everything said above about human dignity and sociality may be considered aspects of the general category of moral anthropology. A comprehensive inquiry into the moral anthropology implicit in the documents of Catholic social teaching would systematically investigate how these texts treat such categories as sin, grace, freedom, responsibility, creaturehood, embodiment, suffering, hope, virtue, individuality and social obligation. The modest goal of this brief section is to describe one aspect of the portrayal of personhood in Catholic social teaching: the transcendent character of human personhood, especially as this claim about human nature issues constraints upon the workings of economic and political systems.

Rerum novarum begins its defense of the rights of workers by arguing that all people, owners and laborers alike, have "spiritual and mental interests" which alongside "property and possessions . . . must be protected." These concerns are immediately placed in the context of Christian cosmology:

> Life on earth, however good and desirable in itself, is not the final purpose for which man is created; it is only the way and the means to that attainment of truth, and that practice of goodness in which the full life of the soul consists . . . . No man may outrage with impunity that human dignity which God himself treats with reverence, nor stand in the way of that higher life which is the preparation for the eternal life of heaven.[31]

---

31. RN 32.

Especially remarkable is how quickly and seamlessly the encyclical moves from the task of situating humankind within the context of its relation to transcendence to the task of outlining guidelines for rather mundane workplace policies. Two sentences after the above citation, the document begins to address the most inner-worldly, even nitty-gritty of concerns such as desirable length of the work week, proper schedules of holidays, child labor and collective bargaining for wage scales. Partly because Catholic social theory is based on a participation metaphysics that defines humans as hylomorphic unities of body and soul, the encyclicals exhibit this extraordinary tendency to move abruptly between perspectives, frequently juxtaposing statements shaped by the long view (concerns about salvation and supernatural destiny) and the short (the human need for material sustenance).

A discourse recognizing a transcendent destiny of human persons need not translate into a discourse about ontology, but Catholic theology makes this translation readily. *Pacem in terris*, for example, shows no hesitation in making robust claims about human nature. It introduces its ground-breaking treatment of human rights with this thumbnail sketch of moral anthropology:

> Any human society, if it is to be well-ordered and productive, must lay down as a foundation this principle, namely, that every human being is a person; that is, his nature is endowed with intelligence and free will. Indeed, precisely because he is a person he has rights and obligations flowing directly and simultaneously from his very nature. And as these rights and obligations are universal and inviolable, so they cannot in any way be surrendered.[32]

A being possessing free will and intelligence is rightly called a subject. Defining subjecthood and analyzing the implications of predicating it to humans is a chief concern of personalism, a loose-knit school of thought prominent in philosophical and theological circles in the twentieth century. The diversity among the many forms of personalism testifies to the many ways in which modern philosophy's "turn to the subject" can be interpreted. Among the most prominent Catholic personalists may be counted Jacques Maritain and Pope John Paul II.[33] Since each has helped shape and interpret Catholic social teaching, a brief look at the contribution of each will assist our investigation of Catholic moral anthropology.

---

32. PT 9.
33. The works of Bernard Häring and Louis Janssens also merit attention, but they focus on personal, rather than strictly social ethics.

Maritain holds out a paradox for investigation: humans are beings of inestimable and inviolable value, transcending any temporal or political order, yet they find themselves and realize their dignity only by participating in (and, in so doing, subordinating themselves to) the community. The human person simultaneously transcends and is subordinate to the common good. The *second* term of this paradox is supported by the Thomistic assertion that "every individual person is as it were a part of the whole,"[34] related to the entire community organically, as one part of the body is to the entire organism. The *first* term is reflected in the Thomistic proviso: "Man is not ordained to the body politic according to all that he is and has."[35] Even in serving the common good as he or she must, the human person is violated if treated merely as a part, or as a means to an end. Maritain was horrified by the atrocities of Nazism and other forms of totalitarianism which trample on individuals. Yet in his desire to safeguard persons, he sought to avoid the divinization of the individual, which could be as blasphemous and destructive as the divinization of the state (to which it may be linked, as the history of totalitarianism demonstrates).

Key to Maritain's analysis is a distinction between "individuality" (which reserves sovereignty to itself) and "personality" (which includes openness to God and a reservation of ultimate sovereignty to God alone).[36] He broke out of the supposed impasse between liberal individualism and communist collectivism by denouncing both as materialistic options unworthy of true "persons," with their immanent aspirations for transcendence. In a judgment that recalls the contents of earlier social encyclicals (and anticipates the contents of subsequent documents of official Catholic social teaching), Maritain insists on the ultimate inadequacy of any social, political or economic system which fails to acknowledge the spiritual nature of persons, possessing as they do aspirations which surpass their temporal needs.[37]

Three of the major social encyclicals appear over the signature of John Paul II. His first, *Laborem exercens*, is in some respects an extended commentary on this brief passage from the Second Vatican Council's *Gaudium et spes*:

> Human labor . . . is superior to the other elements of economic life . . . [for] this labor comes immediately from the person. In a sense, the person stamps the things of nature with his seal and subdues them to his will.[38]

34. *Summa Theologica* II-II, q. 64, a. 2.
35. Ibid., I-II, q. 21, a. 2.
36. Maritain, *The Person and the Common Good*, 1–4.
37. Ibid., esp. ch. 5.
38. GS 67.

John Paul takes this observation in a personalist direction. While using a "labor theory of value" similar to those which led John Locke and Karl Marx to very different conclusions, John Paul identifies the hermeneutical key which for him links the phenomenon of labor to theology and spirituality, namely that "work in its subjective aspect is always a personal action, an 'actus personae'. . . ."[39]

At several places in *Laborem exercens*, John Paul provides an explicit theological rationale (one imbued with a personalist flavor) for rejecting two ideological approaches inimical to the Catholic style of moral anthropology: scientific and economic reductionism. The former had been mentioned by Paul VI in *Octogesima adveniens* as a danger ("a purely quantitative or phenomenological point of view . . . [threatens] to mutilate man and, under the pretext of a scientific procedure, to make it impossible to understand man in his totality"[40]). The latter had been criticized in *Gaudium et spes* ("Many people . . . seem to be hypnotized, as it were, by economics, so that almost their entire personal and social life is permeated with a certain economic outlook"[41]). *Laborem exercens* seeks to counter these distortions with the assertion: "in the first place, work is 'for man' and not man 'for work.'"[42] It extends its argument to generalize about the need to oppose all forms of reductionistic philosophies (economism, scientism, materialism) which reverse the proper order of creation.

> We must emphasize and give prominence to the primacy of man in the production process, the primacy of man over things . . . .Man, as the subject of work and independent of the work he does—man alone is a person. This truth has important and decisive consequences.[43]

Perhaps the most decisive of these consequences is the effect which this personalist interpretation of a central tenet of Catholic anthropology has on the question: how best should we measure social progress? *Octogesima adveniens* had already in 1971 cast doubt on the moral value of a "never-ending, breathless pursuit of a progress" that consists of "a merely quantitative economic growth."[44] Material progress alone is not an adequate yardstick for social advancement. The pursuit of what *Populorum progressio* calls "authentic" and "integral development"[45] must consider

39. LE 24.
40. OA 38.
41. GS 63.
42. LE 6.
43. LE 12.
44. OA 41.
45. PP 14.

spiritual and human values (love and friendship, prayer and contemplation) which neither markets nor governments, no matter how efficient or just, can offer. This criterion constitutes a word of judgment upon both atheistic communism and unfettered capitalism. In calling for a "new humanism,"[46] Catholic social teaching notes that standard definitions of progress can "imprison us" in an "avarice [which] is the most evident form of moral underdevelopment."[47] The result may be a "super-development" which not only leaves central aspects of our lives impoverished, but may be a temptation to idolatry.[48]

This brief glance at how personalist themes add a new "spin" to Catholic moral anthropology demonstrates new criteria and rationales for engaging in the familiar project of carefully balancing the individual and social aspects of human living. On no topic has Catholic social teaching worked out a more developed position on the blend of personal and communal values which best contributes to human flourishing than on the topic of private property.

2. Private property

At several places where they take on questions of distributive justice and the proper arrangement of social institutions, the documents of Catholic social teaching recapitulate an ongoing debate within the history of Christian thought about the nature of property ownership. This debate begins with a shared core of beliefs but soon proceeds to areas of dispute. All Christian reflection on the holding of material goods proceeds from the Biblically based doctrine of creation, which includes the notion that God created the material world for the benefit of all and bestows dominion over all creation to people in common. Christian positions on the possession and use of property are thus shaped by central beliefs about the divine order. These include such notions as: (1) God's permanent lordship over all creation (as sole absolute proprietor, to whom all are accountable); (2) the universal destination of material things (created for the purpose of sustaining life for all); and (3) a moral stewardship (supported by numerous scriptural texts) which necessitates a responsible employment of resources.

In the patristic era, these themes were cited in polemics against avarice, in exhortations for detachment and charity, and in frequent but

---

46. PP 20.
47. PP 19.
48. CA 41.

imprecise attempts to describe the practice of distributive justice.[49] The scholastic era witnessed attempts at a more systematic treatment of the topic of property, as Christian thinkers began to employ several important distinctions. Among these were: (1) the distinction between the use of possessions and their ultimate ownership; and (2) the distinction between God's original intentions for creation (the absolute natural law) and a prudent reliance on those institutions suited for a postlapsarian cosmos (operating under the relative natural law, which governs human behavior after the fall). The key question to be settled, of course, remains the same in the thirteenth century (when property meant primarily land) as in the twentieth (when at stake is control over the means of industrial production and, increasingly, the knowledge and human capital of a postindustrial economy): what type of ownership arrangements can be justified using Christian theological warrants?

Aquinas's treatment of property issues in the *Summa Theologica* II-II, q. 66 ("Of theft and robbery") is worthy of attention for several reasons. First, it reflects the full range of the intellectual traditions the scholastics inherited on this matter; the first two articles (investigating whether it is natural and lawful for humans to possess external things) make explicit reference to numerous passages from Scripture, patristic sources and Aristotle as well as other philosophers. Second, Aquinas here establishes distinctions in the relation of humans to material things which would be indispensable to all subsequent analysis. By distinguishing among the powers of procuring, dispensing and using goods, he advances the notion that ownership consists of a "bundle of rights." Other rights which were subsequently recognized as existing within this bundle include those of occupancy, benefit and alteration. This is a construct which affords a much sharper analysis of property issues by not only theologians, but legal scholars and political philosophers as well.

Third, Aquinas sets the frame for modern Catholic social teaching by introducing a dialectic between two sets of concerns which accord to the institution of property ownership its dual character—as individual and as social. On the one hand, the concern for "the common" which derives from God's original intention that the goods of creation serve the sustenance needs of all imprints the "use" of material things with a social stamp. As Aquinas declares: "with regard . . . to their use . . . man ought to possess external things, not as his own, but as common, so that he is

---

49. An excellent source of texts (primarily from Clement, Basil the Great, Ambrose, John Chrysostom and Augustine) and commentary upon them is Charles Avila, *Ownership: Early Christian Teaching* (Maryknoll, N.Y.: Orbis Books, 1983).

ready to communicate them to others in their need."[50] Aquinas cites scriptural and patristic sources which condemn the coexistence of great wealth and dire poverty as he builds up a case to justify a social obligation for the sharing of earthly goods. If sharing does not occur voluntarily, in situations of extreme need (such as under the threat of starvation) theft by the poor from the surplus of the rich may be defensible.

On the other hand, Aquinas judges that it is not only lawful but necessary for people to have exclusive control over other aspects (besides "use") of property. This is so for the most practical of reasons in this fallen world, where human sinfulness is expressed in such mundane forms as inattentiveness, disorder and conflict. "There would be confusion if everyone had to look after any one thing indeterminately. . ."[51] as when goods are shared by imperfect beings who tend to be overeager to benefit from the contribution of others, but slothful about doing their own share of work. Therefore "human affairs are conducted in a more orderly fashion if each man is charged with taking care of some particular thing."[52] The individual character of material possessions, which we recognize in the institution of private property, is strictly instrumental, since it is primarily a concession to human sinfulness.[53] However, for a fallen world private ownership is defensible as a prudent arrangement. Indeed it emerges as the only practical way for most people to meet their needs for material sustenance, to provide for their future, and thus to insure that God's common gifts of creation are used for their intended purpose.

The documents of Catholic social teaching move back and forth between the poles of this dialectic of social and individual concerns. Because they are historically conditioned by the political atmosphere in which they were written, their analysis of the role of private property in society undergoes significant variation as context changes. Of all the documents of modern Catholic social teaching, *Rerum novarum*, the first of this genre, differs the most from the others in its treatment of property. This encyclical was primarily concerned to counter the appeal among Catholic workers in Europe of a form of socialism which sought to eliminate private ownership of the means of production. In its desire to bolster the case for the necessity of retaining the practice of private ownership, it neglected the Thomistic claim that private property is necessary primarily

---

50. *Summa Theologica* II-II, q. 66, a. 2.
51. Ibid.
52. Ibid.
53. Indeed, all three of Aquinas' justifications for private holdings in this text may be interpreted as measures of prudence in response to the existence of sin in the world.

as a concession to human sin. Charles Curran recounts several ways in which Pope Leo XIII either misinterpreted or drew only selectively from Aquinas's positions on property, dominion and natural law in this encyclical.[54] As a result, *Rerum novarum* portrays private property as a demand of the natural law in the strict sense, an interpretation which leads the document to downplay the social character of property ownership.

The next social encyclical in chronological order, *Quadragesimo anno*, is more authentically Thomistic in its treatment of property and strikes a felicitous balance between individual and social aspects of material goods which is maintained in subsequent documents. It seeks to relativize the property rights it affirms by warning of

> a double danger to be avoided. On the one hand, if the social and public aspects of ownership be denied or minimized, the logical consequence is "individualism," as it is called; on the other hand, the rejection or diminution of its private and individual character necessarily leads to some form of "collectivism."[55]

The "twofold character of ownership, which we have termed individual and social"[56] becomes the overarching framework for all the subsequent efforts of Catholic social teaching to offer moral guidelines for the proper use of wealth. The social dimension of property creates an obligation to measure all uses of material goods in terms of the common good. This criterion constrains individuals in their economic decisions and governments in their policies. The notion of the universal destination of material goods (a Christian belief about the divine order) thus serves as the ethical basis for a number of moral imperatives with profound implications for economic structures, including public policies regarding the poorest members of society.

Quadragesimo anno emphasizes that these injunctions sometimes justify economic intervention on the part of government:

> [W]hen civil authority adjusts ownership to meet the needs of the public good . . . it effectively prevents the possession of private property, intended by nature's Author in his wisdom for the sustaining of human life, from creating intolerable burdens . . . .[57]

Later documents frequently reaffirm this principle (that ownership needs to be "adjusted" so that property serves the livelihood of those in great-

---

54. Charles E. Curran, *Directions in Catholic Social Ethics* (Notre Dame, Ind.: University of Notre Dame Press, 1985) 23–27.
55. QA 46.
56. QA 49.
57. Ibid.

est need[58]) but they seldom offer detailed courses of action. It is beyond the scope of papal social teaching to recommend measures that would specify legislative strategies for such actions as curtailing monopolies, regulating markets, providing poor relief or writing tax codes. When Church leaders feel the need to address such specific policy directions, it most frequently falls to local or national conferences of bishops to apply universal principles to their specific political and economic contexts.[59]

Nevertheless, documents from Rome frequently venture to denounce the extreme positions on property—collectivism for its refusal to recognize the private dimension of property, and extreme laissez-faire liberalism (which features nearly absolute ownership rights) for its refusal to recognize the social dimension of property. The insistence of Catholic social teaching that private property be neither abolished nor given free rein serves as its testimony to the proposition that such "-isms" as liberalism and collectivism never constitute anything more than half-truths—partial insights into the human condition which require correction and supplementation from other perspectives.

3. The role of the state

One especially influential passage from John Paul II's 1987 *Sollicitudo rei socialis* may serve as a conceptual bridge from the topic of private property to a consideration of the role and responsibility of the state as it is portrayed in the tradition of Catholic social teaching:

> The goods of this world are originally meant for all. The right to private property is valid and necessary, but it does not nullify the value of this principle. Private property, in fact, is under a "social mortgage," which means that it has an intrinsically social function, based upon and justified precisely by the principle of the universal destination of goods. . . . The motivating concern for the poor must be translated at all levels into concrete actions, until it decisively attains a series of necessary reforms.[60]

Only some of the morally mandated "reforms" called for are likely to occur through voluntary efforts. Other measures necessary for the enactment of economic justice and the protection of the poor require the active involvement of the instrumentality of the state. Governments legitimately

---

58. GS 70; PP 66; SRS 31.

59. Part Three of the present work examines how the U.S. bishops and some state-level conferences of bishops attempted to apply Catholic social teaching and to exercise their moral leadership on fairly specific aspects of one policy area: social welfare appropriations.

60. SRS 42–3.

execute the powers of regulating economic activity when they act in the public interest through such measures as collecting taxes, instituting environmental and safety regulations, preventing monopolies and providing public services and infrastructure.

The most frequent objection to such economic interventions is the complaint that they require coercive force to be effective. While there are schools of thought (some, like political libertarianism, which are secular in nature and others within religious traditions, including sectarian Christianity) which exhibit a high degree of aversion to the use of governmental coercion, Catholic social teaching defines a number of potential justifications for such interventions. This assigning of tasks to government rests on the Aristotelian-Thomistic tradition of reflection which defines the state as a natural institution for humans as social beings.[61] Whether they use the rubric of "common good" or "public order," the documents of Catholic social teaching follow Aristotle and Aquinas in identifying a package of social goals the accomplishment of which calls for an active role for civil authorities. Jacques Maritain summarizes this pattern of thought with the simple definition: "The state is a part which specializes in the interests of the whole." Its particular concerns are "with the maintenance of law, the promotion of the common welfare and public order, and the administration of public affairs."[62]

This does not imply that governments enjoy a *carte blanche* in extending their control over economic affairs. Since freedom and human rights are prominent among the goods it seeks to protect, Catholic social teaching is aware of a cost accompanying every such intervention. The necessary balancing of "value" and "disvalue" may be described as proceeding according to the traditional principle of *"tantum quantum."* This pragmatic guideline expresses the idea that what is justified is only as much of some measure as achieves the value sought. Coercive action beyond what is required for the end is considered excessive and potentially dangerous. In making use of this mental construct, John Courtney Murray, in his writings on public policy, often repeats the adage: "as much freedom as possible, as much government as necessary."[63] Ultimately, all

---

61. Besides the texts from Aristotle already cited on this point, see Thomas Aquinas "On Kingship," bk. 1, ch. 1. The texts establishing the natural sociality of humans and the efficacy of government in providing for the common good are found in William P. Baumgarth and Richard J. Regan, eds., *Saint Thomas Aquinas: On Law, Morality and Politics* (Indianapolis: Hackett Publishing Company, 1988) 263–7.

62. *Man and the State* (Chicago: University of Chicago Press, 1951) 12.

63. John Courtney Murray, "Leo XIII: Two Concepts of Government," *Theological Studies* 14 (1953) 559. Conceptual borrowing from the liberalism of J. S. Mill and others is readily evident in Murray's desire to maximize freedom as far as is practical.

restrictions of freedom are justified by the goal of increasing the freedom of all. Our decisions to use the coercive apparatus of the state must be guided by the distinction between law and morality; not everything that any given group considers morally good (perhaps as a part of the common good) ought to be the subject of legislation. Government intervention is a self-limiting principle, since "constraint must be for the sake of freedom."[64]

An illuminating example of how this principle has been applied to justice issues in American economic life involves the work of Msgr. John A. Ryan, an important figure in American church history in the early decades of the twentieth century. As the major interpreter of *Rerum novarum* to the American context, Ryan's agenda (explicated in the 1920 Church document, "Bishops' Program of Social Reconstruction") generally converged with that of the Progressive movement. In his later years, he was sometimes referred to as "the Right Reverend New Dealer." Ryan was a proponent of an activist, though limited government oriented toward creating favorable conditions for the attainment of distributive justice, which he defined in terms of insuring that fair shares of economic output accrued to the four sectors which contributed to production: capitalists, laborers, landowners and business managers.[65]

Our judgments about what constitutes the fairness of a given share are ordinarily based on such criteria as inheritance, gift, purchase, first occupancy, productivity, effort, and sacrifice in contributing to the process of production. However, from a moral standpoint, these conventional titles to wealth do not form a complete picture. While providing a fair return for the efforts of those who contribute to the production process is a good worthy of protecting, there are other goods at stake in economic transactions as well, such as the good of preserving lives threatened by destitution. Ryan cites the theme of the universal destination of material goods (the theological claim based on God's original intention that creation serve human sustenance) in order to establish the legitimacy of the distributive criterion of human needs.[66] In order to safeguard the minimum requirements of resources required to lead a reasonably adequate human existence, Ryan proposes a "need" criterion to supplement the conventional bases of claims to goods. Each person is owed access to enough of the goods of the earth to support his or her life.

64. John Courtney Murray, *We Hold These Truths: Catholic Reflections on the American Proposition* (N.Y.: Sheed and Ward, 1960) 160.
65. These four form the outline of Ryan's longest work, *Distributive Justice: The Rights and Wrongs of Our Present Distribution of Wealth* (N.Y.: The Macmillan Company, 1925).
66. Ibid., 304.

Since this access is conditioned upon and becomes actually valid through the expenditure of labor, then those "who are in present control of the opportunities of the earth are obliged to permit reasonable access to these opportunities by those who are willing to work."[67]

The bottom line of Ryan's analysis is the idea with which his name is most frequently associated—the right of workers to a "living wage." In advocating this notion, Ryan engages in a project with at least four noteworthy implications. First, he models for future generations how a general principle from a papal encyclical can be applied to a local or national context. *Rerum novarum* had called for a "family wage," but had left unspecified what this might entail. Ryan does the legwork necessary to spell out the precise ramifications of Pope Leo's challenge within the U.S. economy of his day. Ryan devotes a major portion of his book-length defense of the living wage[68] to such details as regional costs of living and sample family budgets, itemized to provide for reasonable expenses, in the interest of determining with some precision a satisfactory wage level.

Second, in challenging on ethical grounds the Malthusian "iron law of wages" which was the conventional wisdom in the American economic thought of his time, Ryan supplied some of the impetus for a religion-labor alliance which would play an important role in subsequent U.S. labor history. The principle of collective bargaining rests on the assumption that not every free exchange is automatically a fair exchange. This is a point Ryan makes in his indictment of the "starvation wages" that result from an economic regime of laissez-faire in the style of those who entrust the achievement of social justice to the invisible hand cited by Adam Smith.[69] In order to foster fairer outcomes, the bargaining position of labor might be improved by changing the procedures and groundrules governing labor markets. Ryan detected an imbalance in the power equilibrium of early twentieth-century American industrial relations and sought to address it by supporting the establishment of some checks upon the wage-setting practices of employers.

Third, Ryan advances Catholic thought about the role of government in achieving desirable ends. Whereas *Rerum novarum* had argued for the notion of the family wage but had shied away from specifically advocating legislation to enact it,[70] Ryan leaves no uncertainty about the proper

---

67. Ibid., 359.

68. John A. Ryan, *A Living Wage: Its Ethical and Economic Aspects* (N.Y.: The Macmillan Company, 1912) 128–50.

69. Ibid., 12–19.

70. RN 34 argues that just wages should be enforced by private "societies or boards." The state may at most "be asked for approval and protection," but should not be

course of action. He asserts: "[t]he state has both the right and the duty to compel all employers to pay a living wage."[71] This is part of the legitimate function of the state in "promoting the general welfare," a phrase which appears in the Preamble of the United States Constitution and which resonates richly with Catholic social teaching as well. Ryan portrays the living wage as a demand of justice, not of charity alone.[72] He goes so far as to introduce the language of rights ("the laborer's claim to a Living Wage is of the nature of a right"[73]) in an effort to move the argument away from the arena of convention (fixed "just wages" had been a practice in medieval guilds and elsewhere, as Ryan notes[74]) or charitable activity and into the legal-juridical sphere. Voluntary compliance on the part of employers is not an adequate basis to insure that justice is done; legislation mandating the enactment of wage scales adequate for a decent livelihood for workers is imperative. Ryan cites the achievement of minimum wage legislation in other nations such as Australia and New Zealand[75] as a potential model for a U.S. initiative.

Fourth, Ryan demonstrates an adherence to the *"tantum quantum"* approach introduced above. In proposing reforms to remove what he saw as the major defects of the industrial system of his day, Ryan often uses the phrase "an ethical minimum."[76] We may interpret this as a polyvalent term, referring not just to a "minimum" in the literal pay scale, but also in the more general sense of indicating Ryan's desire to introduce the lowest level of intervention in the free economy which would still be effective in protecting the fundamental needs of workers. Instituting a minimum wage does not necessitate a great deal of bureaucracy or government meddling in the affairs of employers; it is more a matter of oversight and regulation than of burdensome interference with the economic management of private enterprise.

In keeping with the pragmatic aspect of the *"tantum quantum"* criterion, Ryan also makes a number of concessions to actual economic conditions which might alter how we apply such principles of justice as the ethical minimum in wage scales. We have already seen that Ryan sets

---

the primary agent of this reform "in order to supersede undue interference on the part of the State."

71. *A Living Wage*, 301.
72. Ibid., 110–22.
73. Ibid., 43.
74. Ibid., 23.
75. Ibid., 315.
76. Ibid., "Author's Preface," viii and passim.

standards for what constitutes a reasonable family budget based on conventions of adequacy which vary over time and location. In fact, Ryan even makes provisions for limiting the scope of living wage regulation to those industries and sectors profitable enough to support such a minimum wage level.[77] In thus exempting some employers from the actual obligation to pay a living wage (at least in the short-run), Ryan cites a general principle which is applied in several other places in his work: the notion that "no one is morally bound to do the impossible."[78] In order to serve as practical guidelines, our notions of moral obligation must link the "ought" with the "can." The discourse of "absolute positive rights" is at variance with this pragmatic consideration, and is not an idiom favored within Catholic social teaching.

Ryan demonstrates a consistent sensitivity to this concern for holding together "ought" and "can." He nuances his use of the notion of rights, holding that even "inviolable moral claims" are "not absolute in extent."[79] Ryan considers several important instances where rights are limited by the conditions in which they might be attained. For example, a nation experiencing absolute scarcity simply cannot enact the standard of a decent minimum (in the form of a living wage or any other distributive mechanism) to protect workers from poverty if that poverty is already an unavoidable general condition.[80] Similarly, the *prima facie* obligation of each person to engage in enough productive work to avoid poverty is suspended when a worker is placed in a position (such as in a loose labor market) where "conditions for which he is in no wise responsible, and which take no account of his human dignity"[81] prevent that worker from escaping destitution. Such a worker cannot be considered morally culpable for the resulting condition of poverty. Neither workers nor employers can be held morally responsible unless they have the freedom to fulfill their obligations. Once again, "ought" implies "can."

From John Ryan's analysis can be gained much clarity about the patterns of thought by which Catholic social teaching addresses the role of government. His writings at once apply the content of *Rerum novarum* to the American context and anticipate the formulations of the later documents. The remainder of this section addresses three concerns that arise not only in the work of Ryan, but whenever the documents of Catholic social teaching (or, for that matter, the statements of any "public church")

77. *Distributive Justice*, 366–70; *A Living Wage*, 249.
78. *A Living Wage*, 249.
79. Ibid., 45.
80. Ibid., 79.
81. Ibid., 244.

turn their attention to the activities of public authorities: (1) limitations upon the scope of government; (2) alternatives to governmental intervention; and (3) adjusting our notions of proper governmental responsibility to the changing demands of new eras.

First, we have already seen some of the implications within Ryan's work of the Catholic position on the nature of the state. Since the state is not the ultimate source of rights,[82] legislation does not create rights but merely recognizes and fosters the achievement of those universal entitlements which flow from the innate dignity of each person. As *Rerum novarum* argues, "man is older than the State," so our "recourse to the State"[83] is always instrumental. It must always be for limited purposes which require specification and justification. *Populorum progressio* uses the pattern of *"tantum quantum"* reasoning in this regard to clarify the conditions under which government programs are justified. "Every program," the encyclical enjoins, "has in the last analysis no other raison d'être than the service of man." This task includes the goal of "free[ing] man from various types of servitude" and "render[ing] the world a more human place in which to live."[84] Modest attempts at the regulation of wages, such as the adoption of living wage legislation, serve the humanization of the economy by helping to insure that property will be used to fulfill its end: the service of human livelihood.

Second, we have already noted Ryan's aversion to excessive governmental intervention, but in examining Ryan's writings we had no occasion to focus on alternative actors and courses of action to bring about such desired ends as the human dignity and the demands of justice. Nevertheless, it seems fair to interpret Ryan's approach as one which turns to government primarily as a last resort, only when the internal operations and interrelations of the four economic sectors he identifies fail egregiously in producing just outcomes. It is important to note that Ryan wrote his major works in the years before the 1931 *Quadragesimo anno* coined the term "subsidiarity." In introducing this awkward but eminently useful term (which the encyclical labels a "fundamental principle of social philosophy"), Pius XI advises:

> [O]ne should not withdraw from individuals and commit to the community what they can accomplish by their own enterprise and industry. So, too, it is an injustice and at the same time a great evil and a disturbance of right

---

82. Ryan addresses this point in *A Living Wage*, 55–66. In this section, he takes issue with Hegel's positivistic notion of the origin of rights in social groups, which Ryan identifies as threatening to deify the state and to violate individual dignity.
83. RN 6.
84. PP 34.

order to transfer to the larger and higher collectivity functions which can be performed and provided for by lesser and subordinate bodies . . . . The State authorities should leave to other bodies the care and expediting of business and activities of lesser moment . . . [85]

Unlike other notions central to Catholic social teaching, subsidiarity is not linked to sources in Scripture or natural law. It is perhaps best characterized, in the words of John Coleman, as "neither a theological nor even really a philosophical principle, but a piece of congealed historical wisdom . . . affirm[ing] the importance of social pluralism and intermediate groups."[86] Subsidiarity is a principle of acting and being which is bipolar in that it seeks to strike a balance between statism and anarchy. It conforms to the *"tantum quantum"* mode of judgment in recommending as much centralization as is necessary for human flourishing, but as little as is possible while pursuing legitimate goals. Government should not usurp the functions appropriate to other levels of activity, but there nevertheless remain important tasks which only government can accomplish.

Implicit in the invocation of the principle of subsidiarity is a distinction between state and society, with the imperative that the latter never be absorbed within the former. This distinction is a crucial one in forestalling the potential for totalitarianism, an ideology which legitimizes the practice of ubiquitous and maximal governmental involvement in all aspects of social life. The controlling metaphor here evident is of society as an organism, a unified whole in which responsibilities appropriate to each part are assigned on a prudential basis. Government intervention is necessitated only when lesser bodies (today we might use the term "mediating structures"[87] to refer to these voluntary grassroots organizations of a for-profit or nonprofit nature) cannot complete their own tasks without assistance. The encyclical *Quadragesimo anno* uses a series of verbs to describe the actions of government in social coordination: "directing, supervising, encouraging, restraining as circumstances suggest or necessity demands."[88] Each of these descriptions supports the core of the notion of subsidiarity: that the state plays its proper role when its ac-

---

85. QA 79–80.

86. John Coleman, s.j., "Development of Church Social Teaching" in Charles E. Curran and Richard A. McCormick, s.j., eds., *Readings in Moral Theology No. 5: Official Catholic Social Teaching* (N.Y.: Paulist Press, 1986) 183.

87. The phrase was popularized by the work of Richard John Neuhaus and Peter Berger in the 1980s. Two hundred years earlier, Edmund Burke described the same phenomena as "little platoons."

88. QA 80.

tions constitute assistance (Latin: *subsidium*) to, rather than replacement of, the efforts of individuals and other groups within society.

Of course, the mere invoking of the concept of subsidiarity, even if all agree on the validity of the principle, does not settle many of the controversial issues raised when government intervention is considered. There are still many prudential judgments to be made about how and when to apply this concept. It has been cited as justification for the positions of groups across the ideological spectrum, from socialists (who perceive some need for government intervention at every turn) to libertarians (who are averse to almost any interference in individual choice). Therefore, this conclusion seems inescapable: subsidiarity remains a formal principle which requires determination in a concrete context, where precise judgments about proper courses of action depend on detailed knowledge of the interplay of the responsibilities of various levels of social actors. Part Two of this study will revisit this topic in considering some of the arguments made about the proper role of charitable organizations in the contemporary debate over U.S. social welfare policy—a controversy which constitutes a case study in the application of the principle of subsidiarity.

Third, John Ryan's analysis raises some important concerns about how and whether it is possible to adjust the lessons of Catholic social teaching on the role of government to new issues that arise with the advent of new historical eras with novel economic realities. Recall that Ryan's work (as well as *Rerum novarum* which it sought to interpret and apply) was part of a larger effort among social scientists and other scholars to adapt their thinking to the demands of an era of large-scale industrialization. This vast economic upheaval had transformed the social and political order of the West in the course of a few generations, raising profound questions about social relationships and political responsibilities never before considered. Ryan saw the notion of the living wage as a novel application of the Church's social commitment necessitated by these new realities:

> Now, the simple and sufficient reason why this general right of the laborer takes the special form of a right to a Living Wage, is that in the present industrial organization of society, there is no other way in which the right can be realized. He cannot find a part of his livelihood outside of his wages because there are no unappropriated goods within his reach. . . . [H]e can effectively realize his natural right of access to the goods of the earth only through the medium of wages.[89]

Part Five below will suggest that the coming of "postindustrial society" constitutes another economic and social upheaval which demands

89. *A Living Wage*, 100.

a metamorphosis in applying Catholic social teaching to the demands of justice in a new context. However, in Church documents published in the 1960s we may detect an example of how Catholic social teaching has already undergone such an adjustment. *Mater et Magistra*, *Gaudium et spes*, and *Populorum progressio* each reflected upon shifts in economic conditions since the onset of industrialization and updated the Church's recommendations for how best to pursue distributive justice amidst these new realities. An examination of the relevant contributions of each, accompanied by a glance of some of the subsequent development of Catholic social teaching, will close this chapter in a way that advances much of the previous analysis.

Mater et Magistra began this process of rethinking the responsibilities of civil authorities when it highlighted the existence within political economy of the trend which is often termed "socialization" (not to be confused with the identical term in developmental psychology nor with its cognate, "socialism"). This word is a shorthand way of saying "the multiplication of social relationships," a phrase which serves as the official translation in English of the original Latin of the encyclical (*socialium rationum incrementa*), although the Italian, French and German versions use cognates of "socialization."[90] After surveying trends of modernization in many fields (technology, economics, politics, etc.), Pope John XXIII in that encyclical noted:

> One of the principal characteristics of our time is the multiplication of social relationships, that is, a daily more complex interdependence of citizens. . . . These developments in social living are at once both a symptom and a cause of the growing intervention of public authorities in matters which, since they pertain to the more intimate aspects of personal life, are of serious moment and not without danger.[91]

This new interdependence is neither good nor bad in itself; however, the response on the part of government which it evokes is subject to judgment by the criteria (such as subsidiarity and the simultaneous promotion of human dignity and the common good) we have seen above. Indiscriminate nationalization of industry is an overreaction to the new facts of interdependence. A refusal of public authorities to enact programs which address the legitimate needs of citizens (for income security, the protection of their rights, etc.) amidst potentially overwhelming economic

---

90. For a detailed discussion of the origin of this term and its subsequent translation, see Donal Dorr, *Option for the Poor: A Hundred Years of Catholic Social Teaching* (Maryknoll, N.Y.: Orbis Books, 1992) 132–35.

91. MM 59–60.

forces beyond their control constitutes an abdication of responsibility. In addressing the challenges presented by these changed conditions within nations and in the international arena, the encyclical explicitly reaffirms the institution of private property,[92] but also offers a new nuance to the tradition's insistence on the social function of property. *Mater et Magistra* notes that, given the present circumstances, social responsibility must now be carried out along a dual track of public and private; the enhanced interventions of governmental agencies must not be considered as replacing private, voluntary and charitable efforts to share wealth and enact concern for the less fortunate. The existence of a new share of "public property" does not absolve the owners of private property from the moral obligations incumbent upon them to exercise regard for the less fortunate.[93]

All the subsequent documents of Catholic social teaching build on this analysis of what John XXIII called "new aspects of the social question"[94] in defining and describing the role of government in this new era. For example, *Gaudium et spes* recommends that public authorities meet their new responsibilities by adopting new objectives and directing renewed efforts "toward providing employment and sufficient income for the people of today and of the future."[95] In its characteristic optimism, this document of the Second Vatican Council makes the judgment that "socialization, while certainly not without its dangers, brings with it many advantages with respect to consolidating and increasing the qualities of the human person, and safeguarding his rights."[96]

The encyclicals of Pope Paul VI reflect a continuation of these same concerns. *Populorum progressio* focuses on several international aspects of the trend toward greater economic interdependence. Systemic solutions, such as greater coordination of international aid, are necessary responses to the need for a humane development. To these ends, there is a legitimate and growing role for public authorities, who alone have the ability to coordinate true development, so long as they avoid the temptations of "complete collectivization or of arbitrary planning."[97] Paul VI's subsequent *Octogesima adveniens* conducts a doleful survey of those categories of people who are harmed by the new interdependence, including among their numbers "the victims of situations of injustice" such as refugees and those marginalized by "racial discrimination" and

92. MM 109.
93. MM 116–21.
94. This phrase serves as the title of Part Three (pars. 123–211) of MM.
95. GS 70.
96. GS 25.
97. PP 33.

"industrial change."⁹⁸ This survey leads to the conclusion that "there is a need to establish a greater justice in the sharing of goods, both within national communities and on the international level."⁹⁹ While this document contains an especially strong denunciation of secular ideological utopias, from Marxism to liberal ideology,¹⁰⁰ it nevertheless finds numerous warrants for public authorities to play a constructive role in helping to create favorable conditions for the flourishing of humanity within the new situation of interdependence.¹⁰¹

The encyclicals of John Paul II complexify the manner in which Catholic social teaching addresses the challenge of socialization. These three documents introduce several new terms which serve to crystallize the previous papal reflections on the political implication of increased economic interdependence. *Laborem exercens*, in focusing its attention on the issue of employment, notes how amidst a situation of increased complexity of social relations, the state has assumed the function of an "indirect employer" with responsibility for various aspects of the labor process:

> The concept of indirect employer includes both persons and institutions . . . and the principles of conduct which are laid down by these persons and institutions and which determine the whole socioeconomic system or are its results. . . . The indirect employer substantially determines one or other facet of the labor relationship . . . . This is not to absolve the direct employer from his own responsibility, but only to draw attention to the whole network of influences that condition his conduct . . . . The concept of indirect employer is applicable to every society and in the first place to the state. For it is the state which must conduct a just labor policy.¹⁰²

The encyclical's affirmation several paragraphs later that "the role of the agents included under the title of indirect employer is to act against unemployment"¹⁰³ is merely a more sophisticated statement of what earlier encyclicals propose in other terms: that the regulation of the conditions of employment is part of the legitimate responsibility of government. As the process of socialization progresses, whether by design or by forces beyond our planning capability, it is incumbent upon public authorities to play their proper role in executing policies which serve workers.

98. OA 15–16.
99. OA 43.
100. OA 26–35.
101. OA 18, 46–7.
102. LE 17.
103. LE 18.

John Paul II is eager to specify criteria for judging how adequately governments respond to the phenomenon of socialization. *Laborem exercens* advises:

> This group in authority may carry out its task satisfactorily from the point of view of the priority of labor, but it may also carry it out badly . . . . We may speak of socializing only when the subject character of society is ensured, . . . when on the basis of his work, each person is fully entitled to consider himself a part-owner of the great work-bench at which he is working with everyone else.[104]

A regime of indiscriminate collectivization does not measure up to these criteria, since it fails in the tasks of "refraining from offending basic human rights" and "associating labor with the ownership of capital."[105] On the other hand, a regime of unfettered "liberal capitalism," as John Paul II claims in a passage from *Sollicitudo rei socialis* reviewed above, "fails to honor the truth that private property is under a 'social mortgage.'"[106]

While government authority can be misused in these and other ways, it nevertheless plays a vital and positive moral function. John Paul II shows an insightful appreciation of the ways in which the irreplaceable tasks of government change from age to age when he includes this observation in *Centesimus annus*:

> It is the task of the state to provide for the defense and preservation of common goods such as the natural and human environments, which cannot be safeguarded simply by market forces. Just as in the time of primitive capitalism the state had the duty of defending the basic rights of workers, so now, with the new capitalism, the state and all of society have the duty of defending those collective goods which, among others, constitute the essential framework for the legitimate pursuit of personal goods on the part of each individual.[107]

In this age of advanced socialization, public authorities are assigned care of what may be called the "social ecology." They are entrusted with the task of protecting those elements of the common good which would "fall through the cracks" if market forces were not thus supplemented. The preservation of collective goods is the proper responsibility of government today.

---

104. LE 14.
105. Ibid.
106. SRS 42.
107. CA 40.

In making such claims, Catholic social teaching is sometimes accused of lapsing into an uncritical statist approach to public policy. This charge formed the centerpiece of the debates surrounding the U.S. bishops' 1986 document *Economic Justice for All: Pastoral Letter on Catholic Social Teaching and the U.S. Economy*.[108] During the months just before and after the publication of the pastoral letter, the bishops were accused of favoring a style of government intervention deemed too activist by a number of observers, including many prominent American Catholics.[109]

There are two possible ways of demonstrating that this interpretation of Catholic social teaching is a misunderstanding of its approach to the proper role of government. The first is simply to cite brief texts from the documents which support the notion that popes and bishops really have in mind a sharply limited role for government. One such text is paragraph forty-eight of *Centesimus annus*, which speaks of "excesses and abuses, . . . malfunctions and defects in the social assistance state" (i.e., the Keynesian-style welfare state). In fact, this paragraph has become a favorite text in recent years among those seeking to "steal" Catholic social teaching for the polemical purposes of the right wing of American politics.[110]

However, a second and more adequate strategy is to gain a comprehensive appreciation of the philosophical and theological underpinnings of the Catholic Church's position on public affairs, especially those intellectual constructs which Catholic social teaching uses to balance the social and personal values at stake in political and economic issues. The Church's stance toward social issues is based on a tradition of reflection which is supported in the first instance by theological beliefs which inform the moral analysis and prudential judgments contained in its documents. Statements about the proper role of government must not be taken out of the context of the theological and philosophical argumentation which drives these teachings about the moral basis of political arrangements.

---

108. Washington, D.C.: National Conference of Catholic Bishops, 1986. This text also appears in O'Brien and Shannon, 572–680.

109. One group, headed by Michael Novak and several others, expressed their disagreement with the bishops by issuing, even before the final draft of the bishops' work appeared, their own version of how the Catholic Church's teaching applies to the American context. See Michael Novak and others, "Towards the Future: Catholic Social Teaching and the U.S. Economy: A Lay Letter," *Catholicism in Crisis* 2, no. 12 (1984) 1–53.

110. Michael Novak, *The Catholic Ethic and the Spirit of Capitalism* (N.Y.: The Free Press, 1993) 125–63; Richard John Neuhaus, *Doing Well and Doing Good: The Challenge to the Christian Capitalist* (N.Y.: Doubleday, 1992) 243–51; George Weigel, "The Virtues of Freedom: *Centesimus Annus*," in George Weigel and Robert Royal, eds., *Building the Free Society: Democracy, Capitalism and Catholic Social Teaching* (Grand Rapids, Mich.: William B. Eerdmans Publishing Company, 1993) 207–23.

It is toward the end of proceeding along this second path that the analysis in the several sections above is offered. Nevertheless, no matter how often the necessary distinctions are drawn (as when it is repeated that "the church does not have technical solutions to offer"[111] and "the church has no models to present"[112]), there will no doubt continue to be controversy generated by those who seek to interpret Catholic social teaching as supportive of their own political agenda—whether that agenda favors or opposes greater levels of economic intervention on the part of government.

111. SRS 41.
112. CA 43.

Chapter 2

Three General Principles for Social Policy

We have already encountered a number of principles cited in the documents of modern Catholic social teaching, in the sources from which it draws (Scripture, patristics, scholastic philosophy) and in the writings of those (Maritain, Murray, Ryan) who seek to interpret and apply it in various contexts. Many more such ethical guidelines could be enumerated. The purpose of this chapter is to identify and examine just three normative principles which are most relevant to the formation of social welfare policy. One factor which complicates this task is the need to extrapolate somewhat from the documents of Catholic social teaching, since they do not in each of the three cases articulate in their precise form the principles we wish to isolate.

A prefatory word about the status of these general principles is necessary, especially since other more specific policy principles will be identified in Part Three below. The task of Christian social ethics is to translate religiously inspired concerns about social relations into judgments about the desirability of various courses of action. Once we agree that communities of faith must have something to say about the moral significance of social behavior, the next step is to seek agreement on how to articulate a set of principles which accomplish several simultaneous goals. Among these goals is: (1) achieving a balance between the generality of the principles we formulate and the specificity of concrete cases; and (2) establishing a clear and credible linkage between core theological beliefs and specific judgments on social issues.

Christian social ethics proceeds most responsibly when it resists a perennial temptation: to pretend to have achieved more moral clarity than is actually possible in a complex world. Even people with similar theological beliefs, when confronted with a practical situation involving multiple parties and complex social institutions, may reach vastly different conclusions about the implications of Jesus' commandment to love our neighbors. "Ambiguity increases with each step toward specificity,"[1] remarks James A. Nash about the task of linking theological beliefs with courses of moral action. It is especially in the ethics of public policy, where "factual disputes and value conflicts block the way" so frequently, that "the linkage is anything but a straight line."[2] Faced with the challenge of sorting out differing opinions about social priorities, strategies and policies, Christian ethicists attempt to discover "satisfactory ways of bridging the gap between the fundamentals of faith and the immediate situation."[3]

In coming to terms with these challenges, Christian ethicists have developed certain useful tools which allow them to distinguish among various levels of ethical analysis and thus to attach the appropriate measure of moral authority to a given judgment. One particularly helpful concept developed primarily by Protestant ethicists facing this challenge is the notion of a "middle axiom." Middle axioms are moral principles of the type which address the "middle ground between general statements and detailed policies."[4] This phrase dates back to the writings of J. H. Oldham in preparation for the Oxford Conference of 1937, and has subsequently been associated with such luminaries as William Temple, John Bennett, Philip Wogaman and Ronald Preston. Preston points out how useful such middle axioms can be, especially in providing a "link between different confessions" and "between Christians and non-Christians in facing a common problem."[5]

Because middle axioms are provisional formulations of Christian social principles, and need not invoke distinctively Christian theological beliefs in staking out ethical positions on worldly matters, they may serve as loci of overlapping agreement, holding the potential to build bridges among social observers of diverse backgrounds. Parts Three and Four of the present study expand upon this claim about the unique power of middle axioms by offering a case study in how they have been used by religious voices in American public life. In Parts Three and Four, we shall explore how the U.S. Catholic bishops' delineation of ethical norms for

---

1. James A. Nash, "On the Goodness of Government," *Theology and Public Policy* VII, no. 2 (1995) 18.
2. Ibid.
3. Ronald Preston, *Explorations in Theology 9* (SCM Press, 1981), ch. 3, reprinted in John Atherton, ed., *Christian Social Ethics: A Reader* (Cleveland: The Pilgrim Press, 1994) 147.
4. Preston, *Explorations in Theology 9*, 146.
5. Ibid., 149.

social welfare policy may serve as a rallying point for the formation of a broader constituency committed to a new and growing consensus on the meaning of distributive justice. The cogency of the bishops' message may be attributed as much to the form of their contribution (namely, through the medium of offering middle axioms) as to the sources of moral wisdom from which they draw (the tradition of Catholic social teaching, as surveyed here in part one).

Ronald Preston does us a further service in voicing a lingering concern about the question of how detailed a statement may be and still remain a "middle axiom." On the one hand, he admits that there are times, such as when a polity is confronted with a clear evil, that a significant level of detail can be included in a middle axiom. Since these principles may contain many details suited to a specific historical moment, Preston advises, "they need to be under constant revision as circumstances change."[6] On the other hand, he characterizes them as benefitting from retaining a measured level of generality, as when he recommends: "For the most part, church bodies as such should hesitate to rush in with a detailed policy on each controversy as it occurs."[7]

The resulting tension may be a creative one, so that the mere existence of some ambiguity in this matter in no way invalidates the general category of "middle axioms" nor any particular one. However, for the purpose of clarity in the present study, it may be helpful to distinguish between middle axioms which are relatively more general (consisting of principles applicable to all societies in all ages) and those which are relatively more specific (policy guidelines appropriate in only certain social contexts). The former will enjoy a higher level of moral authority, since they are conceptually closer to theological sources and universal beliefs that lie at the core of Christian faith. The latter are more provisional and more subject to disagreement and revision, since they are closer to actual policy-making concerns where moral judgments are less clear.

In this chapter, we will consider three principles which fall within the more general category. In Part Three, while investigating the details of the U.S. bishops' involvement in the welfare reform debate, we will examine five principles of the more specific variety. Both sets of principles are grounded in moral analysis contained in Catholic social teaching. Nevertheless, both sets readily display considerable overlap with the social insights of many Christian and even many non-Christian confessions, whether these groups refer to their recommendations as middle axioms, ethical principles, moral teachings or social doctrines.

6. Ibid., 149.
7. Ibid., 148.

1. Social membership must be universal

We have already seen (in our survey of the themes of dignity and solidarity) how Catholic social teaching articulates its version of the common Christian theme of universalism. The inclusiveness of God's love, in creating, redeeming and loving all people as God's children, serves as the proper model for human activity. Social unity is an important good, a constituent part of the common good; it is one of the conditions which is recognized as conducive to the realization of human dignity. As such, the necessity of social unity applies to the national and subnational communities in which people are organized as well as to the universal level of human solidarity. At the very beginning of the century-long documentary heritage of Catholic social teaching, *Rerum novarum* sounds this note when it calls for a social unity that transcends class boundaries: "The poor are members of the national community equally with the rich; they are real component parts, living parts...."[8] When, seventy years later, *Pacem in terris* enumerates the rights and duties that belong to people, it litters its description of the principles of a just social order with recurring words ("all," "every," "each") which leave no doubt about the intention of universal inclusion.[9]

These same two documents may be cited to point out an important tension in the meaning of universal membership: the interplay between equality and inequality. *Rerum novarum*, as part of its effort to combat the appeal of socialism, warns against unrealistic expectations of establishing complete equality among people:

> Humanity must remain as it is. It is impossible to reduce human society to a level. The socialists may do their utmost, but all striving against nature is in vain. There naturally exist among mankind innumerable differences of the most important kind; people differ in capability, in diligence, in health and in strength; and unequal fortune is a necessary result of inequality of condition.[10]

The spirit of this defense of inequality (at least some types of it) seems quite antithetical to the condemnation of inequality found in *Pacem in terris*: "All men are equal by reason of their natural dignity.... Hence, racial discrimination can in no way be justified."[11] The difference, of course, is attributable to the distinction between equality of opportunity and equality of result (or condition). In relying upon this distinction, Catholic social teaching implicitly acknowledges a concomitant distinc-

8. RN 27.
9. PT 8–45.
10. RN 14.
11. PT 44.

tion between those items which are justifiable as morally relevant determinants of distribution (natural endowments, effort) and those items which cannot be justified in this way (such as the effects of racial prejudice) and which should therefore not be tolerated.

The above consideration of morally legitimate *causes* of inequality raises the further question of morally legitimate *levels* of inequality, a matter which touches upon the very possibility of universal social membership. The documents of Catholic social teaching consistently express a concern about the great disparities in wealth and income which prevail in modern society. *Gaudium et spes* decries the tendency for economic development to exacerbate inequalities:

> While an enormous mass of people still lacks the absolute necessities of life, some, even in less advanced countries, live sumptuously or squander wealth. Luxury and misery rub shoulders. While the few enjoy very great freedom of choice, the many are deprived of almost all possibility of acting on their own initiative and responsibility, and often subsist in living and working conditions unworthy of human beings.[12]

Populorum progressio reflects the same concerns in expressing a longing for

> a world where every man, no matter what his race, religion or nationality, can live a fully human life, freed from servitude imposed on him by other men or by natural forces over which he has not sufficient control; a world where freedom is not an empty word and where the poor man Lazarus can sit down at the same table with the rich man.[13]

If universal membership is a fundamental principle of justice, and social unity (its corollary) is an important good, then what public policy strategies might be employed to foster the realization of these worthy goals? Perhaps more promising than any effort of public policy to mandate concrete levels of material accumulation would be the strategy of encouraging the expansion of economic and political participation to all members of society. The theme of participation is increasingly prominent in recent documents of Catholic social teaching. It is frequently portrayed as a remedy for forms of marginalization which undercut human dignity and unfairly isolate segments of the population.[14] The U.S. Catholic bishops gave the concept of participation a central place in their call for a renewed effort to achieve justice within the American economy:

12. GS 63.
13. PP 47.
14. GS 65, 73; CA 52.

Basic justice demands the establishment of minimum levels of participation in the life of the human community for all persons. The ultimate injustice is for a person or group to be actively treated or passively abandoned as if they were nonmembers of the human race.[15]

At stake in the achievement of participation is access to the mainstream of society, the ultimate goal of the primordial Hegelian struggle for recognition. Michael Walzer reminds us that "the primary good that we distribute to one another is membership in some human community,"[16] and to be a genuine member is to enjoy the opportunity to participate in the mainstream. This includes engaging in those social acts which serve at once as sources and as certificates of full membership in society. Judith Shklar identifies two such activities as key to establishing and protecting the status of full adult citizenship in contemporary American society: voting and earning.[17] Although each of these items has a tendency to lose its sense of urgency once it has been attained by a given person or group, nevertheless both remain crucial in enabling someone to be accorded recognition as an independent agent.

Because our concern is with principles which may guide public policies to address economic poverty, we shall put aside the topic of political participation (i.e., voting) and treat Shklar's other item: earnings. The principle of inclusive membership contains important implications for our judgments about the moral dimensions of earning and employment—the practices most central to economic participation in contemporary society. Holding a job takes on added importance when we consider all that is at stake in one's employment status. Clearly, an important way for public authorities to support people's efforts to achieve the good of social recognition is to enhance employment opportunities. This is the public policy strategy which most directly uses legitimate governmental authority to foster self-sufficiency and the other conditions of full social membership. The documents of Catholic social teaching affirm the desirability of government intervention to supplement the private sector in encouraging job opportunities. *Gaudium et spes*, for example, states: "It is the duty of society . . . in keeping with its proper role, to help its citizens find opportunities for adequate employment."[18]

15. EJA 77.
16. Michael Walzer, *Spheres of Justice: A Defense of Pluralism and Equality* (N.Y.: Basic Books, Inc., 1983) 31.
17. Judith Shklar, *American Citizenship: The Quest for Inclusion* (Cambridge, Mass.: Harvard University Press, 1991) 15.
18. GS 67; see also LE 18; CA 52; and EJA 80 (which discusses the right to employment), and 150 (which calls for guaranteeing full employment).

But what about those situations when this path is blocked—when the conditions in job markets or other barriers to employment (such as the existence of full-time family obligations) make the holding of a job impossible or inordinately burdensome for an individual or a segment of the population? Such situations which restrict the ability of potential workers to engage in ordinary methods of earning necessitate reliance upon what economists call "second-best solutions." These are fall-back options which preserve as many of the relevant values as possible. Not all the benefits of paid employment (financial self-sufficiency, participation in the workplace) can in these cases be preserved. Nevertheless, from an ethical perspective it is imperative to preserve those central goods which can be safeguarded: the life, security and dignity of the persons affected and their dependent children. When public authorities act in such a way as systematically to protect citizens from economic insecurity, they are providing what is frequently called a "safety net." The goal of this type of public assistance is to guarantee a dignified minimum of material goods and income security to people affected by unemployment due to age, illness, family situation or economic conditions beyond their control.

Kenneth Boulding notes that "virtually all societies, once they attain a certain stage of development, accept some responsibility for the social minimum below which their members should not be allowed to fall."[19] Catholic social teaching supports this form of income maintenance which protects "the right to security in the event of sickness, unemployment, and old age . . . with benefits sufficient to provide individuals and their families with a standard of living in keeping with human dignity."[20] John Paul II includes this claim within his treatment of the responsibilities that accrue to governments as "indirect employers" in this era of interdependence and socialization:

> The obligation to provide unemployment benefits, that is to say, the duty to make suitable grants indispensable for the subsistence of unemployed workers and their families, is a duty springing from the fundamental principle of the moral order in this sphere, namely the principle of the common use of goods or, to put it in another still simpler way, the right to life and subsistence.[21]

One subcategory of these "unemployment benefits" is the form of income maintenance which in common American parlance has come to

---

19. Kenneth E. Boulding, "The Boundaries of Social Policy," *Social Work* 12, no. 1 (1967) 6.
20. EJA 80.
21. LE 18.

be called "welfare." These are transfer payments and in-kind benefits targeted at low-income families with no other means of subsistence. Unlike Social Security benefits, the provision of such transfers is based upon a means-test, rather than upon a contributory principle which assumes that at least one member of a given family has a history of regular participation in the work force. That these measures have the character of second-best solutions is a truth conveyed by this qualification offered by Brookings Institution economist Robert Reischauer: "The welfare system exists largely as a last recourse, one that picks up the pieces when other systems and institutions fail. Failures in the educational system, in marriages and families, and in labor markets are the major systemic causes of welfare dependency."[22]

People receiving welfare benefits have truly fallen through the cracks in the economic structures of modern societies. Receiving these benefits by no means assures these families access to the mainstream of society, but it offers them at least a decent material minimum so as to keep them from utter desperation. By supplying an income floor which safeguards the lives and health of members of poor families, this assistance serves as a precondition for more substantial progress toward full social participation. A comprehensive solution to the problems of poor families would include sweeping reforms of social systems (especially changes in education and employment opportunities) and perhaps changes in the affected individuals themselves (to prepare them and their family systems to take advantage of whatever economic opportunities do become available). As administered within present institutional structures, welfare is a necessary band-aid, not the full structural solution to the problem of the marginalization of poor families.

There is remarkable overlap between the moral justifications for social provision found within Catholic social teaching and the conceptual frameworks employed by early theorists of the welfare state (Lord William Beveridge, T. H. Marshall, John Kenneth Galbraith, etc.). The historical project of the welfare (or social assistance) state hinges on the assumption by public authorities of responsibility for establishing favorable conditions for national economic performance, including a measure of economic security for all citizens. Key goods are decommodified; social insurance covers the exigencies of life in industrial society, including fluctuations in earnings levels across the life cycle. The people of a na-

---

22. Robert D. Reischauer, "The Welfare Reform Legislation: Directions for the Future," in Phoebe H. Cottingham and David T. Ellwood, eds., *Welfare Policy for the 1990s* (Cambridge, Mass.: Harvard University Press, 1989) 19.

tion are thus granted, on a universal basis (which in many historical cases replaces a class-based system of status) "social and economic citizenship."[23] The recognition of these rights has been portrayed as the latest phase of the historical process which previously accorded to members of Western societies political rights and "civil elements" of citizenship.[24]

Welfare states take many historical forms which vary according to the details of the political developments and class compromises which shaped their central institutions. Some are quite ambitious in their attempts to institutionalize economic planning. Others serve primarily as "broker states," where government plays a greater role in socializing income rather than controlling productive capital. Some, like the U.S., come to rely mostly upon means-tested and categorical rather than universal programs in determining eligibility for social benefits—a situation which tends to stigmatize recipients and to treat those who depend on transfer payments and in-kind benefits as passive clients. But in all cases, the development of welfare states has created powerful instruments for the meeting of "the needs of distant strangers,"[25] an end which is at least *prima facie* compatible with those moral obligations stemming from universal membership as identified by Catholic social teaching. In fact, certain concepts within Catholic social teaching (subsidiarity, socialization and the dual character of property, among others) provide particularly useful insights for welfare states as they grapple with the challenge of simultaneously maintaining adequate entitlement programs and still preserving the human dignity of citizens who are recipients of material assistance.

2. *No person is to be considered a surplus person*

This principle forbidding the exclusion of any is a necessary complement and corollary to the previously examined principle enjoining inclusion of all, for it calls particular attention to the plight of those who are in danger of falling out of the mainstream. The above examination of the call to universal inclusion focused on two central issues in social membership: equality and participation. *Octogesima adveniens* identifies these two as keys to the establishment of a social order conducive to human flourishing ("Two aspirations persistently make themselves felt . . .: the aspiration to equality and the aspiration to participation, two forms of man's dignity and freedom."[26]). The present section will consider some of

---

23. T. H. Marshall, "Citizenship and Social Class," in Tom Bottomore, ed., *Citizenship and Social Class* (London: Pluto Press, 1992) 8.
24. Ibid.
25. Michael Ignatieff, *The Needs of Strangers* (N.Y.: Viking Penguin, Inc., 1984).
26. OA 22.

the implications of the imperative not to frustrate the legitimate aspirations of people for these goods.

We must begin here with the sober acknowledgment that throughout history the relegation of some segment of the population to a status of "unwanted" or "superfluous" has been the rule rather than the exception. Some of these exclusions are based on *ascriptive* status such as membership in despised castes or races which are entered through the accidents of birth. Others rely on *achieved* status (based on behavior attributable to individuals) to justify discrimination. Herbert Gans recounts a litany of terms used to label the classes of people who were judged harshly because of the perception that they filled no socially useful (that is to say, no economically productive) role: defectives, delinquents, paupers, the *Lumpenproletariat*.[27] Perhaps the most telling label is "'residuum,' the prevailing turn-of-the-century English label for the persistently jobless and poor that crowded the cities."[28] An intriguing historical fact (one which underscores how these labels are intimately linked to perceptions of economic usefulness) is revealed in Gans's observation that this label "disappeared almost instantaneously at the beginning of World War I, when the labelled people found jobs in the war economy."[29]

One might hope to discover measures short of waging war to bring such devalued segments of the population into the mainstream. In 1970, Gunnar Myrdal recommended that the United States, faced with its own "residuum," a growing underclass[30] of the unemployed and underemployed, turn to this remedy: "invest heavily and for a prolonged period in the education and the general well-being of its underclass, in order to bring them into the mainstream of the nation's life and work by increasing their ability to become effectively in demand."[31] To the ears of the political realist, such an effort sounds prohibitively expensive, but to Myrdal it is the only alternative to what he calls a "horrible truth": members of the American underclass are so socially distant from the mainstream, and are perceived as such a drain on the resources of the nation, that it would

---

27. Herbert Gans, *The War Against the Poor: The Underclass and Antipoverty Policy* (N.Y.: HarperCollins Publishers, Inc, 1995) 15.

28. Ibid., 21.

29. Ibid.

30. This term was first used in English by Myrdal in his *Challenge to Affluence* (N.Y.: Pantheon Books, 1962) 34. He uses it to describe those whose opportunities for advancement have been closed off by processes beyond their control, and who are consequently "not really an integral part of the nation but a useless and miserable substratum."

31. Gunnar Myrdal, *The Challenge of World Poverty* (N.Y.: Random House, 1970) 407.

be judged a boon in economic and social terms "if all inhabitants of the slums were to vanish."[32]

If Myrdal is correct, this situation stands as a major moral indictment of the nation's failure to achieve an adequate level of social unity. Despite America's celebration of the supposed achievement of political equality, the realities of the social (and increasingly, the geographical) distance between the poor and the mainstream suggest that the U.S. has become a two-tier society, with a significant segment of the population now considered "disposable" by the rest of the society. This situation not only contradicts the ideal of solidarity, but raises profound and troubling questions on the practical level, where we consider the efficacy and stability of our political and social institutions. Aristotle's maxim that political justice is not possible among unequals[33] and the often rediscovered truth that citizenship does not admit of gradations both serve as reminders of how imperative it is to counter the tendency of economic forces to render sections of the population as surplus workers and hence surplus people.

Robert B. Reich exposes new aspects of this problem in his study of the new divisions in the labor force of modern industrial nations. The very nature of the occupations of certain workers serves as a centrifugal economic force, drawing this segment of the workforce away from their fellow citizens. Reich calls them "symbolic analysts," those whose skills allow them to excel in the "problem-solving, problem-identifying and strategic brokering activities" which involve "manipulation of symbols—data, words, oral and visual representations."[34] As the trading of information becomes global, symbolic analysts come to have more commonalities with members of their own class around the world and less to do with their fellow citizens—those with whom they still share, at least in a physical sense, a nation. In actuality, the immediate environment of the residences and workplaces of this elite twenty percent may be separated from their service-worker neighbors by gated community entrances and elaborate security systems; their segregation is physical as well as figurative.

Because of advances in automation and other trends Reich surveys, the affluent are increasingly able largely to avoid daily contact with those who are not in their social group; consequently, this privileged stratum may be less willing to share social activities, invest in public life, and even to make financial sacrifices for those separated from them by such a

---

32. Ibid., 406.
33. *Nichomachean Ethics*, bk. V, ch. 7.
34. Robert B. Reich, *The Work of Nations: Preparing Ourselves for 21st-Century Capitalism* (N.Y.: Alfred A. Knopf, Inc., 1991) 177.

chasm. The ensuing social distance raises profound questions about the future of nation-states and how they may organize social responsibility. Reich poignantly asks: "Are we still a society, even if we are no longer an economy?"[35] The many uncertainties surrounding "the politics of secession" underscore the practical and moral dangers of these centrifugal forces which relegate many to superfluousness.

The documents of Catholic social teaching do not address all these pressing questions about how to arrange social institutions to counter such centrifugal forces, but they do offer a moral compass through at least part of this minefield. We have already seen how they argue for the alleviation of at least certain types of inequality, supplying a moral motivation (if not a detailed strategy) for fostering equality of opportunity for all. We have also seen how Catholic social teaching proposes the advancement of the common good as the rationale for the legitimate use of government intervention. As *Octogesima adveniens* states: "Political power, which is the natural and necessary link for ensuring the cohesion of the social body, must have as its aim the achievement of the common good."[36] Indeed, one passage from the most recent papal social encyclical, *Centesimus annus*,[37] even seems to address some of Robert Reich's concerns about asymmetries in social relations caused by new features of the global labor process:

> Human work, by its nature, is meant to unite peoples, not divide them. Peace and prosperity, in fact, are goods which belong to the whole human race; it is not possible to enjoy them in a proper and lasting way if they are achieved and maintained at the cost of other peoples and nations, by violating their rights or excluding them from the sources of well-being.[38]

There are many thorny issues facing polities and policymakers as they seek to put into practice strategies to prevent social exclusion. Three such issues—each requiring hard-headed prudential reasoning as well as good intentions—seem most prominent. First, the principle which forbids treating people as if they are unwelcome requires specification. What is the proper extent of its application? No matter how generous they are, the people of a given national or subnational community cannot offer membership or assistance indiscriminately to every person on earth, no more than someone with limited resources can extend hospitality to every homeless person seeking shelter for the night. This is a limitation which

35. Ibid., 9.
36. OA 46.
37. Published, intriguingly, in the same year (1991) as Reich's *The Work of Nations*.
38. CA 27.

touches upon matters of immigration policy, the logistics of maintaining control over the boundaries (in both the geographical and figurative senses) of a community, and ultimately the preservation of national sovereignty itself. On such matters, communities must make prudential judgments which are governed by both the attendant practical constraints and the relevant moral principles. As a rule of thumb, the most pressing concerns will ordinarily involve those people who are already physically present within the boundaries of a community; their dignity must be safeguarded before the community reaches out to invite new people into membership.

Second, the principle of inclusion often finds itself undercut by a pernicious psychological dynamic which divides many communities into "givers" and "takers." In receiving those benefits of social membership (such as social provision for material needs) which a given person cannot attain without assistance, that person may also incur a measure of stigma. This is especially so when the person in question is perceived as enjoying these benefits without making sufficient effort to fulfill the corresponding duties and responsibilities of membership as an independent agent. Contributing to stigma is the resentment (in many cases, an arguably defensible reaction) of those who incur great costs and sacrifices in making their own social contribution. Their efforts seem to be mocked by those who receive without giving in return; the uneven distribution of burdens constitutes an offense against commonly held standards of fairness. This is a dynamic which in our age affects a number of U.S. policy areas, including affirmative action as well as social welfare policy. In the practical order, the principle of inclusion runs up against the desire for fairness interpreted as reciprocity. The resulting psychological realities of stigma (attached to recipients) and resentment (experienced by contributors) problematizes the process of extending the social benefits of membership on a universal basis.

Third, the attainment of the ideal of universal inclusion is complicated by human sinfulness. So far, we have not considered any features of persons threatened with exclusion except their humanity and their need. The waters grow murky when we entertain the possibility (indeed, the near certainty) that some of those who are on the margin have committed legal or moral offenses which threaten to disqualify them from greater inclusion. The illegal immigrant, the convicted felon, the single mother repeatedly pregnant with children she cannot support, the unemployed drug addict with no evident ambition to find work—all seem to exhibit behavior which renders them legally or morally culpable to one degree or another. The invidious distinctions which place some in the category of "the undeserving poor" often have persuasive bases in fact, jeopardizing the claim of these needy people to the benefits of membership. Common legal practice allows public authorities to revoke a portion of social benefits (those considered "privileges" rather than "rights") from certain categories of offenders. For example, some convicted felons are not allowed to own a gun, hold public office or qualify for a driver's license. Communities enforce such sanctions against undesirable behavior as methods of maintaining order and as deterrents against future offenses against social standards.

It is, of course, a constant challenge to determine where to draw the appropriate lines in qualifying the benefits of membership to punish past offenders and to deter future antisocial behavior. Since these questions of desert and fairness deal not just with legal infractions but often with moral boundaries (especially in matters of reproductive and work behavior), the task of drawing these lines is properly a moral, not merely a legal one. As a moral task, it invites the contribution of religious traditions and their representatives to apply appropriate theological categories, such as their understandings of sin, grace, mercy, redemption and human dignity. Religious leaders and scholars are seldom experts in all aspects of such policy matters, but their analysis may highlight features of the issues that other observers overlook or fail sufficiently to emphasize.

One example of how a religious perspective may add to a public debate will be explored in detail in Part Three below, but deserves mention here as an example of the complexity of applying the principle that no person be treated as superfluous. Contemporary discussions of welfare policy feature many suggestions for categorical exclusions—cutting off benefits from adults whose behavior society deems undesirable and worthy of censure. Restricting assistance on the basis of such judgments about behavior is defensible from the perspective of strict legal (or retributive) justice. Potentially overlooked, however, is the effect of such policies on those children who are dependent upon these censured adults. It may be just to punish the parents for irresponsibility, but the effects on the innocent children must not be ignored. To deny benefits to otherwise eligible children in this way is to relegate them to the status of surplus people, whose well-being is liable to be sacrificed in the interest of pursuing other concerns, such as meting out justice to offenders.

When religious voices offer a distinctive perspective which lifts up such potentially forgotten concerns as the plight of these children, they recommend to the wider society priorities which grow out of the theological beliefs undergirding their concern for the inclusion of all. Religious voices may also be of service to the wider society by issuing reminders of truths which are universally acknowledged but which are tempting to forget because they greatly complicate policy. In the welfare reform debate, one such truth is captured in the maxim: it is impossible to help innocent children without simultaneously helping their possibly culpable parents.

Even when religious voices are thus consulted, lines excluding some applicants from social benefits will continue to be drawn and offenders will continue to be punished. Nevertheless, by admitting into policy debates some voices shaped by religious sensibilities, we might witness the growth of a greater awareness of the moral hazards of hastily abandoning marginalized groups and of too readily accepting the distinction between "us" and "them." Catholic social teaching is one such voice advocating increased sensitivity to the precarious position of those who, for a number of reasons (some within their control, others beyond it), are in danger of being excluded from vital benefits of social membership. Concerns in the practical order may limit and qualify our personal and corporate responses to the plight of marginalized people, but faith-based voices render the salutary service of keeping the well-being of these persons on the policy agenda.

3. Preferential option for the poor

This principle differs from the previous two in two significant ways. First, it focuses attention not so much on the attainment of the status of social membership, as upon the routine treatment of the least privileged among those already recognized as belonging. The focus shifts from the threat of utter abandonment to marginal adjustments in the distribution of social burdens and benefits. Second, its status within Catholic discourse is different from the previous two principles. Because it has received explicit treatment in numerous documents (albeit only since 1979), there is no need to extrapolate from the documentary heritage of Catholic social teaching in order to crystallize their message in a succinctly phrased, extratextual principle. What remains is the task of identifying some of the central features of the "option for the poor," as well as offering some initial analysis of its policy implications, especially with regard to social benefits and welfare policy.

The use of the phrase "preferential option for the poor" in official Catholic sources begins with the documents of the Latin American Conference of Bishops in Puebla, Mexico in 1979. However, since this theme has conceptual roots in Scripture, it is not surprising to find references to nearly identical notions in previous documents. *Octogesima adveniens* in 1971 offered a paraphrase, "preferential respect due to the poor," in its call for "the more fortunate [to] renounce some of their rights so as to place their goods more generously at the service of others."[39] The opening sentence of *Gaudium et spes* famously identified the Church with the concerns of the poor, but its subsequent calls for the attainment of justice, including the reduction of inequality and maldistribution, contain only faint echoes of the phrase "option for the poor."

The phrase is used and embraced by many official Catholic documents which appear since 1979, including two of the three social encyclicals of John Paul II.[40] *Sollicitudo rei socialis* lists among "the characteristic themes and guidelines" recommended to contemporary persons by the tradition of Catholic social teaching "the option or love of preference for the poor." Immediately upon being named, this priority is linked to concrete actions which are meant to instantiate it:

> This is an option, or a special form of primacy in the exercise of Christian charity, to which the whole tradition of the church bears witness. It affects the life of each Christian inasmuch as he or she seeks to imitate the life of Christ, but it applies equally to our social responsibilities and hence to our manner of living, and to the logical decisions to be made concerning the ownership and use of goods.[41]

Centesimus annus contains a passage in which John Paul II interprets *Rerum novarum*'s nineteenth-century call to improve the condition of workers as a manifestation of "the preferential option for the poor" long before the phrase was coined. Recognizing that the church was engaged in advocacy for the poor in each of these centuries, John Paul notes, provides "an excellent testimony to the continuity within the church of the so-called 'preferential option for the poor'" and to "the church's constant concern for and dedication to categories of people who are especially beloved to Jesus Christ."[42]

It may be somewhat anachronistic to read all the documents of one hundred years of Catholic social teaching through the lens of this recently thematized principle, but it is nevertheless true that the phrase "preferential option for the poor" serves as a succinct summary of a major rationale for the Church's long opposition to inequality and maldistribution. The necessity of advancing the social condition of the poor is a central element in the Church's teachings on such issues as property, the com-

---

39. OA 23.
40. *Laborem exercens* is the exception; in speaking of the "priority of labor," it may suggest but never explicitly refers to the priority of the poor.
41. SRS 42.
42. CA 11.

mon good, and the legitimate use of governmental authority. Its role in defining the agenda of the Church's social involvement has been enhanced in recent years as local and national conferences of bishops have followed the example of the Latin American bishops in speaking more self-consciously of the necessity of arranging institutional priorities so that more of the benefits of social prosperity flow to those who currently possess the least. The growing awareness of the urgency of this priority has, in turn, influenced the Catholic Church's operational understanding of the very word "poverty." Whereas previously it was only spiritual poverty (as in the scriptural phrase "the poor in spirit") which seemed an appropriate concern of the Church, in recent years deep concern for and involvement in the alleviation of material poverty have moved onto the agenda of a broad sector of the Catholic community.

Prominent among these local efforts to explore the implications of the option for the poor is the U.S. bishops' 1986 pastoral letter, *Economic Justice for All*. In a section of the letter entitled "Moral Priorities for the Nation," the bishops specify how such an option should shape American political and economic life. In bolstering the assertion that "the poor have the single most urgent economic claim on the conscience of the nation," the document posits an "obligation to evaluate social and economic activity from the viewpoint of the poor and the powerless."[43] The letter repeatedly calls for a reorientation of economic structures and public policies so that the poor benefit in two ways: first, that their most basic and immediate needs be met; and second, that they are afforded enhanced opportunities to participate in all facets of the life of the mainstream, including dignified standards of living, healthy family life, and greater access to economic power. The bishops' letter is primarily a reformist proposal rather than a call to a radical praxis of liberation. It thus interprets the option for the poor not as an adversarial slogan which endorses class conflict, but as an appeal for social cooperation that will benefit all. It does not recommend the immediate overthrow of structures responsible for poverty, but it does firmly advocate the reform of economic and political institutions that have been complicit in blocking the progress of society's most vulnerable members.

The preferential option for the poor, as a middle axiom, is not specific enough to eliminate the need for prudential judgments about how precisely to achieve the goals it recommends. What forms and combination of governmental and private sector effort are likely to be effective in opening up opportunities? Are the poor helped by attempts at direct

---

43. EJA 86–7.

redistribution, such as transfer payments which provide an income floor, or are such efforts counterproductive because they reduce incentive to pursue other avenues of advancement? Are indirect approaches to redistribution, such as progressive taxation and universal social insurance, more effective in the long-run in lifting the incomes of the most needy? These are clearly matters which depend to a great extent upon empirical data as well as moral principles. But the empirical and the moral must not be portrayed as being somehow in conflict; it is not a matter of choosing between the recommendations of social science and those of ethical analysis. The challenge, rather, is to find creative ways for our moral intentions, guided by such principles as the preferential option for the poor, to achieve effectiveness in the concrete order.

So far, our consideration of the implications of the principle of the preferential option for the poor has been limited to the arena of a domestic economy, where the challenge is to find ways to share the resources of a nation more widely. The same principle may be applied even more inclusively to address the sharing of goods at the global level, where perhaps even greater imaginative resources are required to discern and fulfill mutual obligations among the peoples of all nations. It is this task which John Paul II describes when he reflects on the change in thinking and the re-imaging of the "other" which would be required before the preferential option for the poor could be truly enacted:

> It will be necessary above all to abandon a mentality in which the poor—as individuals and as peoples—are considered a burden, as irksome intruders trying to consume what others have produced. The poor ask for the right to share in enjoying material goods and to make good use of their capacity for work, thus creating a world that is more just and prosperous for all.[44]

Catholic social teaching makes the case for a robust sense of social obligation, different facets of which are expressed by each of the three principles we have examined in this chapter. It is noteworthy that all three of these principles contain an implicit rationale for the distribution of material goods which is grounded in distinctive elements of the Christian tradition. In accord with the Christian affirmation of the dignity of all persons, Catholic social teaching insists that people are owed certain goods (social recognition, a decent minimum) by virtue of who they are, not merely by what they do. In terms of moral anthropology, we might characterize the perspective of Catholic social teaching as one which portrays people as more than exchangers, valued for the goods they produce and the services they perform.

44. CA 28.

In terms of its position on proper criteria for determining distributive justice, Catholic social teaching justifies a principle of (at least some) provision by "need," not just by merit or contribution. John Ryan stated particularly clearly the salience of need as a defensible, indeed an indispensable distributive principle. In contrast to the distributive logic upon which models of pure market economies depend, this Christian perspective judges the needs of people for material subsistence and for social recognition to be morally relevant and legitimate criteria for distributing goods. As Ryan argued in his defense of the living wage, "human needs constitute the primary title of claim to material goods."[45] As Ryan noted, in the practical order, the need criterion is never more than a partial standard, for it becomes impractical unless combined with other titles to goods: distribution according to effort, sacrifice, contribution, etc. Nevertheless, as we turn our attention in the coming chapters to the plight of those whose potential work contributions are not highly valued by society, we will be considering a segment of the population for whom "distribution by need" plays a vitally important role in making possible the pursuit of all social goods, including the preservation of life itself.

Catholic Social Teaching in the American Context

When the Catholic Church in any country addresses issues of public policy, it draws from the rich resources we have surveyed above. In thus acting as a "public church," Catholicism may serve as a catalyst for social change, planting the seeds of a new shared perspective on social policy and broader questions of distributive justice. Of course, the goal is never for Catholic voices to dictate an agenda for institutional reform, but rather to enrich the public debate and offer helpful suggestions for framing a constructive dialogue in which other traditions of moral reflection may make their contributions as well. The ultimate hope is for a convergence of opinion on norms for distributive justice and for an overlapping agreement, at least on the level of middle axioms, about social obligations toward the least fortunate among us.

In order for Catholic social teaching to play this constructive role, it must win a fair and sympathetic hearing in our national dialogue. There is room for optimism on this front, since many of the values proposed in the Church's encyclicals (democracy, human rights, universal economic opportunity and participation) already resonate with many elements of the broad American intellectual tradition. However, there is also cause for

---

45. John A. Ryan, *Distributive Justice* (N.Y.: The Macmillan Company, 1925) 357.

concern about how Catholic social teaching is perceived in the American context. At least three specific objections threaten the credibility of these Catholic resources.

First, the documents of Catholic social teaching might be criticized as being historically conditioned and thus suffering from noticeable lapses of continuity. We have already noted how successive documents adopt positions (such as on the proper role of private property) which vary considerably, and how successive authors add new concerns and frameworks (such as the personalism of John Paul II). As John Coleman writes:

> [T]o see the encyclicals in their historical context is to run the risk of a critical appraisal of papal social teaching . . . . [O]nce we decide to see these documents in historical context, it will not be easy to celebrate them as an absolutely unbroken coherent unity passing from papal mind to papal mind, untouched by the waves of time.[46]

The polyvalence of Catholic social teaching reflects its nature (as a developing moral tool) and its intended purpose of offering modest guidance to the consciences of its hearers. However, this fluid quality may also be perceived as a disadvantage, for it subjects Catholic social teaching to charges of exhibiting a lack of coherence and even of sending contradictory messages.

A second and related objection charges cultural and ideological bias in Catholic social teaching, raising suspicion about the assumptions and purposes of these documents. Even a sympathetic reading of Catholic social teaching cannot ignore questions about how papal social theory reflects the concerns of the specific social location and established power structure within which it originates. Even without suggesting crassly cynical motivations on the part of Church officials, it is possible to view many aspects of Catholic social teaching as products of contingent historical forces and events rather than as elements within a strictly principled system of thought. Catholic social teaching may thus be accused of a misplaced nostalgia for a medieval social order, of a distorted interpretation of the natural law tradition which tends to legitimate an oppressive status quo, and of a systematic avoidance of conflict which undercuts its stated objective to eliminate barriers to the establishment of true justice.[47]

46. Coleman, "Development of Church Social Teaching," 176.
47. A sympathetic reading of Catholic social teaching which nevertheless raises suspicions regarding certain aspects of the Vatican's struggle with post-Enlightenment liberalism is found in Gene Burns, *The Frontiers of Catholicism: The Politics of Ideology in a Liberal World* (Berkeley, Calif.: University of California Press, 1992).

The third and perhaps most serious objection points to internal Church policies and abuses which constitute serious instances of hypocrisy. Catholic social teaching will not receive a sympathetic hearing in the American context if the credibility of the Catholic Church itself is compromised by the perception that its structures and practices institutionalize sexism, clericalism and authoritarianism. As the 1971 Synod of Bishops declared, "anyone who ventures to speak to people about justice must first be just in their eyes."[48] Many American observers detect a dissonance between the public face of the Church (especially in its social teachings which espouse the values of equal human dignity, participatory democracy and collegiality) and what they consider to be lamentable internal Church praxis. While any of a number of ecclesiastical practices might be cited, the most important issue in the context of the United States (as the nation with, arguably, the most advanced feminist movement) is the Catholic Church's achievement of a credible approach to gender equality.

Significantly for our purpose, the documents of Catholic social teaching find themselves in the middle of this arena of contention. Passages from the earliest of the modern papal social encyclicals[49] are often cited as emblematic of the prevalence within Catholic social thought of a static family ideal, organized around male breadwinners and subordinate roles for women, whose social contributions are circumscribed and devalued in ways unacceptable to the dominant sensibilities of contemporary American society. Carol Coston, O.P., an American Dominican, argues cogently that the encyclicals "indicate a definite bias toward keeping women in the home" and fail to acknowledge the features of "women's ways of working," so that "women and their needs as wage-earners [are] not taken seriously."[50] Even the more recent documents tend to ignore the repressive connotations of the lingering legacy of patriarchy and hierarchy in the Church, so the teachings are in danger of sacrificing much of their moral force and persuasiveness when the public at large detects such large disparities between the world of their daily experience and the one portrayed by the documents.

---

48. JW 3.

49. See esp. RN 33 and QA 71 which describe the "proper" role of women as unfolding primarily in the domestic sphere.

50. Carol Coston, O.P., "Women's Ways of Working," in John A. Coleman, S.J., ed., *One Hundred Years of Catholic Social Thought: Celebration and Challenge* (Maryknoll, N.Y.: Orbis Books, 1991) 257, 266.

There is no simple method of response to these serious and often well-founded criticisms. The one sure conclusion we may draw from this survey of concerns is that the future credibility and influence of Catholic social teaching within the American context is inextricably intertwined with the endeavor of ongoing ecclesiastical renewal. Until Church reform addresses these concerns, Catholic social teaching will remain not only a flawed instrument for public policy analysis, but also something of a stumbling block on the path which American Catholicism is following in its effort to become truly a "public church."

Part Two
Welfare Reform in the 1990s: Context, Measures, and Rationales

Chapter 3

The Historical Context of U.S. Welfare Policy

Taken together, chapters three and four examine the welfare reform debate of the 1990s as the context within which Catholic voices, especially the U.S. bishops, contributed their moral analysis. In order to set the stage upon which the most recent episode of welfare reform unfolded, this chapter analyzes just enough of the history and development of U.S. welfare policy to shed light upon the central arguments and novel features of recent policy debate. This chapter concludes with a brief consideration of one of the most frequently debated topics with profound implications for the outcome of welfare reform: the role of private charitable organizations and other voluntary efforts to alleviate poverty.

Because this part of our study is concerned with political and sociohistorical realities rather than theological argumentation, its methodology will be quite different from that of the previous chapter. Rather than justifying certain policy directions through appeals to theologically grounded principles, these chapters attempt to make only the most minimal assumptions in evaluating the feasibility and desirability of policy proposals. As we analyze various policy rationales, we will have occasion to appeal to what is often loosely referred to as "American political culture"—a set of generally shared convictions and commonly revered norms for determining which social practices are fair and desirable. As in any democracy, the convictions prevalent among the American populace play an influential (if not determining) role in public policy formation. Indeed, our public laws may be viewed as a text from which a perceptive observer might glean the underlying social values we share as a nation.

Few Americans would dissent from the small set of convictions which will here be assumed to shape social policy. The most central of these controlling ideas include these propositions: (1) people should earn their living through paid employment if such work is a realistic and available option for them; (2) government should act to shield children from

61

the worst effects of poverty; and (3) public policy should foster the formation and stability of two-parent families. Since conflict among such general guidelines for policy is inevitable, one of the perennial tasks of policymakers is to strike a balance among competing values. For example, a decision to increase welfare benefits bolsters the achievement of the second objective at the possible expense of the first and third; decisions to scale back welfare benefits and restrict eligibility compromise the second objective in the name of pursuing the others.

Another factor complicating policy analysis is that the relative salience and popularity of these shared objectives seem to shift over time, as new eras witness varying climates of opinion among both political leaders and the general populace. This phenomenon seems to constitute at least a partial explanation for the outcome of the most recent reform of the welfare system. While previous rounds of welfare reform produced incremental changes in AFDC program rules, the events of 1994–96 resulted in a radical restructuring of welfare arrangements, including the elimination of AFDC and reductions in many other federal means-tested programs. Although these changes would not have occurred without widespread support among both our political leaders and the general public, it is nevertheless imperative to avoid a false interpretation of the attitudinal shift reflected in the new welfare law. It is not necessarily the case that Americans have simply become less compassionate in their attitudes toward poor families. Alternative explanations are available. It is also possible that the transformation of the welfare debate primarily reflects a general increase in the level of public dissatisfaction with government programs, including greater distrust of the efficacy of federal efforts in fighting poverty.

The present chapter will assume a general continuity in the fundamental desires of the American people in social policy. The nation's support for a new antipoverty strategy (one which strikes a new balance among the social policy goals of enforcing work and providing a floor of income for the "deserving poor") need not be interpreted as an abandonment of the goal of alleviating childhood poverty—the basic objective of six decades of welfare policy. It is upon this item of consensus (viz., some low-income families continue to merit substantial public assistance) that religious voices may construct their future efforts to forge greater agreement about the contours of a principled social policy for a postindustrial America.

The Roots of American Social Policy

A complete survey of the historical developments relevant to contemporary U.S. social welfare policy would include an examination of all private forms of almsgiving and public arrangements for poor relief in all those civilizations that bequeathed a cultural inheritance to twentieth-century America. Even the more modest task of isolating those developments which have most directly influenced the dominant rationales for U.S. social policy would draw our attention at least as far back as the late medieval and early modern English Poor Laws.

Several episodes in the history of English social welfare legislation reveal the consistent tendency for relief arrangements to be conceptually and practically linked with the tasks of establishing discipline within the labor force and developing and sustaining a true market for free labor. The Statute of Laborers, enacted during the reign of Edward III in 1349, attempted to control the widespread practice of begging by restricting the movement and fixing the wages of potential laborers. The measure was a response to the social upheavals of the end of serfdom and the shortage of labor caused by the Black Death.[1] Subsequent Tudor and Elizabethan poor laws "established the principle of a legal, compulsory, secular, national (although locally administered) provision for relief."[2] Those to whom assistance was extended during this era, although presumably unable to work, were nevertheless subject to considerable shame and stigma because of their inability to support themselves. Localities provided a mix of "indoor relief" (in which the unemployed received money and in-kind assistance to help them survive) and "outdoor relief" (which required paupers to take up residence in a poorhouse or workhouse). The need for each, as well as the expense of each, expanded whenever economic conditions worsened.

In 1795, a new poor relief arrangement was tried, first in Berkshire, then more generally throughout England: the Speenhamland system of wage subsidies for farm workers whose earnings left them below the subsistence level. This system of income supplementation had the advantage of shielding agricultural laborers somewhat from the worst effects of the economic upheavals of the dawning industrial age, but it also had the disadvantages of high cost, potential work disincentives and dependency, and complex unintended effects on productivity and mobility which served to forestall the establishment of a national industrial labor market. Thomas Malthus added a new rationale for the repeal of the Speenhamland subsidies. He argued that, according to the supposedly inexorable law of population, overgenerosity could only lead to social disaster by

1. Joel F. Handler, *The Poverty of Welfare Reform* (New Haven: Yale University Press, 1995) 10.
2. Gertrude Himmelfarb, *The De-Moralization of Society: From Victorian Virtues to Modern Values* (N.Y.: Alfred A. Knopf, 1995) 127.

encouraging an unsustainable increase in the number of those living at a level of bare subsistence.[3]

Gertrude Himmelfarb points out that the reforms contained in the eventual New Poor Law of 1834 accepted only some of the recommendations that emanated from Malthusian premises. Rather than repealing all forms of assistance, the new law provided for distinctions to be drawn between those recipients worthy of aid (the "deserving poor," such as the sick, aged or widows with small children) and the able-bodied poor, who did not merit assistance and should be encouraged to become independent. In order to discourage overgenerosity to those not in genuine need and to deter new applicants from seeking relief, the workhouse came to be used as a locus for administering a harsh work-test. Conditions there were to be so severe (indeed, prison-like, as the novels of Charles Dickens attest) that no one would voluntarily choose the terms of poor relief. This rationale for such arrangements is often termed the principle of "less eligibility," whereby the instrument of relief also serves as the test of relief. The New Poor Law became infamous because of the way it degraded and in a sense criminalized the poor, diminishing the freedom and social status of those unfortunate enough to seek out assistance.[4]

Colonial and nineteenth-century American relief arrangements reflected the intellectual legacy of the English Poor Laws. The triumph of the American version of individualism and a distinctive philosophy of economic liberalism failed to challenge (and in fact reinforced) the English tendency for poor relief to serve as a system to denigrate the poor, to draw moral boundaries between worthy and unworthy, and to enforce a rigorous work ethic. The Puritan ethos which constitutes one strand of American intellectual culture gave rise to a "gospel of self-help" which so emphasizes personal responsibility that it eclipses other social values, such as solidarity and compassion, which support public assistance efforts. The desire of these early generations of Americans to relieve the misery of their less fortunate neighbors was no doubt genuine, but was checked by their reluctance to induce the socially destructive consequences that they supposed would accompany overgenerosity. A premium was thus placed on the rigid control of the distribution of social provision, whether by means of "indoor" or "outdoor relief."[5]

3. Karl Polanyi, *The Great Transformation: The Political and Economic Origins of Our Time* (Boston: Beacon Press, 1944), esp. 77–85, 280–8.
4. Himmelfarb, *The De-Moralization of Society*, 131–3.
5. A succinct introduction to this set of cultural issues and categories concerning poverty in America before 1900 appears in Michael B. Katz, *The Undeserving Poor: From the War on Poverty to the War On Welfare* (N.Y.: Pantheon Books, 1989) 9–15.

As members of a frontier society, where opportunity seemed limitless, Americans perhaps found it even easier than their English counterparts to blame the poor for their own poverty. Further, when there are, ready at hand, widely accepted theological justifications to enforce self-reliance and maintain inequality as divinely ordained, there will be a presumption against generous terms of social provision. When prosperity is interpreted as a sign of divine favor, it is morally hazardous to lift economic losers above the level they attain through their own work effort. Against this intellectual backdrop, it was easy for eighteenth- and nineteenth-century American policymakers not only to restrict eligibility and generosity of relief, but also to ignore the structural economic issues which made reliance on social provision necessary for some segment of the population. If poverty stubbornly persists in an increasingly prosperous society, the true need seemed to be for moral reform on the individual level, not for systemic change to address the deeper causes of poverty.[6]

American relief arrangements in this era thus followed the English tradition inasmuch as they reflected serious concern not only for people threatened by destitution, but also for the social goal of maintaining labor force discipline. In the interest of deterring potential workers from dependence on assistance, the institutions and administrators of relief came to regulate the lives of the poor in numerous ways, some of them objectionable on a number of grounds.[7] In her study of how American social welfare policy has affected the cause of gender justice, Mimi Abramovitz recounts the many ways policy has served to regulate the lives and roles of women in particular. The maintenance of a patriarchal family ethic has been an implicit goal of relief arrangements and welfare policy in every era, from colonial times (where the family was considered a "cell of righteousness") to nineteenth-century industrialism (with its moral reform charity efforts to support conventional family life) through the Progressive Era's scientific and environmentalist reform movements and finally to the rise of the casework approach of the social work profession of the current era.[8]

---

6. Katz calls this the "supply-side" view of poverty. He adds that "often despite powerful evidence, [it] has coursed through American social thought for centuries," *The Undeserving Poor* (7).

7. For a compelling account of the interaction among relief-giving, political processes and the threat of civil disorder, see Frances Fox Piven and Richard Cloward, *Regulating the Poor: The Functions of Public Welfare*, updated edition (N.Y.: Vintage Books of Random House, Inc., 1993 [1971]).

8. Mimi Abramovitz, *Regulating the Lives of Women: Social Welfare Policy from Colonial Times to the Present* (Boston: South End Press, 1988).

Relief arrangements as administered by public authorities are not neutral in their social effects, for stigma is attached to all recipients who, for whatever reason, engage in those types of behavior (such as low attachment to labor markets and independence from male heads of families) which policy seeks to discourage. Welfare program rules may be likened to a text which, for better or worse, encodes the values of particular forms of the family ethic and work ethic.[9] In every era, public policy has been not only a means of material assistance but also an instrument of social control which has treated punitively those who flout social standards.

All of these features of welfare policy can be detected in the AFDC program, which came into existence as ADC ("Aid to Dependent Children"), under Title IV of the Social Security Act which President Franklin Delano Roosevelt signed into law as part of the "Second New Deal" on 14 August 1935. Although the Act is rightly considered a major social policy landmark, it would be a serious mistake to view this first comprehensive federal welfare program for families as somehow discontinuous with policy developments preceding it on the state and local levels. Theda Skocpol alerts us of the need to update the conventional wisdom about the narrative of social policy, namely that the New Deal represents a "big bang" of social reform consisting of many unprecedented "extensions of federal power into the country's economic and social life."[10] A less familiar but very influential story is that of the first modern phases of U.S. social provision, which proceeded on two fronts which Skocpol links by noting their common conceptual rationale: they were based upon "solidarities of gender" as opposed to those solidarities of class position which accounted for the development of advanced welfare states in many European nations.[11] The first was a system of generous military pensions for veterans of the Civil War. It was designed to reward soldiers of the Grand Army of the Republic for their service to the nation and to protect them from the indignities of poverty in their old age. The second con-

---

9. In her essay "Women, Welfare and the Politics of Need Interpretation," Nancy Fraser argues than many welfare state program rules, despite a veneer of seeming neutrality, encode an "unmistakable gender subtext" with "a common core of assumptions concerning the sexual division of labor." It is when these assumptions become increasingly counterfactual that programs undergo a legitimation crisis. See Nancy Fraser, *Unruly Practices: Power, Discourse and Gender in Contemporary Social Theory* (Minneapolis: University of Minnesota Press, 1989) 149.

10. Theda Skocpol, *Protecting Soldiers and Mothers: The Political Origins of Social Policy in the United States* (Cambridge, Mass.: Harvard University Press, 1992) 4.

11. Ibid., 528.

sisted of a series of measures which brought the U.S. to the brink of establishing a truly "maternalist" style of welfare state nearly a generation before the New Deal. It included forty-six state-run "Mother's Pension" programs for "deserving" (mostly widowed) single mothers and a federal program (administered from 1921–29 by the Children's Bureau under the Sheppard-Towner Act) to advance the provision of health care for mothers and infants.

These two "precocious social spending regimes" left a legacy of predispositions and attitudes within the collective memory of Americans. As it happened, much of it was negative. Startling levels of patronage and corruption plagued the administration of veterans' benefits. The maternalist programs were discredited by objections to the cost of thus "honoring motherhood" and to the programs' basic rationale, best summarized by the claim that "motherhood creates entitlements."[12] At the very least, these programs demonstrated that political support could be mobilized to enact national social provision for goals identified with the common good of all Americans. The U.S. might still be considered a "welfare laggard" compared to many European nations with developed social assistance programs, but the achievements of the Progressive era had demonstrated that there were possibilities within the American political culture for mobilization beyond what many expected from a nation most frequently characterized as a laissez-faire regime of rugged individualism.

The New Deal and Its Legacy

The centerpiece of the New Deal's social legislation, the Social Security Act of 1935, merits careful attention in any study of subsequent welfare policy. This breakthrough measure may be analyzed in terms of its continuity, as well as several points of noteworthy discontinuity, with previous American social policy. Its provisions for low-income families with absent breadwinners (Title IV) must be viewed against the background of its other measures and within the context of the historical moment that prompted the Act.

If there had been no Great Depression, there would have been no Social Security Act. Sudden economic constriction and destitution on a massive scale in a hitherto prosperous nation prompted a profound rethinking of social policy during the 1930s. The seemingly random distribution of economic misfortune made a mockery of the work ethic which sustained earlier policy approaches. Harry Hopkins's realization amidst

---

12. Linda Gordon, *Pitied But Not Entitled: Single Mothers and the History of Welfare 1890–1935* (N.Y.: The Free Press, 1994), ch. 3.

the severe social dislocations of the depression, that "the poor are not a class apart who are to be pitied, but are . . . just like the rest of us, with the same hopes, aspirations and appetites,"[13] was emblematic of a new appreciation for the structural causes of poverty. New assumptions about the nature of poverty allowed at least some of the poor to be viewed more as victims than as culprits. Individuals or families might suffer dramatic declines in income and wealth for reasons completely beyond their control, as when stock values plummeted, factories closed, jobs were lost, labor markets crashed, crops withered and illness struck. The national emergency sparked a renewed sense of social solidarity similar to the wartime solidarity which prompted the citizens of many European nations to make remarkable sacrifices during armed conflicts and to forge comprehensive social assistance regimes once the struggles had ended.[14]

The "solidarity of emergency" led many to the common conclusion that something must be done to increase income security in the United States. However, many diverse factors came to influence the precise form these measures would take, as Roosevelt's Committee on Economic Security found itself buffeted by ideological and popular pressures on all sides as it attempted to draft what would become the Social Security Act.[15] The major concern of the deliberations was to provide replacement income to the unemployed and elderly poor. These goals were accomplished by the establishment of such programs as Old Age Insurance (popularly called "Social Security"), Unemployment Insurance, Disability Insurance and Workers Compensation. The federal commitment of resources to these programs, based as they are on a contributory principle (in which "attachment to the labor market" serves as the key basis for entitlement to transfer payments), dwarfed in size and scope the grant-in-aid public assistance programs (Old Age Assistance, Aid to the Blind, Aid

---

13. From a speech by Harry Hopkins, 10 May 1935. Quoted in James T. Patterson, *America's Struggle Against Poverty 1900–1980* (Cambridge, Mass.: Harvard University Press, 1981) 46.

14. One contemporary author, looking back upon the drafting during the 1940s of the Beveridge Report which became the cornerstone of the British welfare state, characterizes this development by observing: "Just as there could be no atheists in foxholes, there were no aristocrats in bomb shelters. The common sacrifices of war brought home to the British middle class the unpleasant realities of gross social inequality" (Robert Kuttner, *The Economic Illusion: False Choices Between Prosperity and Social Justice* [Boston: Houghton Mifflin Co., 1984] 32).

15. For a revealing account of these deliberations, especially the racial and gender subtexts which placed pressures on the parties involved, see Gordon, *Pitied But Not Entitled*, chs. 6–10.

to Dependent Children, and their successor programs) which are noncontributory in nature.

There are three especially noteworthy features of this structure set up in the 1930s and still largely in place today. First, it places the American welfare state on a "categorical basis," with distinct programs targeted to address separate categories of need. This characteristic distinguishes the American approach to social policy from those European welfare states with universal programs for guaranteed income maintenance and the provision of basic goods (food, housing and health care) as "rights of social citizenship."[16] In this respect, the Social Security Act displays continuity with the heritage of state-run programs which it largely replaced, for it established a patchwork of programs with varying eligibility requirements, rather than a seamless social safety net.[17]

Second, as already noted, the Act's primary concern was the establishment of a social insurance regime in which the predominant rationale for the distribution of benefits was to support workers through earnings fluctuations in their life cycle (including provision during spells of unemployment, disability, and retirement). This minimized the potential redistributive effects of the legislation and served to support the traditional work ethic. Without a history of attachment to the labor market and contribution to the program funds, individuals could lay claim to benefits only by establishing themselves as belonging to categories of citizens who were not expected to engage in paid employment (the elderly poor, the permanently disabled or blind, and—at least at the time—single mothers with young children).

Third, the system was established in such a way that these latter categories constituted a lower tier or track of a stratified welfare state. The distinction between the entitlements of the upper and lower tiers may be measured in at least three ways. One is in terms of benefit levels. Programs in the upper stratum of social insurance are consistently more generous than the others, providing recipients with a more adequate standard of living than the normally subpoverty level of AFDC benefits.[18] This

16. For a historical and cross-national comparative perspective on modern systems of social provision, see T. H. Marshall, *Social Policy in the Twentieth Century*, third revised edition (London: Hutchinson and Co., Ltd., 1970). An excellent comparison of the features of the welfare-state regimes of most industrialized nations appears in Gosta Esping-Andersen, *The Three Worlds of Welfare Capitalism* (Princeton: Princeton University Press, 1990).

17. Handler, *The Poverty of Welfare Reform*, 20–1.

18. Comparisons of benefit levels across programs are very difficult because of complex factors in the determination of benefit packages, the overlap of multiple benefits and

type of discrimination introduces a peculiar mode of irrationality into the structure of U.S. programs, for it means that children may be divided arbitrarily into categories which receive different treatment. Those "lucky" enough to be the offspring of a formerly working but now deceased parent receive more generous assistance (from the Social Security program) than those unlucky enough to be growing up in one-parent families receiving AFDC.

A second measure is the use of means-testing to limit eligibility for the lower tier of benefits. This criterion introduces earnings disincentives, "notch effects" and other similar complications for welfare recipients. Third, the American welfare state introduces significant stigma into some transfer programs by subjecting recipients to more rigorous, frequent and potentially degrading scrutiny in order to determine initial and continuing eligibility. For example, in the ostensible interest of reducing fraud and establishing more reliable verification of demonstrated need, welfare caseworkers have frequently conducted such intrusive procedures as midnight visits to enforce the "no-man-in-the-house" rule upon single mothers receiving AFDC. The overall effect has been not only to stigmatize recipients of this lower tier of programs, but also to make their very livelihood more precarious by rendering their continued eligibility more conditional and subject to withdrawal than has ever been the case for the upper stratum of programs. In addition, in all three of these instances, the differential effects of these program rules on men and women are quite marked; the highly gendered basis of U.S. social assistance is demonstrated by the fact that women disproportionately find themselves in the lower tier of social program provision.[19]

The Social Security Act surely deserves high praise for institutionalizing an active and constructive role for the state in achieving the social goal of establishing a decent floor of income for many categories of Ameri-

---

variations in state contribution. However, as one benchmark of comparison, consider that in the early 1990s, no state offered AFDC recipients a basic payment that raised their family income above 80 percent of the poverty line. In the lowest-benefit states, the figure is in the range of 40 percent. The average AFDC family of three in 1994 received cash and Food Stamp benefits that bring its income up to two-thirds of the poverty line. These figures are from Sharon Parrott, "How Much Do We Spend on Welfare?" (Washington, D.C.: Center on Budget and Policy Priorities, 4 August 1995). The subpoverty level of AFDC benefits is not the case for most recipients of Social Security benefits.

19. See Gordon, *Pitied But Not Entitled*, ch. 10, for an elaboration of the features of this stratification of programs. The author attributes these features to dominant social attitudes at the time of the institutionalization of the Social Security Act, and laments how their perpetuation has relegated women receiving welfare to second-class citizenship.

cans in a time of dire economic distress. Its implicit acknowledgment of structural causes of poverty was a great step forward, for it challenged the dominant assumption that low incomes result exclusively from the moral failings of the individuals suffering their consequences. Nevertheless, we should not allow the accomplishments of the Social Security Act to obscure its failure to address a number of unresolved issues (such as the needs of groups excluded from adequate coverage) and its tendency to introduce unfairness and even irrationalities into the national system of social provision, as the subsequent history of American social policy attests.

The "Permanent Crisis" of AFDC

As we move now to a brief examination of the lacunae, shortcomings, and unresolved tensions in the American welfare state, we will limit our focus to those items which most directly shaped the recent welfare reform debate, specifically those concerns which prompted the termination of the AFDC program. As we shall see, some of these problematic features of social policy can be attributed to flaws in the original legislation, others to a failure to adapt to changed social contexts, and still others to flawed modes of implementing and amending the Social Security Act. Many of the objectionable aspects of welfare policy in general, and AFDC in particular, may further be attributed to a problematic tendency we already noted in pre-twentieth-century English and American poor relief. This is the tendency for the goal of providing material assistance to low-income families to be compromised by a desire to enlist welfare policy to serve other social goals (such as the enforcement of such moral boundaries as the work ethic and the traditional family ethic) which all too often cut at cross-purposes to the well-being of the economically marginalized.

The seemingly easy task of identifying program goals is complicated by the recognition that policy rationales, social conditions and political cultures change over time. Judith M. Gueron (President of the Manpower Demonstration Research Corporation, an independent agency based in New York), in 1994 testimony before a congressional subcommittee, offered this summary of changes in welfare policy goals over the past sixty years:

> When the federal government got into the welfare business in 1935, the aim was to help poor children. AFDC was intended to give poor mothers the same opportunity to stay at home with their children and out of the labor force that other mothers had. It represented . . . a national commitment to the idea that a mother's place is in the home. Since then, a series of changes—women pouring into the labor market, the increasing costs of

welfare, the growing numbers of single-parent families, and concern about long-term dependency—undermined the 1930s view that welfare should provide an alternative to work and raised questions about the equity of paying one group of women to stay home on AFDC while others were working, often not by choice. The focus shifted toward trying to make welfare a route to work. Welfare reform proposals since the 1970s have sought to balance the original anti-poverty goal against a new anti-dependency goal, always under pressure to minimize costs.[20]

Accompanying this shift in program goals was a corresponding replacement of the original principle of entitlement with a new principle of reciprocal obligation, which gradually subjected recipients to the new expectation that they would engage in either work or activities (such as job training) which would lead to steady employment.

The growth of this new rationale is reflected in the increasing presence within welfare program rules of encouragements for work activity. The 1962 Amendments to the Social Security Act introduced the first work incentives for welfare mothers. It was followed by the institution in 1967 of the Work Incentive (WIN) program which altered benefit formulas to encourage work and mandated that states adopt work incentives for at least a certain percentage of AFDC recipients. Lax enforcement and generous provisions for exemptions prevented these innovations from truly changing the nature of AFDC, despite a series of new regulations and opportunities in the 1970s (under President Carter's Community Employment Training Assistance and the Plan for Better Jobs and Income) and the 1980s (under provisions of the Omnibus Budget Reconciliation Act signed by President Reagan in 1981).

The Family Support Act of 1988 (FSA) was hailed as a promising bipartisan effort to enact a new consensus to transform AFDC from an entitlement into a work-preparation program. However, like previous initiatives, it was ineffective because of a failure to commit adequate resources to making private sector employment feasible and attractive to welfare mothers. In the case of FSA, most of the failure may be attributed to the states, very few of which spent enough of their own funds to draw down their full federal allotment of matching funds under the Job Opportunity and Basic Services (JOBS) program in the years FSA was in effect.[21]

---

20. United States Congress, House of Representatives, Committee on Ways and Means, Subcommittee on Human Resources, *Family Support Act of 1988: Hearing before the Subcommittee on Human Resources*, 103rd Congress, second session, 15 March 1994 (Washington, D.C.: GPO, 1994) 38.

21. An analysis of the failure of these efforts to encourage employment is offered in Gary Burtless, "The Effect of Reform on Employment, Earnings and Income," in Phoebe

Even this sketchy narrative of those events in the history of AFDC which bring us to the threshold of the most recent round of welfare reform indicates the tremendous force of shifting priorities upon program administration. When ADC was adopted, its goal of keeping families intact despite the absence of a male breadwinner was widely accepted, for it reflected family forms and value orientations prevalent in America at the time.

> ADC, along with the Children's Bureau's program for maternal and children's health services, were the least controversial parts of the Social Security Act. To support ADC was, literally, to support motherhood. . . . Almost no one opposed ADC. Its symbolic resonance evoked the most generous emotions among voters.[22]

The alternatives to committing federal resources to social provision for such poor families were considered unpalatable: without some financial assistance, children without resident fathers would be sent to orphanages and single mothers would be forced to enter labor markets on terms considered unacceptable at the time. The status of these recipients as the "deserving poor" was bolstered by the fact that 81 percent of the recipients of ADC in its start-up year of 1935 were widows and their young children, but families started by the birth of an illegitimate child numbered less than 5 percent of recipients.[23]

However, as the makeup of the welfare population changed over the next several decades, AFDC became harder to defend in terms of the maintenance of those moral boundaries drawn by a traditional family ethic. Welfare was increasingly for families sundered by divorce, separation, or desertion. Most recently, a sharp increase in illegitimacy has raised further suspicion not only about the moral quality of the recipients, but about the program itself. AFDC has come to be blamed for acting as a disincentive for work and marriage on the grounds that it cushions the effects of nonwork and promiscuity.

The very nature of these perceptions, as shifting over time, serves to underline a constant in social attitudes among Americans: single motherhood has always been defined as a problem. The tendency to revert to moralistic posturing and "blaming the victim" when this subject is raised may be attributable to a truth articulated in Linda Gordon's observation

---

H. Cottingham and David T. Ellwood, eds., *Welfare Policy for the 1990s* (Cambridge, Mass.: Harvard University Press, 1989) 103–45.
   22. Gordon, *Pitied But Not Entitled*, 254–5.
   23. Ben J. Wattenberg, *Values Matter Most* (N.Y.: The Free Press, 1995) 164.

that "everything about single motherhood is charged with the emotional and moral intensities that saturate social phenomena concerned with sex, reproduction and the family."[24] As long as shared social mores lead Americans to draw sharp moral distinctions between deserving and undeserving poor, our collective social disapproval of single mothers will find eventual expression in political and administrative forms. Even those to whom established programs make a formal offer of social assistance will experience the effects of this "invidious distinction," whether in the form of stigma or the threat that benefits (in any program within the politically vulnerable bottom tier of social provision) will be cut off or made more conditional, as happens anew in every round of welfare reform.

Herbert Gans identifies this type of social disapproval as the underlying but often submerged cause of a periodically renewed "war against the poor."[25] The only real alternative is to institutionalize a true universalism in income guarantees. This is a move which many other advanced industrialized nations have completed (although some have backed away in recent years from particular welfare commitments), but which seems increasingly less likely in the contemporary political atmosphere of the United States. Indeed, the failure of the original Social Security Act to enact universal entitlements to health care, income support and even jobs (as opportunities for earnings and hence the enhancement of social dignity) is sometimes poignantly referred to as "the original sin" of the American welfare state.

Against the background of these reflections on the problematic moral status of welfare recipients, we may interpret the recent upsurge of support for initiatives to move welfare recipients to work in a new light. Welfare-to-work and workfare programs emerge as not just another strategy to assist a needy population, but rather as an attempt to add an entirely new goal and rationale to welfare programs. Alongside the established goals of preventing severe material deprivation and reenforcing social judgments associated with the traditional family ethic, the goal of rehabilitating this population of single mothers is now added. If welfare recipients can be cajoled or even coerced into fulfilling the terms of the work ethic, then programs which encourage and enforce work may possibly drag this segment of society back across the moral boundary, from a status as violators of social mores to one of moral worthiness. The goal seems to be eliminating social deviancy within a family. If this cannot be fully accomplished by adding a male breadwinner, then at least it can be

---

24. Gordon, *Pitied But Not Entitled*, 17.
25. Gans, *The War Against the Poor*, passim.

approximated by forcing single mothers to become self-sufficient breadwinners. Policy affecting single mothers is now oriented not just to establishing "floors" (minimum income entitlements) but also to supplying "doors" (means of escaping poverty through earnings, the strategy of empowerment stressed for other demographic groups in the "War on Poverty" during the 1960s). Increasingly the latter goal is crowding out the former, as politically popular welfare-to-work strategies replace income maintenance approaches to alleviating the poverty associated with single motherhood.

No treatment of the interaction of American welfare policy and social mores could be complete without some consideration of racial issues in policy formation and implementation. U.S. social policy has contained racial as well as gender subtexts in every era, both before and after the enactment of the Social Security Act. State programs prior to 1935 allowed wide discretion to local officials (who enjoyed the prerogative of discriminating between worthy and unworthy recipients) in the distribution of benefits such as mothers' pensions. This situation resulted in great disparities in the assistance white and black families could expect to receive in many states.[26] For a variety of reasons (spanning overt racism, the geography of jurisdictions, social location and employment patterns), African-American women were disproportionately excluded from the category of "respectable widows" who received most of the available assistance in that era.

The Social Security Act, because of political concerns which shaped its provisions and mode of implementation, failed to correct this racial asymmetry. Because President Roosevelt needed the support of influential white Southern Democrats in Congress, he allowed the "weaving [of] racial inequality into his new welfare state."[27] In the upper tier of income maintenance programs, this took the form of excluding domestic and agricultural workers from many programs, measures which achieved the racially motivated goal of preventing public funds from reaching many Southern black workers. In the lower tier of public assistance programs, the desire to prevent black families from receiving welfare benefits led members of Congress from the South to champion a new form of the "states rights" argument. They succeeded in eliminating key clauses in the proposed legislation which set national standards for the ADC program. "Southerners simply would not allow the federal government to dictate

26. Gordon, *Pitied But Not Entitled*, ch. 5; Skocpol, *Protecting Soldiers and Mothers*, 471–9.
27. Jill Quadagno, *The Color of Welfare: How Racism Undermined the War on Poverty* (N.Y.: Oxford University Press, 1994) 20.

standards or set benefit levels. They sought control over any social program that might threaten white domination, so precariously balanced on cotton production."[28] The consolidation of programs in subsequent decades left many racial asymmetries unaddressed, since AFDC has consistently allowed state and local authorities to exercise wide discretion in program implementation. This situation has allowed racial discrimination in welfare administration to persist, varying in its extent from state to state.

It was only with the civil rights movement and "welfare rights explosion" of the 1960s that African-Americans in large numbers began to overcome the systematic discouragement which prevented them from applying for AFDC and receiving the share of benefits to which they are legally entitled. Recent decades have witnessed a closer match between the numbers of black women eligible for benefits and the number actually receiving them; such data constitutes an encouraging sign that we are moving closer to "an equal-opportunity welfare state."[29] While this is certainly evidence of an advance in the level of fairness practiced within program administration, these developments also contain the unfortunate but real peril of sparking a racially motivated backlash against new (though unfounded[30]) stereotype of welfare mothers. In painting the face of welfare black and invoking race to serve as a powerful wedge issue, the program's detractors have contributed to the political delegitimation of AFDC. The racial subtext of the welfare issue is by no means confined to the overt racist motivation of program designers or administrators, but also includes deeply ingrained attitudes of the general public in a racially divided America.

Our consideration of the history of U.S. social policy in this chapter has revealed a number of features of our welfare system which rightly cause concern: the gendered nature of the policy inheritance, a history of racism within programs, and conflicts between such program goals as providing material sustenance to the truly needy, discouraging behavior judged "deviant" by prevalent social mores, and attempting to rehabilitate recipients of AFDC. As America approached the 1990s, only a subset of these concerns from our ambiguous policy heritage rose to prominence in the public eye. Concerns about racial and gender justice were eclipsed by a renewed desire to enforce the work ethic and traditional family norms.

28. Ibid., 21–2.
29. Ibid., 9.
30. Although the percentage of black children receiving AFDC is triple the percentage among white children, blacks constitute a minority (34 percent) of long-term recipients, according to Urban Institute data presented in chart form in "The Long-Term Recipients of Welfare," *New York Times*, 1 August 1996, A23.

These latter goals were converted into new public laws by politicians who openly cited the public's preference for welfare changes which could be accomplished by a partial withdrawal of government from economic life, rather than for policies that would necessitate costly new interventions. The momentum of welfare reform during the 104th Congress was greatly enhanced by such aspects of the contemporary national mood as a renewed desire for budgetary restraint and a rising skepticism about the effectiveness of government in pursuing its policy goals.

The Role of Charitable Organizations in Welfare Reform

In chapter four below, we will examine in detail the provisions of the welfare law of 1996. As a result of this legislation, over the span of the six fiscal years from 1997 to 2002 approximately 54 billion fewer dollars will reach low-income American families through the variety of means-tested federal programs. These cuts in federal spending may be viewed as creating a gap between what poor families had received as income (the sum of their earnings and transfer payments) in previous years and what they will receive in the future. It is never publicly argued that the poor ought merely to accept the lower standard of living resulting from these cuts by reducing their consumption of food, shelter, clothing and other essentials. Rather, attention is usually focused on how low-income families will find new sources of income. Part of the new "income gap" may be filled by increased earnings from enhanced work effort. A second component often touted as the solution to the "income gap" is assistance from private and religious charities.

One clear expression of this "charity strategy" is contained in a policy recommendation from the conservative Cato Institute:

> We should eliminate the entire social welfare system for individuals able to work. That includes eliminating AFDC, food stamps, subsidized housing and all the rest. Individuals unable to support themselves through the job market should be forced to fall back on the resources of family, church, community, or private charity. . . . When it comes to charitable giving, Americans are the most generous people on earth. Every year we contribute more than $120 billion to charity. Surely, we can find private means to assist individuals who need temporary help.[31]

While this prescription of the total elimination of all welfare programs for the able-bodied is extreme, the emphasis on the role of private charity is

---

31. Michael Tanner, "Ending Welfare as We Know It," *Policy Analysis*, no. 212 (7 July 1994) 23.

very much in line with more mainstream recommendations for how the poor may replace the income lost as a result of the welfare reform process. The Republican authors of the "Contract with America" devote an entire chapter of their 1995 follow-up document to outlining an agenda for how private initiative and voluntarism in this "nation of good neighbors" may replace the efforts of a shrunken federal government.[32] The benefits of thus liberating people to engage in civic responsibility may be measured not only in terms of how material needs are met, but also in terms of the spiritual renewal which accompanies broad popular empowerment through the enhanced exercise of individual responsibility. The authors of the "Contract with America" conclude their argument with this look backward and forward in time:

> When we say that we need to rely more on the genius and goodness of all our citizens to foster genuine solutions to our social, economic and moral problems, we are calling for a return to what once was called a "civil society." This is the Jeffersonian notion—long accepted in this nation until the birth of the modern welfare state—that America needed effective but limited government in order to liberate people to engage in civil responsibility. Civic responsibility meant being a good citizen. With amazing clarity of vision, Jefferson predicted that the larger government grew, the more it would crowd out individual responsibility in a civil society.[33]

Of relevance to our investigation of welfare reform are two separate (though related) claims in this account of the role of private charitable efforts. Each has significant bearing on the potential of nongovernmental efforts to be enlisted to fill the "income gap" left by the new welfare law. The first is the invocation of a "golden age" of times past when the flourishing of private charitable works provided for the needs of the less fortunate in society without resort to the impersonal, centralized action of governmental agencies. The second is the claim that government efforts to relieve poverty serve to "crowd out" and displace private initiatives and neighborly assistance. An investigation of the contours and salience of these two assertions, particularly as they pertain to the welfare reform debate, will bring the present chapter to a close.

1. Private compassion and public assistance, past and present

Unlike the second claim about "crowding out" (at least some of the effects of which can be measured in quantitative terms), the "golden age"

---

32. "Empowering Citizens, Communities, and States," ch. 9 of Stephen Moore, ed., *Restoring the Dream: The Bold New Plan by House Republicans* (N.Y.: Times Books of Random House, Inc., 1995) 203–25.

33. Ibid., 224–5.

claim is exclusively a qualitative argument. Nothing will be settled by comparing the relative spending for poor relief by, for example, the American network of "Charitable Organization Societies" at their peak in 1895[34] with the budget of the Department of Health and Human Services in 1995. This matter, on the contrary, is an eminently subjective one, involving the perceived moral significance of the dominant institutional arrangements for poor relief before and after the federal government became involved on a large scale.

It is impossible to deny the difference between the "warm feel" of assistance which is offered and delivered on a "face-to-face" basis and the "cold feel" of that which comes from an impersonal bureaucracy. The former has the advantage of superior responsiveness to particular needs and a personal touch which is more apt effectively to challenge recipients to make sincere efforts toward self-improvement and eventual self-sufficiency. The latter runs into the limits of the organizational cultures of rational bureaucracies which are rule-based rather than outcome-oriented[35] and which seek to standardize expectations and routinize performance, often with disheartening consequences. For example, administrators and even caseworkers within large-scale poor relief programs generally limit their efforts to assist their clients to the narrow parameters of their official job descriptions, such as determining eligibility and processing applications for benefits. All too frequently, the behaviors which perpetuate the dependency of recipients are assumed rather than challenged.

A *Wall Street Journal* editorial column, in the course of pressing an argument for the privatization of welfare, further explicates this contrast:

> Under government entitlement programs, beneficiaries do not have to explain how they plan to change their behavior or even to show a willingness to change. By contrast, the best private charities often make assistance conditional on behavioral changes. Overall, the private sector has shown that only through hands-on management—direct, personal contact between aid giver and recipient—can we help the poor without encouraging dependency.[36]

---

34. For a description of the activities of this distinctive form of nineteenth-century charity, see "Part Three: The Gilded Age" in Paul Boyer, *Urban Masses and Moral Order in America, 1820–1920* (Cambridge, Mass.: Harvard University Press, 1978).

35. On this point, see Lisbeth B. Schorr, "What Works: Applying What We Already Know About Successful Social Policy," *The American Prospect*, no. 13 (1993) 47.

36. John C. Goodman, "Welfare Privatization," *Wall Street Journal*, 28 May 1996, A18. The same author's fuller treatment of this contrast appears in "Why Not Abolish the Welfare State?," *Common Sense* 2 (winter 1995) 63–72.

In a volume frequently cited in the welfare reform debate, Marvin Olasky portrays as a "tragedy" the progressive substitution of depersonalized dependence for genuine compassion within American relief arrangements. This alleged failure is made especially poignant when Olasky points out that the root meaning of the very word "compassion" denotes a sense of "suffering with" the needy—something largely impossible within the context of a bureaucratic approach to poor relief.[37] Perhaps the root problem is precisely that bureaucracies must treat the people they serve as "clients" rather than neighbors. The possibilities for personal challenge and moral uplift come to be sacrificed by the necessity in this context of eschewing moral judgmentalism, guaranteeing professional standards and insuring uniform operating procedures.

Olasky's work serves as an instructive reminder of the virtues of an ethic of private initiative, on the one hand, and of the dangers of the "helping conundrums" or "Good Samaritan dilemmas" that accompany indiscriminate giving (a risk perennially encountered in large-scale programs, whether public or private), on the other. Nevertheless, it remains impossible to turn back the clock and pretend to live in simpler times, when neighbor-to-neighbor assistance constituted (what some dubiously claim to have been) an adequate response to social needs. The most constructive approaches in this regard, then, are those which seek to translate Olasky's insights into an agenda for incremental improvement in the actual system of social provision we have inherited.

In this project, Michael Walzer supplies a useful orientation. His analysis of how the framework of contemporary relief arrangements can be improved proceeds from two complementary starting points. First, he acknowledges the constraint that "bureaucracy is unavoidable given the size of contemporary political communities and the range of necessary services."[38] Second, he insists that "some modern substitute is sorely needed" for the essential "mobilization of altruistic capacities" which characterized social provision in earlier times, before the "professionalization of social work" displaced efforts which proceeded on a voluntary basis.[39] If we cannot duplicate the virtues associated with a system of exclusively private giving once we enter an era where necessarily public ef-

---

37. Marvin Olasky, *The Tragedy of American Compassion* (Washington, D.C.: Regnery Gateway, 1992), esp. 192–7. See also Olasky's subsequent work *Renewing American Compassion: How Compassion for the Needy Can Turn Ordinary Citizens into Heroes* (N.Y.: Free Press, 1996).

38. *Spheres of Justice* (N.Y.: Basic Books, 1983) 94.

39. Ibid.

forts are financed by such impersonal, coercive means as taxes, we can at least hope to approximate these virtues.

Walzer's suggestions for how state action might be able to recapture the vital and beneficial aspects of mutual aid are described in his later essay, "Socializing the Welfare State."[40] Nationalization of social provision need not cancel out such goods as local empowerment and voluntary involvement in distributive arrangements, as long as the political system remains committed to the principle of broad participation in the processes of decision-making and delivery of welfare services. Such desirable elements as hope, care, accountability, discernment and involvement can be preserved, Walzer maintains, within the context of "a lively and supportive welfare society framed, but not controlled, by a strong welfare state."[41]

Walzer is not alone in articulating a "both/and" rather than an "either/or" approach to the roles of government and private agencies of civil society in poor relief. While recent years have witnessed prominent politicians[42] staging legislative and even electoral campaigns based on the principle that charitable voluntarism could serve as a substitute for government antipoverty efforts, it is more common to encounter the opinion that government assistance plays an irreplaceable role. A number of editorial writers and other commentators have accused Olasky and his disciples of a false nostalgia for an era of compassion that never existed.[43] It has frequently been argued with considerable cogency that private philanthropy and compassion were no more adequate in the time of Charles Dickens or Herbert Hoover than they would be today in the absence of government assistance.

Regardless of one's interpretation of this aspect of history, we can draw from this discussion at least one helpful clarification: a new appreciation of the distinction between what is *desirable* in social provision and what is *necessary* (i.e., what is experienced as an inevitable though regrettable constraint). In the former category belongs, among other items, an enhancement of the healthy role which "mediating structures" play in American life. Ideally, relief arrangements would follow

---

40. In Amy Gutmann, ed., *Democracy and the Welfare State* (Princeton: Princeton University Press, 1988) 13–26.

41. Ibid., 26.

42. Including Lamar Alexander, William J. Bennett and Senator Dan Coats. Each has proposed tax credits to reward philanthropy and encourage the privatization of compassion.

43. For an overview of these critiques of Olasky's work, see Joseph P. Shapiro, "Marvin Olasky's Appeal: A Golden Age of Charity," *U.S. News and World Report*, 9 Sept. 1996, 52–3.

the contours of the voluntary associations (churches, neighborhood groups, professional and charitable organizations, etc.) which form the texture of civil society. Provision for the neediest members of our society would spring organically from the structures which nourish the whole of social life. However, in the complex, large-scale, increasingly mobile society of the present, informal and voluntary arrangements would simply be unable to supply the accountability necessary to distribute fairly and widely the sacrifices necessary to provide for the needy. Unless the mechanism of universal taxation continues to enforce individual contributions to this necessary social function, members of society will surely yield to the temptation to become "free riders" on the sacrifices of others. Without the accountability which only government can insure, citizens would face no effective sanctions against evading their share of responsibility for the least fortunate. Without government involvement in social welfare provision, it would become a certainty that many of the neediest would fall through the cracks.

It is hardly original to argue for the necessity of balancing the contributions of local/voluntary efforts and national/public oversight. The need constantly to reaffirm this equilibrium is partially responsible for the writing of the Preamble of the U.S. Constitution, with its list of social goals which, history demonstrates, only a strong national government can successfully pursue. It likewise forms the basis for the Roman Catholic principle of subsidiarity, the prudential guideline (introduced in chapter one above) for the sharing of authority at various levels. Attention to the necessity of this equilibrium is also quite evident in Protestant social thought, particularly in post-Calvinist federalist theory. Communities enact care for their members through a variety of instruments, both public and private in nature. Social responsibility is adequately exercised only when several avenues of assistance to the needy remain open.

2. Does government "crowd out" private charitable activities?

Is it true, then, that government programs "crowd out" the efforts of private charities, discouraging the voluntary efforts of citizens (acting as individuals or in nonprofit organizations) to come to the relief of their neighbors? If so, then should we accept the corollary of this claim, namely that the withdrawal of federal funds will spark a flood of new giving which will fill the "income gap"? Or is it more accurate to say that government efforts serve an indispensable role which nonprofit charitable organizations can at best hope to complement? How shall we evaluate "Olasky's law," that "bad charity" (impersonal government assistance) drives out good (private neighbor-to-neighbor help)?[44] On this set of questions, unlike the previous inquiry, it is possible to compile some conclusive quantitative data which support certain courses of action over others suggested in the context of the welfare reform debate.

One relevant set of data involves the sums spent by government and by private charities on poor relief each year. According to estimates from the Congressional Budget Office,[45] government at all levels spends $290 billion each year on the entire panoply of programs to assist low-income people. Of this amount, $208 billion comes from Washington, representing 15 percent of all federal outlays. By contrast, charitable donations nationwide hover around an annual level of $120 billion. Of course, these raw figures are only marginally helpful for our analysis, since each includes many types of resource flows not at all relevant to the welfare system. For example, the government budget figures include spending (38 percent of the total) on means-tested medical aid and some categories of assistance (such as energy subsidies) to those living at levels well above the poverty line—items peripheral to welfare reform. In fact, based on 1994 statistics, only 5 percent of all federal entitlement spending actually reaches AFDC families, which are the focus of the welfare reform debate. Conversely, very little of the total figure for charitable donations is targeted for social services and income maintenance for the poor. Most private donors earmark their contributions to their favorite charities, which most often include the arts, hospitals, medical research, universities, private schools and a variety of other institutions and causes which hardly benefit the welfare population at all.

While the above figures are instructive in providing a general sense of the magnitude of the challenge private charities would face if asked to replace the federal social safety net entirely, a more precise gauge of the actual new demands on charities would limit its focus to the size of proposed government spending reductions on the poor. Several studies published during the 104th Congress suggest that it is unrealistic to expect charities to meet this additional burden. Research conducted by Independent Sector, a coalition of nonprofit foundations and charities, indicates that the array of federal cuts (at least those proposed during 1995 budget deliberations) in assistance to the poor could not be replaced by private

---

44. This parallel to Gresham's law is introduced in D. Eric Schansberg, *Poor Policy: How Government Harms the Poor* (Boulder, Colo.: Westview Press, Inc., 1996) 153. Chapter 15 of this work is a spirited defense of Olasky's strategy for seizing the moral high ground in the welfare reform debate.

45. The figures cited in this paragraph are from 1992 and are compiled in Parrott, "How Much Do We Spend on Welfare?," 3–13.

nonprofits, even if the level of contributions doubled. A Twentieth Century Fund study entitled "Patterns of Generosity in America" similarly found it highly implausible that the "income gap" created by proposed federal cuts would be filled by resources generated by private giving. While the level of donations to charities in the U.S. has in recent decades remained fairly constant, at around 2 percent of personal income, replacing the lost federal funds would require this figure to make a huge and unprecedented leap to 5 percent of income.[46] The numbers simply do not support the claims of Olasky and his followers that the private sector can be expected to make up the difference. These conclusions are confirmed by some calculations published by Rev. Fred Kammer, president of Catholic Charities USA. If the religious community alone were expected to make up for the proposed cuts in government social spending over the next several years, the task of replacement would require an average annual increase of $225,000 in resources devoted to charitable works from each of the nation's 258,000 churches, synagogues and mosques. As a point of comparison, the average total budget of a congregation is only $100,000 per year.[47]

A final set of statistics must be considered in evaluating Olasky's theory that government spending displaces private charitable efforts. Some key figures regarding the budgets of nonprofits suggest that government assistance itself is an indispensable resource for the providers of charitable social services. These statistics establish that private charities are not as "private" as is frequently assumed, but rather draw a large share of their operating budgets directly or indirectly from government funding. Of the $87 billion which private charities project they will spend in 1996 for social services (such as homeless shelters, soup kitchens, foster care for children, refugee resettlement, training programs for the unemployed, etc.), half (50.1 percent) comes from federal funding.[48] Each of the nation's three largest religious-affiliated social service agencies (Lutheran Social Ministries, Catholic Charities USA, and Jewish Federations) receives between 54 and 62 percent of its operating budget from

---

46. The findings of both of these reports are summarized in Peter Steinfel's, "As Government Aid Evaporates, How Will Religious and Charity Organizations Hold Up as a Safety Net for the Poor, the Sick and the Elderly?," *New York Times*, 28 Oct. 1995, 11.

47. This and other assessments of the future role of religious organizations in social services are reported in Joseph P. Shapiro, "Can Churches Save America?," *U.S. News and World Report*, 9 Sept. 1996, 46–51.

48. Figures are from a study by Independent Sector, as reported in Milt Freudenheim, "Charities Say Government Cuts Would Jeopardize Their Ability to Help the Needy," *New York Times*, 5 Feb. 1996, B8.

government sources.[49] To an extent which often exceeds public awareness, Washington relies upon private charities to serve as an important component of the delivery system it utilizes in providing many types of social services to needy individuals and families.

These data reveal the existence of a delicate private-public partnership in America's poor relief arrangements. What emerges is a more complex picture of the present and potential role of charitable organizations than is allowed for in the less nuanced claims of "Olasky's law." Not only will private charities be unable to substitute for government cuts such as those in the new welfare law, but their existing antipoverty efforts will be seriously undercut by even a partial abdication of the federal commitment to the poor. Government should not be perceived as an alternative to private charities, much less as a hostile force threatening to drive them out of operation, but rather as a partner and important funding source which allows nonprofits to perform the tasks which they do best.

By supplying the income maintenance measures which constitute the basic social safety net, government empowers religious and charitable organizations to provide the subsidiary services (counseling, community development, skills training, family crisis assistance) which they deliver most effectively. If the federal government withdraws significantly from this delicate partnership, private charities would surely be swamped with massive new demands for food, shelter and other basic needs, and the distinctive contributions they currently make to the poor would be compromised. At stake is not only the reliability of vital social services for the needy, but the very character of these charitable groups. If forced by drastic welfare cuts to shift their focus toward primarily material and emergency needs, these organizations risk becoming just the type of impersonal mechanisms for resource distribution which government bureaucracies have become.

Another concern which demonstrates that the privatization of social services is not a realistic alternative touches upon the matter of the distribution (by geography, ethnicity and category of need) of assistance. When it enacts the principle of entitlement (or at least means-testing on a universal, color- and place-blind basis), government serves as a guarantor that, by and large, all material needs will be considered on an equal basis. A government withdrawal from social provision which would cede the primary responsibility for poor relief to private organizations would constitute a danger to racial and other demographic groups whose needs might easily be overlooked. One of the principle features of private,

---

49. Ibid. The income figures are from 1994, as reported by Independent Sector.

voluntary giving is that, for better or worse, donors choose their recipients. No matter how well intentioned, any movement toward privatization is bound to overlook or underserve some social groups—segments of the population identified on the basis of ethnicity, region or other criteria. One sociologist reports these findings of her research on the behavior of wealthy donors to philanthropic causes:

> Such people do not necessarily choose institutions that are the "best" or most needy, or by weighing philosophical arguments. By its very nature, the urge to give does not respond to social issues in a balanced and equal way. This means that organizations whose work may not correspond to the concerns of wealthy benefactors will be at a disadvantage, regardless of their quality or importance. Many groups fear that they will be unable to find enough money to fill the gaps left by cut-backs.[50]

Not only would it be impossible for private charities to substitute for a massively diminished federal role in social services, but few observers would welcome the effects of this substitution even if it were possible. A federal withdrawal would exacerbate existing inequities, present new insecurities to the poor, and compromise the desirable characteristics of religious and private philanthropic organizations.

Support for the privatization of poor relief is part of the larger argument we will evaluate in the next chapter: that radical welfare restructuring such as the dismembering of AFDC is in the long-term interest of low-income Americans, so that it will benefit the poor to be liberated from a government-run welfare system which traps them in poverty. This pattern of thought features a defense of the necessity of short-term hardship in the hope that it will actually help the poor in the long run by altering their behavior. As we shall see, this approach to welfare policy supplies the underlying assumptions behind the major features of the new welfare legislation.

---

50. Francie Ostrower, "The Rich Don't Give Block Grants," *New York Times*, 11 Jan. 1996, A25.

Chapter 4

The Welfare Law of 1996

By the early 1980s, the perception that the welfare system was in crisis was almost universal. A litany of statistics and disturbing trends—including rising AFDC rolls, program costs, and rates of illegitimacy—were frequently cited as proof that the system was broken. The incremental reforms of the previous decades, including the most recent federal welfare legislation, the Family Support Act of 1988, seemed ineffective in the face of the huge challenge. The status quo had almost no defenders remaining; even many liberal Democrats cheered candidate Clinton's 1992 promise to "end welfare as we know it." In the face of this crisis of legitimacy of AFDC and its allied programs, the question facing politicians was no longer whether to undertake ambitious reforms, but rather precisely how to go about a dramatic restructuring of U.S. welfare policy.

The intellectual underpinnings of drastic versions of welfare reform had been supplied during the 1980s by the writings of Charles Murray, Lawrence Mead, George Gilder and others. However, the actual agents of welfare reform turned out to be the new Republican congressional majority, elected in 1994 on the strength of its "Contract with America," a document which included a welfare plank entitled "The Personal Responsibility Act." To keep their promises on welfare, Speaker Gingrich and his allies speedily introduced their welfare proposal into the 104th Congress as bill H.R. 4 in January 1995. This plan of the Republican House leadership quickly eclipsed a number of rival bills (including Clinton's own long-delayed proposal which had languished in Congress since June 1994, even while he enjoyed a Democratic majority). The original version of H.R. 4 passed the House within Gingrich's first hundred days as Speaker, but it took sixteen more months, two vetoes and a number of revisions and amendments before it was signed into law by President Clinton on 22 August 1996. Despite the compromises and changes the bill underwent during a series of legislative battles (at the committee level, in the full Senate and in interhouse conference committee), the welfare bill's basic provisions remained basically the same. They were described by this list which appeared in a March 1994 document of the Republican Party:

1. Require work for benefits.
2. Turn back most of welfare to the states to encourage experimentation and cost-effectiveness.
3. Stop subsidizing illegitimacy.
4. Make welfare a temporary safety net, not a lifetime support system.
5. End the open-ended entitlement feature of welfare by block-granting programs to the states and establishing enforceable spending caps.
6. Renew the vital role of private institutions, such as charities, Boys and Girls Clubs, and neighborhood groups to serve as support networks.[1]

The organizing principle of the present chapter is based upon this list, altered slightly by combining allied items two and five, appending some miscellaneous considerations in four added sections and dropping item six which was considered in the previous chapter. Much vociferous public debate, both within government and in numerous other forums and media, has subsequently revolved around the eight features of the welfare reform legislation to be analyzed below: (1) block-granting; (2) time limitation of benefits; (3) work requirements; (4) anti-illegitimacy measures; (5) other new conditions on benefits; (6) nonwelfare provisions of the new law; (7) the law's probable effects; and (8) what is missing in the new law.

In each section, the task will be to describe the provisions of the new welfare law and to characterize the social, behavioral and philosophical assumptions behind them. These provisions, diverse as they are, constitute a unified welfare policy strategy. For the purposes of the moral analysis of subsequent chapters, we will be interested to contrast this newly adopted strategy to the policy it replaces, which included categorical income guarantees for poor families. By investigating the rationale behind the new law, we will gain some insight into the content and framing of the welfare reform debate to which religious voices, particularly the U.S. Catholic bishops, sought to make a constructive contribution.

1. The block-granting of welfare

This aspect of the new welfare law is not just one item among the others on the list of reforms, but constitutes the framework of all the other policy innovations. Block grants have for decades served as a mechanism

---

1. Stephen Moore, ed., *Restoring the Dream: The Bold New Plan by House Republicans* (N.Y.: Times Books of Random House, Inc., 1995) 170.

for standard-setting and financing, one of several arrangements (alongside the more targeted categorical grants and the less restrictive general-purpose grants) for project management and revenue sharing between the federal government and state and local jurisdictions. The topic of "the new federalism" had appeared sporadically on the national agenda for decades before the "Contract with America." Presidents Nixon and Reagan had developed initiatives under this rubric to alter the sharing of roles and funds between the various levels of government.[2]

The rhetoric supporting block grants suggests that a devolution of funding and decision-making authority toward lower levels of government improves efficiency and responsiveness to local needs. To reverse the trend toward centralization, it has been argued, is a prerequisite to serving people more effectively than the federal bureaucracy is able. However, as research conducted by Michael J. Rich demonstrates, within redistributive programs with funding and authority shared by multiple levels of government, "the balance between accountability and flexibility" is a highly complex phenomenon.[3] Careful consideration of the history of those arrangements which constitute alternatives to block grants suggests that it is by no means a foregone conclusion that Washington is a poor partner for states in their efforts to assist low-income citizens, as proponents of block-granting to reduce the federal role would contend.[4]

By 1995, newly elected majorities of Republicans in Congress and in the statehouses (speaking through the influential National Governors' Association) were registering their support for transforming the funding and administrative structure of AFDC. The program had for decades been a cooperative venture between states and the federal government in the form of an open-ended matching grant. According to this arrangement, the states were required to match federal expenditures, with the matching rate varying somewhat according to a state's fiscal capacity.[5] In the interest of increasing state flexibility and discretion in its programs for poor

---

2. See Timothy Conlan, *New Federalism: Intergovernmental Reform from Nixon to Reagan* (Washington, D.C.: The Brookings Institution, 1988); Paul E. Peterson, *The Price of Federalism* (Washington, D.C.: The Brookings Institution, 1995).

3. Michael J. Rich, *Federal Policymaking and the Poor: National Goals, Local Choices and Distributional Outcomes* (Princeton: Princeton University Press, 1993) 341.

4. An influential and spirited statement of the arguments for governmental decentralization is found in Newt Gingrich, *To Renew America* (N.Y.: HarperCollins Publishers, Inc., 1995), ch. 2. In this bestseller, the Speaker of the House not only lists the fiscal and spiritual advantages of dramatically curtailing the role of the federal government, but mounts a case for devolution by citing the Tenth Amendment to the U.S. Constitution.

5. Poorer states with traditionally low AFDC benefits thus received a greater federal matching share than high-benefit states. Despite this sliding matching formula, low-

families, welfare reformers were calling for replacing the matching grants (the mechanism which gave AFDC its entitlement nature) with block grants, a system which distributes a fixed sum to each state in a given year according to a predetermined formula. Under a block grant system, there is generally no requirement that states match federal funds, although the new welfare law includes provisions requiring states to demonstrate a "maintenance of effort" by spending at least 75 percent of what they previously spent on poor relief.

The final version of the new welfare law in effect abolishes AFDC and replaces it with a new form of federal-state cooperation. States will receive capped block grants called TANF (Temporary Assistance for Needy Families). At the time of the bill's passage, Congress determined the actual shares (out of a combined annual TANF pool of $16.4 billion) which each state will receive through 2002. States enjoy increased freedom from federal oversight to design their own programs, but are still required to submit annual reports to the Department of Health and Human Services to document how they have used these federal monies to support poor families with benefits, education, jobs programs, social services, and program administration. Other block grants for child care and social services will also continue to be divided among the states, which retain some discretion to transfer fixed percentages of funds among these categories. States will compete for some additional funds, called "high performance grants," which reward those states which achieve the highest success rates in meeting such program goals as reducing illegitimacy and moving welfare recipients to work. While the new block grants are far less "categorical" (in the sense of being targeted for narrow purposes and containing uniform federal standards for program administration) than previous welfare funding, they nevertheless introduce some new restrictions. For example, states are in some cases discouraged (by financial penalties) and in other cases legally prohibited from using funds to assist some newly ineligible recipients (as described below).[6]

---

income children in Mississippi (the lowest-benefit state) received only 20 percent of the federal matching funds reaching similar children in the most generous state, Connecticut. The disparity in the actual federal dollars per capita which a state "draws down" under such open-ended matching grants as AFDC is due to widely varying spending commitments made by the states themselves. The above statistics and analysis are from Robert D. Reischauer and R. Kent Weaver, "Financing Welfare: Are Block Grants the Answer?" in R. Kent Weaver and William T. Dickens, eds., *Looking Before We Leap: Social Science and Welfare Reform* (Washington, D.C.: Brookings Institution, 1995) 23.

6. Two excellent sources providing summaries of the new law are: Jeffrey L. Katz, "Welfare Overhaul Law," *Congressional Quarterly Weekly Report*, 21 Sept. 1996, 2696–2705;

Much controversy has been generated by the proposal to write into law this transition from the entitlement-based system of AFDC to a block grant system which shares fixed federal TANF grants with states. A 1995 study conducted by the Brookings Institution[7] uses the following four policy goals as a framework to evaluate the advantages and disadvantages of shifting to a block grant approach for federal welfare policy.

First is the goal of promoting innovation and evaluation of possible improvements in welfare policy. It has been argued that the use of block grants would free states to experiment with new approaches for encouraging the social goods of work effort and family stability. The successes of pathfinder states might then be repeated on a national scale. In response to this suggestion, opponents of block grants emphasized the risk involved in such broad removal of federal oversight from welfare programs. The Clinton administration sought to accomplish the same goal through an alternative means: by approving a series of waivers (granted though the Department of Health and Human Services) allowing states the ability to experiment with novel welfare program features according to state requests. By expediting the waiver process (forty states had received at least one waiver by the time the welfare bill was finally signed), Clinton sought to accomplish the policy goal of encouraging state experimentation in a more incremental way even before the block grant approach was adopted into law. Opponents of block-granting welfare cite this as evidence that the goal of experimentation and innovation is not incompatible with retaining the entitlement nature of AFDC, and does not require new funding mechanisms with unknown effects.

A second policy goal is preventing what has been widely called "a race to the bottom." One risk associated with the block grant proposal is that this new funding arrangement may create incentives for states to reduce welfare spending (by restricting eligibility and lowering benefit levels) in order to make its welfare programs less attractive to present and potential recipients. High-benefit states fear becoming "welfare magnets" as a new funding system exacerbates previous disparities in benefit levels and threatens to trigger interstate migrations of recipients. Concern about this troubling prospect prompted Congress to include the "state maintenance of effort" provisions in the new law. Critics argued that only a

---

and David A. Super and others, "The New Welfare Law" (Washington, D.C.: Center on Budget and Policy Priorities, 14 August 1996). The analysis above draws from both.

7. Reischauer and Weaver, in Weaver and Dickens, *Looking Before We Leap*, 13–26. The authors conclude that the shortcomings of a block grant approach greatly outweigh any advantages it might offer.

"maintenance of effort per capita" (a measure never seriously considered for inclusion in the final bill) would truly protect poor residents of budget-strapped states once low-income families had been stripped of their federal entitlement. Of all the concerns about the potentially dangerous effects of devolution, the "race to the bottom" may be the most serious and hardest to predict.

A third policy goal is the equitable distribution of funds to states and individuals. Efforts to pursue this objective are motivated by the common desire to establish some limits in the state-to-state variation of benefit levels. There have always been high-benefit and low-benefit states, even under the previous AFDC funding mechanism which utilized a system of open-ended matching grants which tied federal contributions to state funding commitments. In the congressional bargaining over TANF grant distribution, the states hammered out a distributional formula which perpetuates most of the inequities in per capita federal funding reaching poor residents of each state. As a result, there is still far more federal money available for the average poor child in Connecticut, for example, than there is for a similar child in Mississippi. Additional inequities will surely accrue to residents of states with higher than average rates of population growth, despite some efforts in the final versions of the bill (including the establishment of a contingency fund for financially pressed states) to correct for this variability. Nevertheless, any block-granting formula which divides aid to states on any criteria besides the actual level of need of the poor families in a given state is based on a principle of justice which is counterintuitive.

A fourth goal of welfare funding mechanisms is to pool the risk of economic difficulties, such as the hardships which accompany cyclical or regional recessions. When recessions reduce the number of jobs available, they increase the need for public funds for poor relief. Unfortunately this usually occurs at precisely the time when state revenues drop off because, in reducing earnings and production, recessions also reduce a state's tax base. Because of its entitlement nature, AFDC served as a countercyclical measure in the tradition of neo-Keynesian macroeconomic policy, for it expanded government spending to match whatever level of need might be generated by recessions. Since TANF block grants are capped, they cannot exhibit this flexibility to adapt to changing economic conditions. No new federal wefare funds flow into a state during a recession, whether of the cyclical or regional variety.

In order to deal with this concern (i.e., that the new welfare system will be unable to transfer the harmful effects of recession to any place besides states or poor families themselves), the authors of the bill included two measures designed to alleviate this risk. First, a contingency fund will make available to states with high rates of unemployment and poverty a total of up to $2 billion over the span of the law's first five years. Second, states will be eligible to borrow, with a series of restrictions and terms upon repayment, from a $1.7 billion "Rainy Day" loan fund to finance emergency social service needs. Critics of the bill claim that the federal commitments to these measures, even if they should be augmented by additional recession-triggered federal block grants, would remain minuscule compared to the immense increases in poverty which accompany even mild economic recessions.

Proponents of a new federalism cite several cogent arguments in arguing that block grants constitute an improved pattern of program funding and control. The states may indeed be better loci for some programs, serving as "laboratories of democracy" more accessible to common people as devolutionists claim. However, to make this argument convincingly requires a consistent commitment to a wider agenda of change. Why did the 104th Congress chose to block-grant only those programs in the "lower tier" of the American welfare state, preserving the security of "upper tier" programs for the middle class according to an entitlement principle? In the interest of equity, there must be a principled rationale supporting such sweeping changes in how the broad array of government programs and functions will be reassigned to the federal, state or local levels. Without such a plan for comprehensive rethinking of the management of all programs, the argument to subject welfare alone to devolution is susceptible to charges of opportunism or bad faith.

The opponents of block-granting AFDC cite a number of objections to this innovation. On the practical level, some observers express concern that many states do not possess adequate administrative or computer capacity to implement their enhanced responsibilities for monitoring and serving recipients under the new block grant system. Accounts of debilitating confusion in state welfare offices in the early months of the new welfare law deepen such concerns.

Opponents also cited more fundamental reasons, on the level of program design and philosophy, to support the argument that block grants are singularly inappropriate for broad income maintenance programs. Throughout the debate, Senator Daniel Patrick Moynihan frequently cited the unfairness of a block grant distribution formula that would lock into place existing disparities in state commitments to their poor. Moynihan renewed his previous calls to move policy in the opposite direction, toward greater equity across the states. Several years earlier, he had argued: "AFDC should be a national program, with national benefits that keep pace with inflation, in exactly the same way that Survivors' Insurance is a national program with national benefits."[8]

Poverty researcher Katherine McFate raises another objection to block-granting AFDC: the likely differential effects of such policy innovations upon distinct geographical and racial groups. McFate fears that further disproportionate harm will accrue to certain segments of the population which have traditionally suffered from the lack of national uniformity in program standards:

> The purpose of our federal welfare system is to insure some kind of support is available to needy families with children regardless of their residence. The poor are not evenly distributed across the United States. States in the Deep South have higher rates of poverty, especially black poverty, than states in other regions of the country, for obvious historical reasons. The majority of AFDC recipients in all the states in the Deep South are black; the majority of southern state legislators are white conservatives. It was largely because southern states lacked the resources and political will to provide assistance to their needy citizens that the federal government originally began applying more federal standards to assistance programs. Although the proponents of block grants argue that state governments have improved their operations dramatically over the past 30 years, benefit levels in the South remain much lower than in other areas of the country.[9]

Other commentators have linked the impetus for block granting to larger historical trends in U.S. policy. Carl T. Rowan notes how this new movement for states' autonomy recalls the earlier pre-civil rights era when the phrase "states rights" served as a codeword for racism and justified states' decisions "to cut people off" (from civil rights as well as social assistance) by covering over a hidden racist agenda with seemingly pragmatic arguments.[10] Looking ahead to a future which threatens to become an era of racial exclusion and "the politics of defensive localism," Margaret Weir views the retreat of the federal government from many aspects of social policy as part of a distressing "fragmentation of the public sphere." The more policy prerogatives fall upon local jurisdictions, the easier it will become for social policy to come under the sway of "thinly

---

8. Daniel Patrick Moynihan, "Welfare Reform: Serving America's Children," *Teacher's College Record* 90 (spring 1989) 340.

9. Katherine McFate, *Making Welfare Work: The Principles of Constructive Welfare Reform* (Washington, D.C.: Joint Center for Political and Economic Studies, 1995) 33.

10. Carl T. Rowan, "Back to 'State's Rights,'" *Washington Post*, 5 Nov. 1995, C7.

veiled exploitation of racial fears and antipathies."[11] Bureaucracies based in Washington may have their drawbacks, but federal partnership in social programs serves a vital function as a guarantor of social safety nets and as a counterweight to the tendency of local forces to segregate and neglect low-income people, especially the minority poor.

2. Time limitation of benefits

As we have seen, a basic goal and effect of the new welfare law is to give states new flexibility, including the freedom to deny aid to any poor family or category of poor family. However, somewhat paradoxically, the law also contains a number of restrictions on how states may spend their federal TANF block grants—provisions which serve to tie the hands of state and local governments. The legislation explicitly disqualifies certain categories of people from receiving this assistance. A number of these restrictions, which came to be referred to as "conservative mandates," were proposed at the beginning of the welfare reform debate; only a fraction of them were actually incorporated into the final version of the legislation. This section examines the rationale behind the most important of these new restrictions: the exclusion from further assistance of people receiving benefits beyond a specified time period.

Since states may exclude any category of recipients, they are free to adopt a time limit as short as they wish. At the time of the new law's passage in the summer of 1996, through the HHS waiver process permitting states to experiment with the AFDC program, "at least thirteen states had already sought federal approval to implement time limits of shorter than five years, and ten states have time limits of two years or less."[12] However, the law does set an upper time limit of five years duration for TANF benefits, specifying that no block grant funds may be used for any adult who has received five years of welfare assistance. Three clarifications about this funding restriction must be made. First, those who exceed the time limit may still qualify for local, state and other federal funds (besides TANF grants). Second, the time limit applies only to adults, so time spent as a child in a household receiving AFDC (or its successor TANF) does not count against the record of an adult applicant. Third, through what is called a "hardship exemption," states are allowed to exempt up to twenty percent of their caseload from the five-year time limit.

11. Margaret Weir, "Urban Poverty and Defensive Localism," *Dissent* (summer 1994) 338.

12. Center on Budget and Policy Priorities, "Urban Institute Study Confirms that Welfare Bills Would Increase Child Poverty" (Washington, D.C.: Center on Budget and Policy Priorities, 26 July 1996) 4.

It is difficult to evaluate the arguments for and against time limitation of benefits in isolation, since this principle is only one part of a larger package of policy measures. One of its major effects and goals is to increase the incentive of welfare recipients to search for and retain jobs—activities which are profoundly affected by other work incentive and work requirement measures (such as workfare) which individual states will adopt. But even before we consider how time limitation interacts with the work requirements (the topic of the section immediately below), it is necessary to describe two aspects of time limitation: (1) the forms it may take; and (2) the rationale behind these measures.

Two forms of time limitation were considered in the public debate of the early and mid-1990s: "hard" and "soft" time limits. Each won a number of supporters after it became evident that the efforts of the Family Support Act of 1988 to facilitate the employment of adults receiving AFDC (mostly through enhanced job training and placement services) had fallen far short of its goal. In the early 1990s, welfare rolls were growing and costs were rising. The work incentives and requirements enacted by a series of laws and amendments over the previous three decades of social policy were being undermined by the existence of so many categories of exemptions that they were reduced to mere paper formalities. Hard time limits were proposed as the simplest way to enforce the end of long-term recipiency; no exceptions would be made for recipient families headed by able-bodied adults once they had exhausted the fixed time limit. Proponents of soft time limits preferred to apply this same principle more flexibly, by making exceptions for those participants in work preparation programs whose sincere efforts to find employment nevertheless left them jobless after the time limit had expired.

The Republicans' "Contract with America" advocated hard time limits, arguing that any half-measure would only serve to muddy the waters by sending the same mixed signals which had frustrated earlier welfare reform efforts. Several amendments considered in the Senate deliberations on successive versions of the welfare bill sought to modify this provision, but they never seriously challenged the basic framework of the Republicans' bill (H.R. 4). On the state level, Governor Tommy Thompson of Wisconsin emerged as a pioneer in adopting the principle of hard time limits through his "Wisconsin Works" (or "W-2") program.

Bill Clinton's 1994 welfare reform bill was something of a hybrid between hard and soft versions of time limitation. The Clinton plan included the sanction of reducing benefits to recipients who did not cooperate with welfare-to-work programs, but it counted various work preparation activities (including education and job training) as equivalent to work effort. It also included provisions for creating thousands of public sector jobs of last resort and subsidizing private sector jobs for recipients who had reached the time limit, although not nearly enough funding was made available for work slots for all who would likely apply for them. Consequently, Clinton's plan was criticized by "time limit hawks" for invoking the rhetorical force of the phrase "two years and out" without imposing the strict measures which would make this outcome a reality. It was also criticized by "time limit doves" for not following through on Clinton's 1992 campaign promise (the often forgotten second half of his pledge to "end welfare as we know it") to guarantee work opportunities to all able-bodied adults who had exhausted their eligibility under the time limit rule.[13]

A purer example of soft time limits is "Project Zero" sponsored by Michigan Governor John Engler[14] and presented to HHS early in 1996 as part of a waiver request. It allows for the continuation of assistance to families whose adult members, because of labor market conditions, learning disabilities and other extenuating circumstances, are unable to find private sector jobs despite sincere efforts toward work preparation during the period of ordinary welfare eligibility. Engler's program emphasizes reciprocal responsibilities between government and recipients. It places Michigan "among the few states that acknowledge the basic need to take care of welfare parents who do everything the state asks but still cannot find a decent-paying job."[15] Because recipients who exceed the five-year time limit are no longer eligible for federal TANF funds under the new welfare law, any benefits they receive (beyond the 20 percent of cases receiving hardship exemptions) in "soft time limit states" like Michigan must come directly from state and local taxes.

---

13. The 1994 Clinton plan required $9.3 billion in additional government spending over five years, much of it for the creation of public sector job slots and for services (child care and job training) that would make welfare-to-work plans feasible. Despite the high cost, the administration's own estimates were that the AFDC caseload would drop by no more than 20 percent by the year 2000. Clinton administration officials had earlier floated ideas for a far more expensive program to create 1.3 million public sector jobs for former recipients, but scaled that number back to 400,000 jobs over a six-year period. The high costs and low payoffs soured many observers on the Clinton plan, but served as a sobering reminder of the difficulty of translating welfare reform slogans into effective work-based programs. In this task, neither hard nor soft time limits constitute "silver bullets."

14. Its name derives from the goal of eliminating unemployment among welfare recipients. For details see Jason DeParle, "Aid from an Enemy of the Welfare State," *New York Times*, 28 Jan. 1996, Section 4, p. 4.

15. "John Engler, Welfare Maverick," *New York Times*, 21 March 1996, A24.

Both hard and soft versions of time limits depend on the common rationale that justifies drastic measures in order to break a supposed "cycle of dependency" in which America's poor find themselves. The account of dependency which has most influenced the welfare reform debate is that of Charles Murray. The central claim of Murray's most influential work, *Losing Ground: American Social Policy 1950–1980*,[16] is that the paradox of the persistence of poverty in the affluent, opportunity-filled United States can largely be explained by the perverse incentives created by public policy, especially by means-tested social programs. Overgenerous welfare policy has built a "poverty trap" which creates an environment in which less advantaged citizens experience disincentives to engage in responsible behavior regarding work, sexuality and family life. By cushioning the effects of failure for this segment of our population, we reward and reinforce dysfunctional values which perpetuate the cycle of dependency. Despite their good intentions, expensive social programs send all the wrong signals; they de-stigmatize irresponsibility and punish achievement. Only a dramatic restructuring of social policy (Murray recommends the total abolition of AFDC) will adequately change this incentive structure and liberate those trapped in the cycle. If we really wish to help low-income Americans, we will enforce the tough-minded discipline which will serve them better in the long-run than the myopic compassion which has damaged their ability to become self-sufficient. Murray concludes his work with the assertion: "When reforms finally do occur, they will happen not because stingy people have won, but because generous people have stopped kidding themselves."[17]

One of the central assumptions of Murray's analysis is that people are rational calculators seeking to maximize short-term gain, choosing courses of action solely on the basis of cost-benefit analysis. The decisions of people with low economic prospects to avoid work, stay on welfare, refuse to marry and bear illegitimate children are based on the fact that such behaviors pay better than the alternatives. Murray borrows principles from the "rational choice" school of economic theory in presenting a series of "thought experiments" which demonstrate the salience of the perverse incentives which exist within the American legal system and educational institutions as well as social policy. In all these cases, the lines of causality run from economic incentives, through the coldly calculating minds of individuals, and finally to socially destructive behavior.

Murray's portrayal of the causes of poverty stands in stark contrast to two alternative theories of the "poverty paradox"—approaches which

16. N.Y: Basic Books, 1984.
17. Ibid., 236.

rely on significantly different anthropological assumptions. The first is the "culture of poverty" school of thought which dates from the work of ethnographer Oscar Lewis. The most important feature of the poor is not the measurable economic variable of low income, but qualitative cultural differences which render part of the population socially distant from the mainstream. The subculture of the poor is marked by certain shared values and patterns of behavior (low work motivation, sexual promiscuity, a proclivity toward escapism, present-time orientation and immediate gratification). These patterns have the adaptive advantage of helping the less privileged cope with the daily pressures and deprivations of their environment, but they also serve to stigmatize those who display them, reinforcing their social isolation.[18] As an explanation of the cause of poverty, the "culture of poverty" has been used in a number of ways: as a neutral set of descriptive categories, as an opportunity to romanticize the alternative cultural practices and values of the poor, or as a reason to blame the poor for what are perceived to be their dysfunctional values.[19]

In all these versions of the "culture of poverty," a cultural explanation is posited to lie at the root of the disadvantages faced by certain groups. Murray's approach, by contrast, deliberately brackets off the need for complex cultural explanations for the persistence of poverty, replacing such potentially controversial claims with a simpler narrative about economic costs and benefits. Social programs and other public policies establish the contours of the social environment, setting "the rules of the game"[20] and creating the perverse financial incentives which explain the prevalence of dysfunctional behavior among the poor.

The second alternative to Murray's theory of poverty is an approach shared by a loose-knit school of thought on the determinants of socioeconomic status which is often termed "structuralism." Its most noteworthy proponent is William Julius Wilson, whose influential works[21] seek to explain the persistence of poverty among residents of minority groups and inner-city neighborhoods in terms of the limited economic opportunities available to them due to forces beyond their control. Such forces

---

18. Michael B. Katz explicates these concepts succinctly in *The Undeserving Poor* (N.Y.: Pantheon Books, 1989) 16–35.

19. One work in this last category is Edward Banfield, *The Unheavenly City Revisited* (Boston: Little, Brown and Co., 1974).

20. Charles Murray, *Losing Ground*, 9.

21. *The Declining Significance of Race: Blacks and Changing American Institutions* (Chicago: University of Chicago Press, 1978); *The Truly Disadvantaged: The Inner City, the Underclass, and Public Policy* (Chicago: University of Chicago Press, 1987); *When Work Disappears: The World of the New Urban Poor* (N.Y.: Alfred A. Knopf, Inc., 1996).

include the lingering effects of historical racial discrimination, geographical barriers to employment, deteriorating job prospects in changing labor markets and declining opportunities for education, stable marriage and social mobility. Structuralism shares one set of common assumptions with Murray's theory of poverty: it too explains the persistence of low incomes primarily in terms of economic, not cultural forces. This accords structuralists like Wilson much room to hope for change, since improvement depends primarily on changing certain key economic conditions, not on somehow altering the cultural inheritance or personal characteristics of the poor. However, in other ways, the perspectives of Murray and the structuralists are precise opposites. Whereas Murray's agenda for improving the lives of the poor is to urge government to scale back its counterproductive economic interventions, Wilson calls for more ambitious governmental efforts to shape the economic environment so as to reduce the unfair barriers to economic opportunity for the least advantaged.

Because of their contrasting assumptions about the causes of long-term poverty, Murray and the structuralists judge the principle of time limitation in directly opposite ways. Since Murray sees welfare benefits as part of a system of governmental over-generosity which traps people in an intergenerational cycle of poverty, a drastic step such as cutting off eligibility for benefits is a necessary step to establish new "rules of the game." Structuralists like Wilson judge this to be the wrong medicine for the ailment of inter-generational dependency. Since their diagnosis is that massive economic forces have locked some sectors of the population out of the possibility of upward mobility, the proper prescription is not to withdraw continued income support from disadvantaged people, but rather to commit greater resources to extend more universally real opportunity for economic advancement and eventual self-sufficiency.

The divergence in these theories of poverty began as a scholarly disagreement over the interpretation of economic data, but when policy-makers turned their attention to the adoption of time limits during the welfare reform debate of the 1990s, the theories of Murray and the structuralists assumed high public profiles. Charles Murray was often cited explicitly by Speaker Newt Gingrich[22] and other supporters of time limitation. Their arguments for reducing open-ended eligibility for AFDC as one way of replacing the "culture of dependency" with an "opportunity society"[23] frequently invoke concepts (such as "the welfare trap" and "perverse moral signals"[24]) introduced by Murray. Conversely, the argu-

22. See his *To Renew America*, 78.
23. Moore, ed., *Restoring the Dream*, 59–61.
24. Ibid., 193.

ments of Wilson and other structuralists were frequently cited by opponents of time limits. They generally argue that it is the existence of systemic barriers to employment, not some perverse desire to pursue a lucrative "welfare career path," which accounts for most welfare recipiency. The alternatives to time limits most frequently proposed include structuralist measures to assist marginalized people in their efforts to join the economic mainstream.[25]

Without doubt, the idea of time-limiting welfare benefits has gained considerable support among the American populace.[26] The enactment of time limits in the new welfare law seems to suggest that, at least in this round of the debate over social policy, Murray's analysis proved more widely persuasive than that of the structuralists. Care must be taken, however, in interpreting the significance of this victory. Welfare reform is a complex process involving numerous clusters of values and competing modes of social analysis, so the resulting legislation must not be characterized as a referendum on the tenability of a single theory of poverty. Murray offers a simple (indeed monocausal) explanation for persistent poverty: the rules of social programs create an alluring trap. The widespread embracing of time limits suggests that American audiences, at least up to the present, have for the most part been satisfied with this seemingly straightforward explanation of the causes of long-term dependency. Americans have not yet felt the need to dig for the more complex answers to the question of "why long-term poverty" offered by structuralist analysis. None of this precludes the possibility of changed public perceptions in subsequent rounds of welfare reform.

3. Work requirements

Because the new federal welfare law devolves authority for program design and administration to the state level, its provisions for work requirements contain few details of specific arrangements. Instead, they take the form of mandates to the states which include: (1) a series of conditions which must be fulfilled in order for states to receive their full share of the allotted TANF grants; and (2) a specification of the penalties

---

25. One fine example of such structuralist argumentation against time limits appears in "Report and Recommendations on H.R. 4, 'The Personal Responsibility Act of 1995,'" *Record of the Association of the Bar of the City of New York* 50 (June 1995) 493–521.

26. See R. Kent Weaver, Robert Shapiro and Laurence Jacobs, "Public Opinion on Welfare Reform: A Mandate for What?" in Weaver and Dickens, *Looking Before We Leap*, 109–28. This study collects data from ten public opinion surveys conducted between Nov. 1993 and April 1995. Each indicates support for the time limitation principle by a substantial majority (generally between 74 and 92 percent) of the public.

for noncompliance. States are free to develop work programs and "individual responsibility plans" for welfare recipients in whatever form they choose, as long as their use of TANF funds follows three sets of rules.

First, to avoid penalties such as the forfeiture of part of their block grant, states must enforce minimum work participation rates for their welfare caseloads. The annual participation rate starts with an initial 25 percent in 1997 and rises by increments to 50 percent in 2002. Second, the law lists twelve categories of activities in which recipients may engage in order to be counted toward their state's work participation rate. Included are an "upper track" of seven categories of direct engagement in work (in the private or public sectors, including community service and subsidized on-the-job training) and a "lower track" of work preparation activities (attending secondary school, vocational education programs, and job skills training). No more than 20 percent of a state's recipients may count toward its work participation rate through this second category of work activities. Third, the law sets a minimum number of hours per week for participation in these activities in order for recipients to count toward the state's work percentage goals. This requirement starts at twenty hours for single parents and rises in stages to thirty hours after 2000.

No matter what specific programs states adopt to meet these goals, the new law certainly introduces innovative elements which constitute a quantum leap in work requirement enforcement over previous federal law. In the three decades since AFDC rules first included work incentives and requirements, never have such strict regulations enforced work as a condition for receiving welfare benefits. The growing appeal of work requirements over these decades represents the triumph of a set of attitudinal assumptions that favor an "employment strategy" over a "guaranteed-income strategy" as the best way of assisting poor families. A consensus has developed which sees work as the primary answer to the problem of welfare dependency.

The evolution of the "workfare" principle from these new assumptions is traced by Richard Nathan, who describes an initial period of opposition to this new synthesis of policy thought and administrative practice before its ascendancy after 1980:

> In the seventies the word workfare was used in a narrow way to refer to the idea that . . . welfare recipients should be required to work, even in make-work jobs, in exchange for receiving their benefits. Liberals on social policy issues—and this included most welfare administrators—heaped abuse on this idea, calling it 'slavefare' and rejecting it out of hand.[27]

---

27. Richard P. Nathan, "Will the Underclass Always Be with Us?" *Society* 24, no. 3 (March/April 1987) 61.

In few states[28] did workfare really get off the ground (in terms of program development and widespread implementation) until its terms of reference changed—away from the punitive enforcement of a *quid pro quo* and toward a commitment of public resources that offered poor families opportunities for real advancement. The occasion for the birth of this "new-style workfare" was the establishment in 1981 of the Community Work Experience Program which provided participants with "an array of employment and training services and activities, job search, job training, education programs and also community work experience."[29] Numerous studies of the effectiveness of such workfare programs, both before and after the 1988 Family Support Act restructured the federal commitment to them, indicate generally modest but occasionally (in the most carefully administered programs) promising results.[30] It remains debatable whether the high cost per participant of these workfare programs and their allied services is justified by the levels of increased earnings and reduced welfare dependency they produce.

As states scramble to set up their expanded workfare programs to comply with the new federal welfare law, they will without doubt scrutinize the lessons and experience of previous workfare programs. The expanding state initiatives will probably reflect at least two key assumptions which contributed to earlier rounds in the development of workfare: (1) single mothers should be expected to work because of the psychological satisfaction and emotional benefits associated with a job; and (2) an employment strategy is in the best interest of poor families because it enhances their long-term prospects for self-sufficiency and membership in the mainstream of society.[31] However, the new phase of workfare may also be shaped by another, much harsher set of assumptions about human behavior and the role of public policy in enforcing such social virtues as the traditional work ethic. These ideas constitute the "new paternalism" advocated by Lawrence Mead.

Although both share the common assumption that a refusal of the poor to work is the major cause of welfare dependency, Lawrence Mead

28. A notable exception was California under Governor Ronald Reagan.
29. Nathan, "Will the Underclass Always Be with Us?" 61.
30. A detailed and balanced analysis of the findings of dozens of such studies conducted by the Manpower Demonstration Research Corporation appears in Judith M. Gueron and Edward Pauly (with Cameran M. Lougy), *From Welfare to Work* (N.Y.: Russell Sage Foundation, 1991).
31. Robert D. Reischauer lists additional elements of this consensus (at least as it existed in 1987 when he wrote) in "Welfare Reform: Will Consensus be Enough?" *Brookings Review* 5 (summer 1987) 3–8.

and Charles Murray reach dramatically different conclusions about how to improve the American welfare system. Murray's primary recommendation is the de-funding of welfare programs as a means to restoring the normal incentive structures to which poor families will presumably respond by leading lives of self-sufficiency. Murray's goal is to make the virtue of work once again a necessity for the welfare poor. Mead, by contrast, reflecting a rather punitive version of the "culture of poverty" thesis, thinks that the members of a "behavioral underclass"[32] have been so pathologically damaged by the prevalence of an "entitlement mentality" that they no longer have the psychic ability to respond to economic incentives intended to encourage greater work effort. Mead claims that "it is less and less apparent that self-interest alone would lead recipients to work."[33] The only true solution to the entrenched habits of dependency is the active enforcement of work discipline by government. Social policy must largely surrender its previous (and counterproductive) goals of extending greater freedom and opportunity to less fortunate citizens. It must now pursue the very different goal of changing the lives of a deviant class within society.

Mead advocates radical reassessments of: (1) the role of social policy; and (2) the nature of workfare. On the first count, a new "authoritative social policy"[34] would function as one arm of a "tutelary regime"[35] seeking to instill in citizens those desirable qualities which will produce acceptable behavior. This goes much further than ordinary "civic conceptions" of the role of government, a long tradition of thought which links "statecraft" with "soulcraft" and recognizes a legitimate role for government in fostering certain kinds of virtues.[36] Since, from Mead's viewpoint, government can no longer assume basic social competencies, it must take a maximal approach to the task of communicating social expectations, using social policy as a tool to force its citizens to comply with basic rules of what Mead calls "social functioning."[37]

Second, Mead's understanding of workfare stands in sharp contrast to the "new-style" workfare which seeks to commit new resources to en-

---

32. Lawrence M. Mead, *Beyond Entitlement: The Social Obligations of Citizenship* (N.Y.: The Free Press, 1986) 22.

33. Ibid., 90.

34. Ibid., 11.

35. Lawrence M. Mead, *The New Politics of Poverty: The Nonworking Poor in America* (N.Y.: BasicBooks, 1992) 181.

36. For one recent representative, see George F. Will, *Statecraft as Soulcraft: What Government Does* (N.Y.: Simon and Schuster, 1983).

37. Mead, *Beyond Entitlement*, ch. 3.

hance opportunity and mobility. In the "custodial democracy"[38] advocated by Mead, workfare becomes a primary way for government to exercise "the social obligations of citizenship."[39] In order for acceptable levels of social discipline to be restored, low-wage work must come to be seen as a duty of the dependent poor, no longer as an option to which they might be enticed by economic incentives.

The "new paternalism"[40] Mead advocates contains this paradox: the struggle against dependency requires not a reduction of government intervention, but actually justifies greater intrusion by public authorities into the lives of those accused of shirking responsibilities. In attributing long-term poverty to deeply ingrained behavioral problems of the poor, Mead cannot be content with a social policy which merely decreases welfare benefits (as Murray's brand of laissez faire recommends). Rather, Mead seeks to couple public assistance with rigorously enforced work obligations.

It is not difficult to imagine numerous objections to Mead's claims. William Julius Wilson articulates one pivotal criticism from a structuralist perspective:

> Despite Mead's eloquent arguments the empirical support for his thesis is incredibly weak. It is therefore difficult for me to embrace a theory that sidesteps the complex issues and consequences of changes in American economic organization with the argument that one can address the problems of the ghetto underclass by simply emphasizing the social obligations of citizenship.[41]

Besides these objections concerning the causes of the social problem of nonwork are serious questions about the practice of work enforcement Mead recommends. Will there be any checks to insure that this work is performed on favorable terms which respect the rights of the workfare participants? Will any types of barriers to employment (disabilities, family obligations, lack of aptitude or skills) be considered legitimate excuses for not engaging in workfare activities? By what rationale is the largely unpaid work of childcare systematically excluded from Mead's accounting of the social obligations of citizenship? Perhaps most importantly, where will the new work positions come from? If work is not

---

38. Mead, *The New Politics of Poverty*, 183.
39. Ch. 11 ("The Common Obligations") of *Beyond Entitlement* lists four further obligations alongside work. They are: supporting one's family, fluency in English, learning enough in school to become employable, and abiding by the law.
40. Mead, *The New Politics of Poverty*, 183.
41. Wilson, *The Truly Disadvantaged*, 161.

needed in the private sector, why should a polity create an artificial situation of full employment (via make-work public sector jobs) if the labor of some sector of the population is truly not required for purposes of useful economic production? These questions raised by critics of Mead have the potential to touch off an important debate that transcends merely technical matters (such as data on job availability and work behavior of the poor) to include a reevaluation of the traditional work ethic in societies experiencing a diminished need for paid labor.

It is difficult to judge how much influence the thought of Lawrence Mead has exercised on the welfare reform debate of the past decade. The notoriety of his writings suggests that at least his appeal to certain cultural values (accountability, reciprocity, the work ethic), if not his actual recommendations for enforcing work discipline among the members of a dependent underclass, has found considerable resonance among the American public and policymakers. The fact that the original welfare bill was entitled "The Personal Responsibility Act" indicates something about the rationale behind the agenda that produced the new law. However, since the new federal law remains a skeletal framework for the state programs which will actually enact new work requirements and workfare arrangements, it is impossible to measure the precise level of Mead's influence upon new social policies. Nevertheless, it is undeniable that the effect of the new legislation will be to enforce an unprecedented increase in work obligations among welfare recipients.

4. Anti-illegitimacy measures

The new welfare law contains some provisions to discourage extramarital births; however decisions on the precise form these measures will take are left to the states. Although bills featuring a wide array of very strict measures to punish illegitimacy were introduced into the 104th Congress (family caps and teenage mother exclusions were among the measures often called "conservative mandates"), the final bill contains only modest restrictions. States were given the option of denying assistance to children born to those already receiving welfare (a group with a high illegitimacy rate) and of denying aid to unwed parents under the age of eighteen, who are now eligible for welfare only if they live with a parent or guardian and attend school. The law also provides states with a modest financial incentive to enact their own anti-illegitimacy programs; the five states which demonstrate the largest decline in the proportion of illegitimate births (without increasing abortions) between 1999 and 2002 will receive a $20 million bonus from Washington. Finally, the legislation allocates $50 million per year (starting in 1998, as part of the Maternal and Child Health Block Grant) to promote sexual abstinence through education.

Opponents of these measures (and of others which were not included in the final version of the law) characterize the effort to discourage illegitimate births as a dangerous foray into social engineering, and even as a potential violation of the reproductive rights of low-income single women.[42] In general, however, support for proposals to use social policy as a tool to fight illegitimacy has deepened in American politics in recent years, extending to most parts of the political spectrum. On the right, the most recent writings of both Charles Murray and Lawrence Mead indicate a shift in their chief social concern, from fighting nonwork to battling illegitimacy.[43] Further to the left, Marian Wright Edelman[44] and Jean Bethke Elshtain[45] each argue for greater anti-illegitimacy efforts by citing the ample data demonstrating a correlation between better outcomes for children and the presence of two parents in a household. No one any longer doubts that high social costs are associated with illegitimate teen pregnancy. A 1996 independent study estimates that government spends at least $7 billion each year dealing with the consequences of teen pregnancy.[46]

---

42. Christopher Jencks and Kathryn Edin, "Do Poor Women Have a Right to Bear Children?" *American Prospect*, no. 20 (1995) 43–52; Iris Marion Young, "Making Single Motherhood Normal," *Dissent* (winter 1994) 88–93.

43. Murray wrote in 1994: "These observations have led me to conclude that illegitimacy is the central social problem of our time." This assessment appears in his article "What To Do About Welfare," *Commentary* 98 (Dec. 1994) 27. An essay Lawrence Mead contributed to a 1996 volume on welfare reform demonstrates a concern for family structure not found in his earlier writings. See Mead's essay, "The Poverty Debate and Human Nature," in Stanley W. Carlson-Thies and James W. Skillen, eds., *Welfare in America: Christian Perspectives on a Policy in Crisis* (Grand Rapids, Mich.: William B. Eerdmans Publishing Company, 1996) 209–42.

44. "Adolescent parenthood is no longer a viable option for thriving and progressing in society. . . . Teenage pregnancy is a problem because it very often precludes the completion of education, the securing of employment, and the creation of a stable relationship. . . ." (Marian Wright Edelman, *Families in Peril: An Agenda for Social Change* [Cambridge, Mass.: Harvard University Press, 1987] 56–7).

45. "We also know, from . . . dozens of other reliable sources, that children growing up in single-parent households are at greater risk on every index of well-being: crime, violence, substance abuse, mental illness, dropping out of school, and so on" (Jean Bethke Elshtain, "Single Motherhood: Response to Iris Marion Young," *Dissent* [spring 1994] 268).

46. The study was sponsored by the Robin Hood Foundation, a charitable organization based in New York. It measured increased government costs associated with the approximately 175,000 births annually to mothers age 15–19, 72 percent of whom are unmarried. The $7 billion figure is dominated by medical care, AFDC, foster care ex-

However, the existence of a consensus that something should be done to prevent extramarital births should not be allowed to cover over an ongoing disagreement among policy analysts over the causes of illegitimacy. The key question for our present purposes is to what extent welfare contributes to the problem of illegitimacy in America. While all observers acknowledge that out-of-wedlock births are generally increasing,[47] and are more common among low-income women than the general population, disagreement remains about how to interpret this data. If a causal relationship can be established, the case for revising welfare policy in order to address this social problem would be bolstered.

Conservatives favor an economic interpretation. Charles Murray, in an argument reflecting his new concern about illegitimacy, ventures the frank claim that "welfare causes illegitimacy," since he interprets recent statistics as indicating that "the generosity of welfare benefits has a relationship to extramarital fertility."[48] He predicts that illegitimacy would decline by 50 percent if welfare were eliminated. William F. Lauber and Robert Rector of the Heritage Foundation posit an ever tighter linkage between welfare recipiency and the conscious reproductive behavior that precedes illegitimate births. They claim:

> Most unwed teen mothers conceive and deliver their babies deliberately rather than accidentally . . . . [T]hey are very much aware of the role welfare will play in supporting them once a child is born. Thus, the availability of welfare plays an important role in influencing a woman's decision to have a child out of wedlock.[49]

George Gilder labels welfare a "promiscuity entitlement" which discourages marriage by displacing the economic role of the father of the illegitimate children it encourages.[50] Arguments such as these inspired the attempt to enact teenage mother exclusions and family caps in the wel-

---

penses and opportunity costs from lost productivity and tax revenues. See Steven A. Holmes, "Public Cost of Teen-Age Pregnancy Is Put at $7 Billion This Year," *New York Times*, 13 June 1996, A19.

47. Census Bureau statistics indicate a steady rise in recent decades of the percentage of births which take place outside of marriage. The 1990 rate was 28 percent; in 1994 it was 32.8 percent (Robert J. Samuelson, "For Better or Worse," *Washington Post*, 31 July 1996, A24).

48. Murray, "What To Do About Welfare," 29.

49. Robert Rector and William F. Lauber, *America's Failed $5.4 Trillion War on Poverty* (Washington, D.C.: The Heritage Foundation, 1995) 27–8.

50. George Gilder, "End Welfare Reform as We Know It," *The American Spectator* (June 1995) 26.

fare bill—items proposed as drastic but necessary efforts at behavior modification. The final legislation's more modest measures regarding illegitimacy are only a remnant of a broader agenda (which individual states may still implement), but the arguments behind the largely defeated "conservative mandates" supply the contours of their rationale.

Liberals and structuralists favor an interpretation of the data on illegitimacy which is more cultural than economic. They attribute illegitimacy to complex social causal factors rather than calculations of gain on the part of potential welfare recipients. In their view, the linkage between family structure and poverty is not as simple as it may appear at first glance. The lines of causality run primarily from a starting point of economic disadvantage through collective social mores to an endpoint of welfare recipiency, not, as many conservatives contend, from overgenerous welfare benefits directly to undesirable behaviors such as promiscuity and illegitimacy.[51] In support of these claims, numerous studies may be cited which demonstrate no correlation between the levels of welfare benefits and rates of illegitimacy over time or across geographical jurisdictions.[52] Rather, illegitimacy is portrayed primarily as one effect of enormous cultural shifts which influence the attitudes and behaviors of all social groups, not just those with low incomes. The effects of the sexual revolution, trends toward delayed marriage, increased female economic independence, new patterns of schooling, work and parenting—all these factors contribute to the surge in extramarital births.[53] The salience of noneconomic explanations for this phenomenon suggests that welfare re-

---

51. The conservatives' claims about the calculation behind the birth of illegitimate children is contradicted perhaps most directly by evidence that teenage mothers are frequently, as one recent study phrased it, "the abused prey of older men" who deserve legal protection rather than demonization. See Mireya Novarro, "Teen-age Mothers Viewed as Abused Prey of Older Men," *New York Times*, 19 May 1996, 1, 18.

52. Much evidence could be cited to support this claim, including numerous studies conducted in direct response to the analysis of Charles Murray. The data from dozens of governmental and independent sources, the great majority of which find virtually no demonstrable causal link between welfare and single-parent families, are summarized in "Statement on Key Welfare Reform Issues: The Empirical Evidence" (Medford, Mass.: Tufts University Center on Hunger, Poverty and Nutrition Policy, 1995).

53. For an analysis of how these social trends interact with rates of marriage and illegitimacy, see Robert D. Mare and Christopher Winship, "Socioeconomic Change and the Decline of Marriage for Blacks and Whites," in Christopher Jencks and Paul E. Peterson, eds., *The Urban Underclass* (Washington, D.C.: The Brookings Institution, 1991) 175–202. Other essays in that volume offer corroborating observations about the causes of the behavioral patterns of one social group of specific concern: urban "underclass" teenagers.

form measures aimed at reducing illegitimacy will not be effective, and will serve only to punish single mothers and their children already caught in difficult circumstances.

Given these disagreements over the relationship between welfare and illegitimacy, it is not surprising that the new federal law draws back from staking out a definitive anti-illegitimacy strategy but instead leaves this task to the states. By highlighting family structure as one of the relevant concerns in social policy, the law reflects the consensus that welfare program rules should address reproductive as well as work behavior as part of an agenda of enforcing personal responsibility. Amidst growing awareness that (1) a high percentage of "welfare spells" begin with the birth of a child out of wedlock,[54] and (2) children in two-parent households experience developmental advantages over others, public policy can no longer afford to remain neutral on matters of family structure. However, disagreement persists over which policy strategy best achieves the desired goals without sacrificing other established objectives of welfare (such as income maintenance). Family caps and other anti-illegitimacy measures thus remain policy options about which our nation is deeply ambivalent. Heretofore, it has largely been left to the states to decide whether to embark on an experiment in behavior modification by adopting these new and harsh strategies to discourage extramarital births.

5. Other new conditions on benefits

This section considers three sets of new welfare measures: changes in child-support enforcement, withdrawal of benefits to legal immigrants, and the imposition of "Learnfare." These three disparate measures, targeted at quite different populations, share a common approach. Each attempts to accomplish social goals through a strategy of offering incentives and disincentives ("carrots and sticks") to modify problematic human behavior.

The least controversial of the three is a series of measures which empower states to facilitate enhanced collection of child-support payments. Under the new law, states are required to implement new, tougher policies (including sanctions such as suspending drivers' and professional licenses in cases of noncompliance) to punish nonresident parents whose child-support payments are in arrears. Federal assistance is offered to states in setting up registries of child-support orders and enforcing col-

---

54. 1993 government statistics indicate that 30 percent of welfare families enter the AFDC rolls upon the birth of an out-of-wedlock child. By contrast, 45 percent enroll in AFDC because of divorce or separation, 15 percent because of a drop in earnings. For further analysis and statistics, see *Let's Get Real About Welfare*, Occasional Paper No. 5 (Silver Spring, Md.: Bread for the World Institute, 1995) 18–22.

lection of these payments, including the establishment of a Federal Parent Locator Service and a system of income withholding for violators in interstate child-support cases. The new welfare law institutes new formulas for determining eligibility for welfare benefits when child-support payments from absent parents are received. These measures to expedite enforcement and establish uniform procedures represent not true policy innovation, but merely an extension of successful provisions of such previous legislation as the Family Support Act of 1988.

There are few serious objections to these attempts to hold accountable "deadbeat dads" (as parents who do not comply with child-support awards are frequently called). Child-support system improvements which could recover the $34 billion in awards which annually go uncollected hold the inviting promise of eliminating the need for a significant portion of current welfare expenditures.[55] Controversy arises, however, when policies intended to implement these goals turn to specific strategies, such as the mandatory establishment of paternity as the basis for future child-support payments. The new welfare law includes a variety of measures which encourage the states to document the paternity of each newborn on a voluntary basis (by recording social security numbers of both parents on birth certificates) or through genetic testing of babies and suspected parents if circumstances warrant. For those who apply for welfare, the new federal law specifies some mandatory practices; states must invoke a penalty equal to at least 25 percent of welfare benefits upon families which do not cooperate with state authorities in establishing paternity and child-support orders. The rationale behind these measures is to use the threat of financial sanctions in order to secure compliance from welfare mothers hesitant to identify absentee fathers.

As one welfare administrator admitted: "The whole goal is to make it her problem in addition to the government's problem."[56]

This is where strenuous ethical objections arise. Such requirements may place custodial parents in impossible situations, especially when single mothers come under the pressure of threats from the men who fathered their children. The well-established possibility of physical or emotional harm in such cases suggests that there is often more at stake than

---

55. See David T. Ellwood, *Poor Support: Poverty in the American Family* (N.Y.: Basic Books, 1988) 163–74; also Robert I. Lerman, "Child-Support Policies," in Phoebe H. Cottingham and David T. Ellwood, eds., *Welfare Policies for the 1990s* (Cambridge, Mass.: Harvard University Press, 1989) 219–46.

56. The statement is from Michael Henry, Director of the Virginia Division of Child Support Enforcement, quoted in Peter Baker, "Virginia Targets Welfare Moms In Effort to Track Down Absentee Dads," *Washington Post*, 31 July 1995, A1, A12.

meets the eye in invoking the threat of sanctions in order to "improve the memory" of a welfare mother. Because paternity identification may create unreasonable burdens on the women and children involved, there is a need to make prudential exceptions to regulations requiring the establishment of paternity. Sometimes neither the "carrot" nor the "stick" seems capable of addressing all relevant needs and concerns in an appropriate way; policy measures based on principles of behavior modification run the risk of treating human motivation too simplistically. Program rules must remain flexible enough to accommodate the complexities of real-life human families and their interactions. While encouraging paternal responsibility may be an indispensable part of welfare reform, this provision of the new law is too blunt an instrument to suit its purposes.

A second "carrot and stick" measure, "Learnfare," receives no explicit attention in the new welfare law. However, under the new law's revocation of the entitlement status of welfare, states are now free to impose behavioral conditions upon the receipt of welfare assistance. One of the conditions likely to be imposed in many states is the compiling of a satisfactory school attendance record by minors in families which receive welfare assistance. Families which do not meet these requirements will be subject to penalties, including reductions in the cash assistance they receive.

Even before the new law, at least twenty-three states had already, under the federal waiver system, conducted preliminary attempts to link welfare benefits to school attendance. One of the earliest programs started in Wisconsin in 1988. The results of this Learnfare experiment have been intensely scrutinized. A 1992 study by researchers at the University of Wisconsin's Employment Training Institute found that "it has not changed attendance patterns of low-income families."[57] One commentator described the results in more dramatic fashion:

> Learnfare was a disaster. In the first year of the program, the drop-out rates actually increased in Milwaukee, where most of the Learnfare sanctions occurred. Errors in record-keeping and lack of follow-up meant that many families lost their benefits for no reason at all. A Federal judge issued an injunction against the program in 1989. In the injunction order, he wrote: "This is a situation where the survival and dignity of individuals and families are involved. These people should not be made homeless and hungry in the name of social experimentation."[58]

57. Ellen Nakashima, "Learnfare Starts off Slowly in Virginia," *Washington Post*, 12 Feb. 1996, D1, D5. For a summary of other studies of similar programs, see Dirk Johnson, "Wisconsin Welfare Effort on School Is a Failure, Study Says," *New York Times*, 19 May 1996, 20.

58. Ruth Cuniff, "Big Bad Welfare," *The Progressive* 58 (Aug. 1994) 20.

Other states, most notably Connecticut,[59] have instituted similar measures only to reap such disappointing results that Learnfare was abandoned. Nevertheless, we may expect the new federal law to encourage further state experimentation with Learnfare measures, if only because the temptation is so strong to attempt quick fixes which seek to accomplish several goals at once. In this case, the laudable goals of encouraging good parenting practices, punishing truancy and lowering welfare costs are attractive enough to lure states into Learnfare experiments. However, even aside from its failure to demonstrate statistical improvements in school attendance, Learnfare may be criticized on ethical grounds. It stigmatizes welfare recipients, imputes unproven motives and behaviors to low-income citizens and holds families' essential lifeline of assistance hostage to conditions beyond the control of at least some members of the family. Like a parallel initiative called "Immunofare,"[60] Learnfare is objectionable because it arbitrarily singles out low-income families with the implicit suggestion that poorer parents will neglect their children unless coerced to do otherwise.

A third new set of restrictions on welfare benefits involves legal immigrants. Even before the welfare reform debate began, *illegal* (or undocumented) immigrants had already been ineligible for most means-tested entitlement benefits. The new welfare law further specifies the narrow conditions under which the undocumented are eligible for emergency medical care and other special assistance from federal agencies. *Legal* immigrants will for the first time be denied assistance from Food Stamps, Medicaid and Supplemental Security Income (or SSI, the means-tested program for the elderly and disabled). The only exceptions are for U.S. military personnel, veterans, political refugees, those granted legal asylum, and those who have worked for ten years in this country. All other immigrants would have to become U.S. citizens before becoming eligible for these safety net programs. Nearly half a million beneficiaries, mostly elderly or disabled poor, lost their eligibility when the law took

---

59. See Jonathan Rabinovitz, "Welfare Cuts For Truancy Are Stalled: Task Force in Hartford Finds Problems in Plan," *New York Times*, 7 May 1996, B1, B4.

60. "Immunofare" programs in some states sanction welfare families for failure to maintain adequate child immunization histories. Jill Duerr Berrick points out the faulty premises of this policy: "The effort is based on the assumption that low-income women are not aware of the importance of vaccinations and that they are not concerned about the health of their children" *(Faces of Poverty: Portraits of Women and Children on Welfare* [N.Y.: Oxford University Press, 1995] 156). Berrick further argues that there is no evidence to suggest that low incomes or welfare recipiency are correlated with willful neglect of the needs of children for schooling or vaccines.

effect; the Medicaid restrictions will leave at least that same number without health insurance within five years.[61] States retain the prerogative of offering some of their TANF grant funds to eligible immigrants who arrived before 1996, but no state assistance to subsequent arrivals may include federal funds. States and localities will have to bear the full cost of any other aid, even most emergency assistance, they choose to offer to noncitizens.

Numerous overlapping goals and strategies prompted these measures. Certainly, a major motivation was the cost savings of these restrictions: approximately $22 billion over five years, or 40 percent of the overall budgetary savings from the entire welfare bill (despite the fact that immigrants comprise only 5 percent of the recipients of affected programs). Yet, these immigrant provisions of the new welfare law may have been equally strongly motivated by the desire to advance "the personal responsibility agenda" by which lawmakers seek to encourage socially constructive behavior. This rationale is evident in additional provisions of the law which "increase the circumstances under which an immigrant's sponsor would be considered financially responsible for that individual."[62] All these aspects of the legislation may be viewed as attempts to use sanctions to modify behavior so that all groups become less dependent upon government assistance.

Within this perspective, immigrants represent a special case. For this distinctive group, the rules of social policy may be used as an instrument of behavior modification not only to motivate them to be financially independent, but also to deter them from arriving in the U.S. in the first place. It is not necessary to impute racism, nativism or xenophobia to the proponents of these policies in order to recognize the new law's intention: to function as a deterrent against dependency by the immigrants deemed most likely to take advantage of U.S. government generosity. Ample public evidence reveals this purpose. In July 1996 Senate deliberations on the final version of the bill, Senator Rick Santorum of Pennsylvania openly cited the argument that elderly legal immigrants take advantage of their eligibility for social benefits and use the U.S. as a "retirement haven."[63]

---

61. These statistics are C.B.O. estimates reported in Super and others. Calculations are complicated by: (1) slight differences between the way the law treats new arrivals after 1996 and those who arrived earlier; and (2) new spending by some states to offset severe hardships.

62. "Provisions of the Welfare Bill," *Congressional Quarterly Weekly Report*, 3 August 1996, 2193.

63. Quoted in Robert Pear, "Senate Votes to Deny Most Federal Benefits to Legal Immigrants Who Are Not Citizens," *New York Times*, 20 July 1996, 9.

Governor Pete Wilson of California praised the new law as "the kind of step that needs to be taken to prevent Federal taxpayers from being inundated with people who come, especially late in life, and become public charges."[64] In sum, supporters see these measures as a needed response to a distressing pattern by which legal immigrants, drawn by the lure of generous benefits, have taken unfair advantage of the U.S. system of social provision. By restricting such assistance, U.S. social policy implements a principle captured in an often-repeated comment of Senator Phil Gramm of Texas: "Immigrants should come . . . with their sleeves rolled up, ready to go to work, and not with their hands out, ready to go on welfare."[65]

Opponents of these measures cite numerous practical concerns, such as the fear that severe burdens may be imposed upon local hospitals and social service agencies which will have to fill the gap in the safety net left by the eliminated federal assistance. Opponents also question the prevailing assumptions about the motivations of legal immigrants in coming to the U.S. As one legal advocacy group protesting these measures contended:

> There is no evidence to support either the thesis that large numbers of immigrants come to the U.S. seeking welfare, or that immigrant benefits constitute a large portion of total welfare expense. Immigration and Naturalization Service data establishes that the vast majority of both legal and illegal immigrants come to the U.S. to work, join family members or to flee persecution, not to seek welfare benefits. Overall, 95 percent of immigrants support themselves or are supported by family members and/or sponsors. Only 2.3 percent of immigrants who entered the U.S. during the 1980s from nonrefugee countries received public benefits, a welfare receipt rate approximately 30 percent lower than that of U.S. citizens.[66]

The immigrants most likely to apply for means-tested benefits are the elderly and political refugees, two subgroups who are hardly likely to be jolted into self-sufficiency by the threat of withdrawing benefits. If a greater deterrent is indeed desired to prevent future immigration of those most likely to become dependent on means-tested benefits, then the blunt tool of eliminating categorical eligibility for programs should be replaced by more precise instruments of policy. Perhaps what is called for is more careful case-by-case determination of immigration permission or improved screening of immigrants' sponsors by immigration officials already charged with this task.

64. Quoted in Tim Golden, "If Immigrants Lose U.S. Aid, Local Budgets May Feel Pain," *New York Times*, 29 July 1996, A1, A12.
65. Quoted in ibid.
66. Association of the Bar of the City of New York, "Report and Recommendations on H. R. 4," 510.

6. Other provisions of the new law

The welfare overhaul legislation (PL 104-193) includes a number of provisions besides those which reform welfare *per se* (in the narrow sense of means-tested cash assistance to families). Here we investigate changes in six categories of assistance which are related to welfare insofar as they tend to serve the same low-income families. The six programs are: (1) Food Stamps; (2) federal assistance in child care services; (3) child nutrition programs; (4) Supplemental Security Income for Disabled Children; (5) Medicaid; and (6) Social Services Block Grants. Most underwent funding reductions and program rule changes, as described below.

Despite several proposals to transform it into a system of capped block grants, the federal Food Stamp program retains its status as an open-ended entitlement to all who qualify. However, it has been significantly scaled back. Cost reductions will accrue from a number of changes: across-the-board cuts in benefit levels (allotments per recipient meal fall from eighty to sixty-six cents), tougher eligibility standards (fewer deductions are allowed in means-test calculations), less generous indexing of benefits to inflation, the imposition of new work requirements, and new efforts to reduce fraud in the program. It is estimated that these measures will reduce the cost of the program by $28 billion over six years, amounting to a 20 percent cut when the new law's provisions are fully implemented.

The two innovations which most change the nature of the Food Stamp program are a pair of related measures which parallel the major changes in the cash welfare program: time limitation and work requirements. Both apply to able-bodied food stamp recipients between eighteen and fifty years of age who do not receive an exemption (as do pregnant women, those who live in areas with over 10 percent unemployment and, in some states, parents of children under age six). Nonexempt recipients are limited to three months of eligibility over any three year period; after three months, applicants may continue to receive food stamps only if they are working at least twenty hours per week or are enrolled in a workfare or training slot. Although states enjoy some increased discretionary power in administering food stamps under the new law, states have no authority to issue hardship exemptions for food stamp recipients with regard to these rules. Because no new funds are set aside for the creation of work or training slots for affected people, this provision has the effect of denying food stamp assistance to people who are willing to work if given the opportunity.[67] This is an especially harsh provision,

---

67. C.B.O. estimates that in an average month, one million individuals will be in this situation (i.e., denied food stamps because of an inability to find work). See Super and others, "The New Welfare Law," 17–23.

since food stamps is the sole safety net program for which many individuals in these categories are eligible. A series of alternative proposals would have protected recipients from having their food stamp benefits terminated unless they had been given the opportunity to work, but each was defeated in Congress.

Second, the new law changes the funding structure of federal assistance to child care services. It creates a single child care block grant to the states, replacing previous programs which had provided federal funds for child care for three categories of children: (1) those considered "at risk"; (2) those in AFDC families which required this service in order to participate in work or training programs; and (3) those in families in the first year of transition from AFDC to employment. The latter two programs had provided assistance on an open-ended entitlement basis, so that the federal government matched state spending on child care with no upper limit. By contrast, the new law creates a capped Child Care and Development block grant, a consolidated fund over which states exercise a high level of discretionary control. Only a few federal guidelines apply to the use of these funds, such as the stipulation that at least 70 percent of each state's allocation be used for low-income, single-parent families. The abolition of the entitlement status means that, at least in some states, a parent who cannot afford the daycare required to participate in a work or training program may be cut off from TANF assistance when the time limit is reached.

To its credit, the new law increases the actual level of federal funding for child care. Over six years, the consolidated block grants include a base allocation of $7.2 billion (to be divided among states based on past spending patterns) and additional grants to qualifying states of up to $6.7 billion, for a total of $13.9 billion. However, a series of studies conducted by the C.B.O. raises serious doubts whether these new funds will be adequate to meet the increased demand for child care as expanded work requirements and time limits take effect. If states meet their new work requirement percentage targets, the child care funding would run $1.8 billion short in fiscal year 2002, assuming the continuation of current patterns of need for such assistance.[68] The new child care needs of the flood of single parents forced into workfare and similar work arrangements would simply overwhelm even the enhanced system of federal assistance for daycare. Only a funding mechanism based on open-ended entitlements is flexible enough to meet such increased needs for child care assistance, but this is precisely what the new law revokes.

68. For details, see Super and others, "The New Welfare Law," 12–4.

In a third category of federal spending, child nutrition programs, far fewer changes were made. Despite long deliberations during which a capped block grant approach was seriously considered, the school lunch program and the Women, Infants and Children (WIC) nutrition program remained practically untouched by the new law. However, an estimated $2.9 billion in savings over six years will be realized through modest reductions in two programs: the Child and Adult Food Care Program which subsidizes meals provided to children in day care centers; and the Summer Food Service Program for Children which supplies meals in low-income areas when school lunches are not available.[69]

The cuts in a fourth category, Supplemental Security Income for Disabled Children, will cause more hardship because they are concentrated on a small number of children who will lose their eligibility for any assistance at all under this program. The new law restricts the types of disabilities (especially in categories which previously considered the combined effect of several minor disabilities) which qualify children for this program. According to the C.B.O., approximately 22 percent of previously eligible low-income children will no longer qualify; by 2002, 315,000 children who would have been eligible for assistance under the previous rules will be denied benefits. The estimated six-year cost savings are $7 billion. This measure is largely a response to the perception that this program had been abused through fraudulent claims and inappropriate allowances. A study by the National Academy of Social Insurance acknowledges that this is a legitimate concern, but recommends some prudent alternative steps to address abuses. Instead of implementing sharp reductions in the rolls by mandating stricter adherence to a fixed "List of Impairments," the program would be more responsive to true need if it retained doctor-administered "individualized functional assessments" as a tool to determine eligibility for benefits to sick, low-income children.[70]

In the fifth category of federal assistance, Medicaid coverage for the health needs of low-income families, sweeping changes were narrowly averted in the final weeks of welfare reform deliberation. Medicaid benefits have been automatically tied to recipiency of AFDC; now that the guarantee of welfare assistance was revoked under the TANF block grant system, Medicaid coverage for millions of poor women and children could have been placed at risk. This danger was averted when congressional leaders accepted an amendment to the emerging welfare law which

---

69. For details, see ibid., 22–3.
70. See ibid., 29–30; Jeffrey Katz, 2699.

linked eligibility for Medicaid to the AFDC rules in effect in each state as of July 1996. Thus, regardless of how a state uses its TANF funds or how it implements the new time limitation and work requirements, low-income families will continue to receive Medicaid on the same basis as they did under AFDC.

The sixth change involves the Social Services Block Grant, a long-standing method of federal revenue sharing with the states. The new law trims the size of these allotments by 15 percent, so that in each year from 1997 to 2002, only $2.38 billion is available. Of all the features of the new welfare law, this provision attracted perhaps the least attention, but will have powerful and immediate impact upon the actual delivery of social services. In previous years, these appropriations have been used "for hundreds of purposes, typically to help the elderly poor stay out of nursing homes, to pay for shelters and day care, to rehabilitate juvenile criminals, and to rescue children from parental abuse or neglect."[71] Unless states make up for the funding cut of $420 million annually, they will be in the difficult position of having to choose which subgroups of the poor they will continue to serve and which social service programs will be eliminated.

7. Probable effects of the new law

We have already noted several likely effects of the new welfare law; these spring from qualitative changes in program structures and eligibility criteria, as well as quantitative changes in the level of federal financial commitment to programs for the poor. A frequently cited summary of the combined effects of these changes appears in a report released by the Urban Institute (an independent Washington-based research center) on 26 July 1996, just as the last details of the bill were finalized in congressional conference committee. The study estimates that the bill's provisions would push 2.6 million people below the poverty line, including 1.1 million children. This represents a 12 percent increase in childhood poverty. When all the law's measures are implemented, the annual poverty gap (the total amount of income that would be required to lift all poor families with children exactly to the government-defined poverty line) will increase by $4 billion (a 20 percent increase).[72] Some house-

71. Peter Kilborn, "Little-Noticed Cut Imperils Safety Net for the Poor," *New York Times*, 22 Sept. 1996, 1, 16.
72. Figures are from a timely summary of the report ("Urban Institute Study Confirms That Welfare Bill Would Increase Child Poverty") published by the Center on Budget and Policy Priorities (Washington, D.C.: 26 July 1996). The accuracy of these figures has not been seriously disputed.

holds will see dramatic decreases in income; the 8.2 million families most affected by the law will lose an average of $1,300 annually. The report's accuracy is confirmed by how closely its estimates match figures from the C.B.O. and the Clinton administration.[73] In fact, the Urban Institute used the most conservative possible assumptions in its calculations,[74] so the poverty effects of the law when actually implemented may be significantly higher than these figures.

The key source of uncertainty in predicting the effects of any social legislation concerns how people will respond to incentives written into laws. In the case of the new welfare rules, the poverty increase is a function of three factors: (1) lost benefits; (2) replacement of these benefits by increased work effort (largely by single mothers who reach the time limit); and (3) the formation of fewer single-parent families requiring assistance (under the assumption that anti-illegitimacy measures have some effect). The Urban Institute study assumes that two-thirds of mothers who lose welfare eligibility will get jobs and another quarter will qualify for an exemption. Both these estimates depend upon unconfirmed assumptions about how individuals and states will respond to new federal policy. One certainty, however, is that even finding a job is no guarantee of being lifted above the poverty line. Millions of American families (the "working poor") subsist on subpoverty wages supplemented by such programs as Food Stamps. The Urban Institute report finds that the new welfare law contains bad news for this group as well; over half of the eleven million families whose incomes will decline as a result of the legislation already contain at least one working member.[75]

Uncertainty about behavioral responses to the new legislation also affects assessments of potential geographical dimensions of the welfare changes. We have already noted the possibility that a "race to the bottom" will be ignited when devolution of programs to the state level threatens to make some states especially stingy with benefits in order to avoid be-

73. Although the administration's Office of Management and Budget chose not to conduct a study of the poverty effects of the final legislation, its Nov. 1995 report on the welfare bill (in the slightly different version being considered at that time) predicted nearly identical effects. See Alison Mitchell, "Greater Poverty Toll Is Seen in Welfare Bill," *New York Times*, 10 Nov. 1995, A27.

74. The researchers assumed that: (1) all states would adopt the longest possible time limits allowed under the law (five years); (2) no state would reduce basic benefit levels except to the extent that the capped federal block grants proved insufficient to maintain current benefit levels; (3) states would not withdraw resources from income support and work programs (although the law allows them 33 percent reductions); and (4) no economic recession will occur.

75. Center on Budget and Policy Priorities, "Urban Institute Study Confirms," 5.

coming "welfare magnets." The "maintenance of effort" provisions in the new law only partially respond to these concerns. States retain the prerogative to shift up to a third of their federal welfare funding away from direct income support, so that existing state-to-state benefit differentials may be exacerbated under the new law.

Further, the time limitation principle introduces an entirely new set of concerns about the geography of poverty. Even assuming a model of human behavior in which people would relocate to higher-benefit states, it is safe to say that no people will change their place of residence in order to receive benefits for which they are no longer eligible. Rather, the concern is that, as one commentator fears, "we will have created a 'welfare dust bowl' in our inner cities."[76] Facing an inadequate supply of jobs and greatly eroded income support programs, inner cities may lose large shares of their population, as people flee to areas with more employment opportunities. This potential exodus from areas with high welfare recipiency and declining job bases (mostly large cities in the Northeast and Midwest[77]) to suburban and sunbelt areas would surely cause hardship and dislocation, as a few regions struggle to absorb an unprecedented flood of internal migration.

A related potential effect of the new welfare law involves its disproportionate impact on racial minorities, especially African-Americans. Although one-fifth of all U.S. children live in families with incomes below the poverty line, approximately one-half of black children experience poverty, so the new law will push a disproportionate number of blacks even further into poverty. A corollary (even if completely unintended) effect of the law involves its impact upon minority and inner-city neighborhoods, where much of the economic activity depends upon income derived from means-tested government programs. Although it is notoriously difficult to measure the economic fallout of such policy changes on the imprecise units we call "neighborhoods," evidence from the recent experience of public assistance cuts in New York suggests a significant impact "on the street level" due to lost income from welfare and other

76. Mark Alan Hughes, "Welfare Dust Bowl," *Washington Post*, 25 Sept. 1995, A23.
77. There is also the possibility that some depressed rural areas will experience similar out-flows of population due to this same combination of factors. One account of the new predicament of the rural poor (Jon Jeter and Judith Havemann, "Rural Poor May Seek Greener Pastures: Welfare Recipients Face Relocation As a Result of Work Rules," *Washington Post*, 14 Oct. 1996, A1, A18) describes efforts already underway in several states to encourage and assist the rural poor to relocate to areas with higher job availability. Although only one-quarter of welfare families live in rural areas, the dearth of transportation and local work opportunities compounds the barriers to employment there.

transfer programs.[78] The families which replace these losses with income from new earnings are the residents least likely to remain in these neighborhoods, so hoped-for gains from work are unlikely to drive substantial economic recovery in these neighborhoods. As these dynamics unfold within low-income communities, it will be necessary for public policy to be more attentive to the racial and geographical dimensions of social spending reductions which have differential impacts on demographic groups.

The data above concerning child poverty suggest several possible scenarios for how children will be affected by the new law. To be sure, the lives of some welfare children will be improved, as their parents respond to the incentives to leave welfare and take advantage of whatever economic opportunities become available. However, conditions will worsen for children in families which run up against the time limits without finding work which pays more than welfare, especially in states which make fewer efforts to provide opportunities for training and work. Two possibilities seem most likely.

First, in families where some of the lost welfare income is replaced (by some combination of earnings from work, child-support payments, charitable assistance and gifts), the ability to raise children in a healthy and positive environment will be compromised, although not completely eliminated. Such families will make sacrifices that include moving into smaller apartments in less desirable neighborhoods, foregoing nonessential health care and eating a less balanced diet.

Second, those families completely unable to adjust to the new conditions will bear the full brunt of a drastic reduction in income, including likely eviction from their homes and complete reliance on the social service system of private and government-run emergency shelters and soup kitchens. The final terminus of children following this path of hunger and homelessness is the child protection system, including foster care and similar institutions. Former welfare children will enter the system when their parents voluntarily admit an inability to care for them or involuntarily surrender them to legal authorities. Several recent accounts of the new challenges to family preservation[79] confirm the arguments about the necessity of an "orphanage solution" as advanced by Newt Gingrich during 1995 welfare reform deliberation. Recall that the original intention of

78. Joe Sexton, "The Trickle-Up Economy: Poor Neighborhoods Fear a Disaster if Welfare Is Cut," *New York Times*, 8 Feb. 1996, B1, B9.

79. See Nina Bernstein, "Do Plans to Restructure the Welfare System Pose a Burden for Foster Care?" *New York Times*, 19 Nov. 1995, 1, 26; Judy Mann, "Welfare Cuts: Making Children Pay," *Washington Post*, 6 Dec. 1995, C26.

the welfare program was to keep hard-pressed families intact through the strategy of income maintenance. With the abolition of AFDC's income guarantees, an influx of children into the costly and already overburdened child protection system will serve as eloquent testimony that this policy goal has been largely abandoned.

Finally, the new welfare law will affect conditions in labor markets. While the effects cannot be predicted with precision, some basic calculations indicate the direction of changes in the supply and price of labor (i.e., in the size of the workforce and prevailing wage levels) resulting from this legislation. Nearly four million adults (mostly single mothers) live in households which received AFDC when the new law took effect (October 1996). Assuming that states will meet targets for work participation, by 2002 (when the law mandates that 50 percent of this number be working) there will be approximately two million new workers in the low-wage end of the labor market. This rapid infusion of new job-seekers represents a large increase in the supply of labor, which will exert a significant downward pressure on wage levels.[80]

Alternatively, it is possible that these labor market changes will be diminished or non-existent because the states will not meet the work participation quotas. The difficulties of reaching the quotas are numerous, especially when the ambitious mandates for welfare-to-work transitions are compared to the cumulative experience of programs assisting welfare recipients to overcome their barriers to employment. Even the most successful experiment, the Riverside, California, GAIN (Greater Avenues for Independence) program begun in 1985, has yielded very modest success rates; approximately 23 percent of its participants made "income exits" (sustained over three years) from welfare.[81] Even the C.B.O. acknowledges that the legislation's work goals are not realistic; Senator Daniel Patrick Moynihan offers this summary of a C.B.O. report on the final version of the bill: "Given the costs and administrative complexities in-

---

80. Using the idiom of neoclassical economics, this represents an outward shift of the labor supply curve, causing a new market equilibrium at a point further down the labor demand curve, at a higher quantity but a lower price. In other words, within the affected occupational groups, more people will be working, but at lower prevailing wages. The relative size of the changes in price and quantity of labor employed depends on the elasticity of the supply and demand curves.

81. See U.S. General Accounting Office, Report to the Chairman, Committee on Finance, U.S. Senate, "Welfare to Work: Current AFDC Program Not Sufficiently Focused on Employment" (Washington, D.C.: GAO, 19 Dec. 1994), esp. 19. The 23 percent figure appears less impressive when it is noted that 18 percent of a control group not participa-

volved, C.B.O. assumes that most states would simply accept penalties rather than implement the work requirements."[82]

Aside from the prospects for private sector employment, labor market conditions will also be affected by workfare practices, the public sector employment alternative. Workfare raises a number of serious concerns for regular employees of local governments. Will their jobs be displaced, devalued or otherwise adversely affected by the sudden presence of a new category of lower-paid worker beside them? Will their bargaining positions in future contract negotiations be eroded because of new labor "competition"? These concerns are reflected in the opposition many municipal union leaders (most notably in N.Y. among transit workers[83]) have expressed toward the expansion of workfare.

The looming "politics of workfare" is fueled by the prospect that regular workers will be intimidated into passivity and eventually replaced by the cheap (frequently, sub-minimum-wage) labor of workfare program participants. Workfare thus reveals its potential to be another face of the general tendency of poor relief arrangements to serve as an instrument of disciplinary control over the labor force. This perennial function of welfare was described a generation ago by Frances Fox Piven and Richard A. Cloward: "Relief arrangements are ancillary to economic arrangements. Their chief function is to regulate labor."[84]

8. What is missing in the new welfare law

The new law significantly restructures America's poor relief arrangements. The termination of the entitlement principle changes welfare from an income-support system into a work-based system in which the limited role of transitional assistance is to encourage people to take advantage of employment opportunities. An appropriate measure of the new system is the extent to which it makes this type of opportunity ef-

---

ting in the program's activities also experienced similar sustained "work exits" from welfare. The difficulty of trimming welfare caseloads (which fell by only 10 percent) and raising job earnings (which increased only 26 percent for the "successes") in even this relatively successful program demonstrates the dependence of these job placement efforts on external factors, such as the general health of the local economy. See Robert A. Moffitt, "The Effect of Employment and Training Programs on Entry and Exit from the Welfare Caseload," *Journal of Policy Analysis and Management* 15 (winter 1996) 32–50.

82. Quoted in Bob Herbert, "Welfare Hysteria," *New York Times*, 5 Aug. 1995, A17.

83. One controversy is described in Steven Greenhouse, "New York Union Leader Urges Halt to Broadening Workfare," *New York Times*, 23 Sept. 1996, A1, B5.

84. *Regulating the Poor: The Functions of Public Welfare*, updated edition (N.Y.: Vintage Books of Random House, Inc., 1993 [1971]) 3.

fective in practice. Does it provide the conditions that will (1) make work available, and (2) make work "pay" for America's poorest families? If it does not perform these tasks satisfactorily, the new system of workfare and transitional assistance will simply be enforcing a renewed obligation to work without making work an acceptable and realistic possibility for the population whose work behavior it targets.

On the first count, making work available, the new law is clearly inadequate. In the contemporary economic environment, where prolonged spells of unemployment face those lacking the marketable skills valued in increasingly automated workplaces, private sector work is not widely available for those leaving welfare. In order to address the disadvantages which lock millions of former welfare recipients into poor employment prospects, massive additional resources will be required—in education, skills enhancement, job training and placement services. At various stages of the welfare reform process, American leaders indicated an awareness of the need for such investments in "human capital," although this insight is not reflected in the actual provisions of the new law. For example, while campaigning in 1992, President Clinton frequently repeated his promise

> to provide people with the education, training, job placement assistance, and child care they need for two years—so that they can break the cycle of dependency. After two years, those who can work will be required to go to work, either in the private sector or in meaningful community-service jobs.[85]

Support was found to be lacking for one policy option to advance these goals: an ambitious public-sector work program which would serve as a government-guaranteed source of "jobs of last resort." William Julius Wilson is one of the few public voices to champion such an approach,[86] as he advocates a proposal modeled on the New Deal's Works Progress Administration programs for the unemployed. More modest federal measures to support employment seemed initially to be within the realm of possibility as an outcome of the welfare reform process. Here is one account of the magnitude of this unmet need and the failure of a new federal effort to materialize as part of welfare reform:

> As recently as 1994, there was a general consensus that additional measures were needed if the welfare system was to be converted to a work-

---

85. Quoted in Berrick, *Faces of Poverty*, 149.
86. *The Truly Disadvantaged*, 150–1. Wilson calls for a variety of government action to "improve the job prospects" of low-skilled people, including "the creation of a macroeconomic policy designed to promote both economic growth and a tight labor market."

based system. The original Contract with America provided $10 billion over five years in funding for work programs. Although the new legislation places states under stringent requirements to put an increasing proportion of recipients receiving aid under the TANF block grant in work activities, funding for work programs in the bill falls short of what is needed to meet the bill's work requirements. CBO projects that the cost of meeting the work requirements, excluding child care costs, will reach $5.6 billion in 2002 . . . . Furthermore, according to CBO, the legislation falls $12 billion short of what will be needed over the next six years to meet the work requirements, excluding child care costs.[87]

The rhetoric of "empowering people to escape the trap of dependency" has frequently been invoked to describe the goal of welfare reform. The strategy chosen by legislators in pursuit of this goal is to encourage an increase in the work effort of those formerly on welfare. What is missing from the final law, however, is the allocation of adequate resources to make this "work-based solution" into an effective and realistic "jobs-based solution." David T. Ellwood's calculations illustrate this lacuna:

> When the dust settles, there would not be much money for welfare reform at all. States would get block grants to use for welfare and work programs. But the grants for childcare, job training, workfare and cash assistance combined would amount to less than $15 per poor child per week in poor Southern states like Mississippi and Arkansas. Moving people from welfare to work is hard. On $15 a week—whom are we kidding?[88]

True empowerment involves more than encouraging "personal responsibility" through stricter program rules. It is also a matter of "social responsibility" in which society, acting through government, makes available to its members the resources necessary to overcome disadvantages (such as barriers to employment) and improve their lives through work or other means.

Second, the new welfare law does little to "make work pay." Reasonable legislation will not only enact measures to enforce socially desirable behavior, but will also create a structure of incentives which communicate the message that this desirable behavior will be rewarded in ordinary social and economic interaction. On this count, the new welfare law comes up short once again. The legislation fails to exhibit a unified pro-work message for the population it targets (mostly unemployed

87. Super and others, "The New Welfare Law," 10–1.
88. David T. Ellwood, "Welfare Reform in Name Only," *New York Times*, 22 July 1996, A19.

single mothers) because it does nothing to address the plight of another group whose prospects are relevant to this debate: the working poor. At best, the unemployed welfare parents who respond to the law's time limitation provisions by finding work (in the types of low-wage jobs for which most of them are qualified) will join the ranks of the millions of Americans who remain below the poverty line despite holding full-time jobs.[89]

Some of the new law's effects on the working poor have already been noted. Because of cuts in Food Stamps, SSI, assistance to immigrants and other programs, millions of families with working members will experience a loss of income.[90] We have already noted one of the indirect ways the new law harms the working poor; because workfare arrangements may flood the low end of labor markets with millions of new workers, unionized and nonunionized low-wage workers may lose some of their bargaining power. Another indirect effect is the potential loss of child care subsidies for the working poor who will find themselves at the end of long waiting lists for these subsidies, since former welfare recipients transitioning to work will be given preference for this limited funding under the new law.[91] This situation is emblematic of a new atmosphere in the provision of social services in the post-entitlement era. Depending upon how states choose to allocate and administer their capped federal funding, various categories of the poor will find themselves competing against each other for limited quantities of services and material assistance.

While other legislation in recent years (the expansion of the Earned Income Tax Credit,[92] and increases in the minimum wage) have strengthened the position of some working poor, major improvements to "make work pay" would have to occur before their situation would serve as encouragement and incentive for those leaving welfare for work. Perhaps the most significant issue to be faced in this regard involves health insurance. In the absence of substantive health care reform, tens of millions of

---

89. On the imperative for welfare reform to address the plight of the working poor, see Sar A. Levitan and Isaac Shapiro, "What's Missing in Welfare Reform," *Challenge* 30 (July/Aug. 1987) 41–8.

90. For example, the 2.3 million food stamp households with a worker will lose an average of $355 in 1998. See Super and others, "The New Welfare Law," 18.

91. See Peter Finn, "Welfare Shifts Tax Child-Care Funds: Area's Working Poor Caught in Child-Care Bind," *Washington Post*, 7 Oct. 1996, B1, B5.

92. The new law leaves EITC unchanged. The earlier version of the bill vetoed by President Clinton in Jan. 1996 would have mandated large cuts in this form of income assistance for the working poor.

Americans in working families will remain uninsured, since not all jobs include health care benefits. The plight of uninsured workers and their dependents serves as a deterrent against efforts to leave the public assistance rolls, since recipients typically lose Medicaid eligibility within months of leaving welfare. While the new law does retain the transitional Medicaid benefits already in place, it fails to address this "notch effect." Former welfare recipients will continue to face the high probability of poverty despite increased work efforts.

What is most fundamentally lacking in the new law is a comprehensive approach to the economic problems of the most disadvantaged American families. Because of the narrowness of its focus on increased work effort as the solution to poverty, the law emphasizes "pushing" former recipients into work (by imposing heavy sanctions on non-work) rather than "pulling" them into the economic mainstream (by committing new resources to work preparation). It relies upon a pro-work strategy which consists of "mostly stick, little carrot." Welfare recipients may well have no choice but to comply with its provisions, but, because the plight of the working poor remains unaddressed, the new law does not offer them the kind of reasonable incentive structure that will encourage them to pursue a better life for their families through a process of self-directed empowerment.

A more comprehensive approach would include the types of measures which other developed nations have adopted under the rubric of "family policy."[93] Such legislation supports family life in general (and poor families in particular) by providing income security as well as enhancing economic opportunity. Family policy is a set of measures which complement welfare policy by creating an entire social ecology more friendly to low-income families. While family policy utilizes the usual impersonal tools of government (particularly the taxation system), at its best it can respond sensitively to such particular concerns of families as the need for flextime, emergency medical leave, special forms of health care and other pressures on family life relating to the nurturance of children. It is only within the larger context of the development of a more conscious pro-family legislative agenda that welfare policy in the post-AFDC era will be able to advance all of the original objectives of the AFDC program.

---

93. For a comparative perspective, see Sheila B. Kamerman and Alfred J. Kahn, eds., *Family Policy: Government and Families in Fourteen Countries* (N.Y.: Columbia University Press, 1978).

By any accounting, AFDC as it stood in the early 1990s needed to be revised and adjusted to new social conditions and expectations. However, the pressures for change have resulted in legislation which, in abolishing the entitlements of the troubled AFDC program, also wiped away our nation's major tool for pursuing a critical national objective: strengthening family life by providing income security for our most vulnerable neighbors.

Part Three

The Bishops' Contribution to the Welfare Reform Debate

Chapter 5

A "Public Church" Addresses Welfare Reform

The goal of Part Three is to explore how Catholic social teaching was utilized to stake out a position in recent U.S. welfare reform debates. We will rely on the American bishops, as those who hold the highest offices in the Catholic Church in the U.S., to serve as faithful interpreters and teachers of Catholic social teaching.[1] In attending to the U.S. bishops' statements on welfare, we implicitly identify them as authentic carriers of the tradition of Catholic social ethics in the American context.

This chapter examines the documents of the bishops and allied spokespersons of the American Catholic hierarchy, placing them within the context of key developments in the welfare reform debates of the years 1986–96. Just enough descriptive and narrative background will be included to provide a glimpse of how the bishops' activities regarding social policy over the past decade constitute a conscious effort to advance the "public church" dimension of their ministry. The next chapter will explicate (with some reworking in the interests of clarity and conciseness) five principles the bishops have advanced concerning directions to pursue in contemporary American social welfare policy. These five guidelines may be considered specifications of the more general principles of Catholic social teaching reviewed in Part One above.

Although our primary interest is in investigating the principles contained in these documents, we must devote some prior attention to the process through which the bishops produce these documents and the general method by which the American Catholic Church speaks on matters

---

1. We thus opt for a stance primarily of observation as opposed to alternative methodologies, such as conducting an independent scholarly application of Catholic social teaching to U.S. social policy. Such an investigation into the policy recommendations a "Catholic position" might include could reach conclusions at variance with the bishops' contribution.

of public policy. In one sense, the pedigree of the documents relevant to our study goes back to the Bishops' Program for Social Reconstruction, the groundbreaking effort of the American bishops in 1920 to join their voices in advocating measures for the attainment of a more just economic order. This landmark document has been followed by a flood of others, published by the bishops on an ad hoc or a regular basis (such as the long series of Labor Day and pre-election statements on political and economic issues).

The United States Catholic Conference (USCC) in Washington, D.C., is the nonprofit public policy agency serving the American bishops, who themselves are organized into another closely related entity called the National Conference of Catholic Bishops (NCCB). The USCC is comprised of several committees and offices which perform the "public outreach" tasks for the bishops; it includes a department dedicated to "Domestic Social Development." This department serves a number of functions: as the lobbying arm of the bishops, as a resource for the drafting of documents on social and economic policy "authored" by individual bishops or groups of bishops, and as a liaison to the social justice offices of the Catholic dioceses in the U.S.[2]

The "New Welfare Consensus" of the 1980s and the Bishops' Demurral

Any listing of documents from the Bishops' Conference with import for welfare reform must begin with the 1986 encyclical letter, *Economic Justice for All*. Paragraphs 186–214 of this document consist of a set of seven "guidelines for action" to address the problem of American poverty. The final item on this list calls for a "thorough reform of the nation's welfare and income-support programs."[3] In five paragraphs, the bishops advocate a series of measures to accomplish two tasks: (1) to improve the welfare system as it existed in the 1980s; and (2) to go beyond that system through new initiatives to make welfare arrangements better fit the values of family, work and community.

In the first category fall the bishops' suggestions for national eligibility standards and uniform minimum benefit levels for AFDC recipi-

---

2. The phrase "Bishops' Conference" will be used as a general term to cover the activities of the professional staff of the USCC as well as the NCCB. The latter term is properly applied only to the body of over 200 U.S. bishops as they assemble three times a year; at other times, it is actually the "Administrative Committee of the NCCB" (a subgroup of appointed bishops) which speaks for the larger body in a timely manner.

3. EJA 210.

ents, measures designed to eliminate distressing state-to-state disparities in safety net provision. As indicated in Part Two above, the variability of welfare benefits and eligibility criteria constitutes a great unfairness to recipients in low-benefit states. These state-to-state differences are not correlated to substantial differences in the level of need of low-income families in these states, but rather are the legacy of unfair racial bias and other forms of ethnic and gender discrimination. The bishops name as a serious injustice the tendency of state governments to encode in their social policy a number of agendas (such as racism and the unrelenting enforcement of labor market discipline) which impede the goal of maintaining an adequate income for vulnerable families.

In the second category are the bishops' suggestions to redesign public assistance programs so that they will henceforth "assist recipients, wherever possible, to become self-sufficient through gainful employment."[4] Some concrete measures to fulfill this goal are listed; they include job creation programs for welfare recipients, coordinated with such services as job training, placement, counseling and child care. The bishops also mention the need to address "notch effects" which discourage people from leaving the welfare rolls. This occurs when, for example, "under current rules, people who give up welfare benefits to work in low-paying jobs soon lose their Medicaid benefits."[5] By implementing such changes in program rules, the U.S. welfare system would move closer to abiding by a prudential rule of thumb identified by the bishops: "Individuals should not be worse off economically when they get jobs than when they rely only on public assistance."[6]

Although the bishops' treatment of welfare in 1986 was relatively brief and was folded into a long and wide-ranging document, it was not overlooked in policy circles. The welfare reform bill which was passed during the next Congress, The Family Support Act of 1988, includes numerous measures which reflect the same concerns and some of the same strategies embraced by the bishops. This bipartisan legislation amended AFDC program rules in several ways. It eliminated some of the most egregious "notch effects" (through provisions for transitional Medicaid benefits and more generous "earnings disregards" in determining eligibility for cash benefits) and made new federal resources available to states for services (such as child care and job training) designed to ease the transition from welfare to work. Although the 1988 law espoused an

4. Ibid., 211.
5. Ibid.
6. Ibid.

enhanced "work strategy" which increased work incentives and introduced new work expectations for nonexempt AFDC recipients, it resolutely reaffirmed the principle that the federal government should commit resources to unemployed single parents. The FSA thus represents a firm response to the assault on welfare spending during the "mean season" of the 1980s, when pressures for sharp cuts in AFDC had arisen from the more extreme voices heard during the Reagan years. The "welfare consensus" of the late 1980s thus constituted a "positive" welfare consensus (one committed to continuing the desirable elements in the existing programs and making improvements, even at substantial cost), not a solely "negative" one (focused on cutting budgets and introducing punitive measures into the welfare system).

There is no simple way to assess the place of the bishops' welfare recommendations in *Economic Justice for All* in the welfare reform process of the late 1980s. Without doubt, the end of the Reagan years witnessed a noteworthy convergence of opinion across the political spectrum in America on how best to approach the topics (family, dependency, work obligation, teen pregnancy) that most directly frame welfare as a policy issue. The findings of several blue-ribbon commissions and scholarly studies sponsored by private groups and government agencies indicated the existence of the "new consensus" which was implemented through the 1988 FSA.[7] This consensus centered around a growing conviction that paid employment rather than cash transfers should be the primary strategy to raise the incomes of needy families. A convergence of opinion along these lines justifies a greater commitment on the part of federal and state governments to adopt programs (such as job training and subsidized child care) which will empower single mothers to make the transition from welfare to work—precisely the policy goals which the FSA sought to achieve.

Social ethicist Philip Land, s.j., devotes an entire volume to identifying the precise contribution which the bishops, in publishing *Economic Justice for All*, made to this new convergence of opinion. Land sees enough similarities between the bishops' recommendations and the FSA

---

7. The recommendations of several such studies are summarized in a report of The Working Seminar on Family and American Welfare Policy, sponsored by the Institute for Family Studies at Marquette University. The volume, *The New Consensus on Family and Welfare*, was co-published by Marquette University in Milwaukee and the American Enterprise Institute for Public Policy Research in Washington, D.C. in 1987. The study's ten policy recommendations, drawn from the findings of several earlier commissions on welfare, are much more moderate than the welfare recommendations contained in the Republicans' "Contract with America" written eight years later.

to warrant his claim that the bishops did indeed play a significant role in shaping the eventual policy outcome. He also notes that basic tenets of Catholic social teaching lead the bishops to espouse certain distinctive positions about the proper role of government in pursuing the common good in modern societies—positions seldom reflected in partisan policy debates. Although much overlap exists between the positions of the bishops and those of liberals and conservatives who joined together in a temporary consensus on welfare in the late 1980s, the bishops harbor significant reservations about many popular policy directions. Land concludes:

> The Bishops hold a middle ground between conservatives and liberals on the welfare function of the state. But it is a proper ground of its own, and not simply a picking of ideas from one side and the other . . . .
> Quite apart from the Bishops' position within the consensus on welfare reform, the Pastoral holds foundational views about welfare. While being the object of severe attacks from within and outside the Catholic community, these views are both defensible and a powerful contribution to welfare policy in general.[8]

Among these distinctive "foundational views on welfare," Land lists some themes and principles of Catholic social teaching we have already seen: the preferential option for the poor, subsidiarity, the recognition of the phenomena of "socialization" and interdependence, and the challenge of fostering economic democracy.[9] However, there is one area of Catholic social teaching not treated in the analysis of chapter one above which provides the basis for the U.S. bishops' most prominent point of disagreement with the "new welfare consensus" of the late 1980s: the issue of family life and, more specifically, how best to shape welfare policy so that it preserves the dignity of single-parent families.

The prevailing bipartisan wisdom which shaped the Family Support Act of 1988 and (in more dramatic fashion) the new welfare law of 1996 is that the well-being of female-headed families will unambiguously be advanced by moving single mothers into work outside the home, through whatever arrangements will expedite this transition. Both laws thus contain provisions which permit, encourage and even require the states to develop programs (such as workfare and mandatory participation in job training or work activities, combined with fewer hardship exemptions) which force mothers to leave their young children in daycare while they either: (1) take a job in exchange for welfare benefits; or (2) accept pri-

---

8. Philip S. Land, s.J., *Shaping Welfare Consensus: U.S. Catholic Bishops' Contribution* (Washington, D.C.: Center of Concern, 1988) 157.
9. Ibid., 145–51, 171–84.

vate sector employment which will move them out of welfare entirely. The former AFDC program rules, whereby mothers with children under the age of three were generally exempt from work requirements, have been abrogated by the 1996 law, which now allows states to impose work requirements upon new mothers as soon after delivery as they wish. These program rule changes are supported, of course, by widespread awareness of the cultural trend by which nonwelfare mothers, single as well as married, more frequently opt for paid employment (part- or full-time, with the ensuing reliance on daycare for their children) rather than devoting themselves full-time to caring for their own children in their homes.

In *Economic Justice for All*, the U.S. bishops' most substantial demurral from the new welfare consensus is their rejection of welfare rules which, according to their alternative interpretation of what is good for families, weaken family life because they force single mothers with preschool children to work outside the home. While the bishops offer no opposition to programs and policies which encourage (through incentives and transition assistance) single mothers to work, they view it as a violation of the dignity of these families to force mothers of young children into paid employment. The bishops write:

> [S]ociety's institutions and policies should be structured so that mothers of young children are not forced by economic necessity to work outside the home. The nation's social welfare and tax policies should support parents' decisions to care for their own children and should recognize the work of parents in the home because of its value for the family and for society.[10]

This particular element of the bishops' own version of a "family values" argument echoes the concerns of a key passage in the first chapter of the same pastoral letter: "The economic and cultural strength of the nation is directly linked to the stability and health of its families . . . . When families are weak or break down entirely, the dignity of parents and children is threatened."[11]

When the bishops thus explicitly link public policy with "the ability of families to fulfill their roles in nurturing children,"[12] they are drawing from a long tradition of concern for family life in papal encyclicals and other Vatican documents. Frequently, the ability of mothers to remain at home to nurture their children in the early years of childhood is a focal point of this concern. For example, *Quadragesimo anno* in 1931 identi-

---

10. EJA 297.
11. Ibid., 18.
12. Ibid., 206.

fies this concern as part of its rationale (within the dominant patriarchal family model of the time) for supporting the notion that the "wage paid to the workingman should be sufficient for the support of himself and his family." Only under this condition can we hope to counteract "the abuse whereby mothers of families, because of the insufficiency of the father's salary, are forced to engage in gainful occupations outside the domestic walls to the neglect of their own proper cares and duties, particularly the education of their children."[13]

Vatican documents in recent years have added some measure of gender sensitivity and an awareness of the changed economic role of women, even while retaining this basic commitment to the idea that there is intrinsic value in full-time parenting. In the face of the massive entry of women (many of whom are mothers) into the paid labor force of many industrial societies, the argument increasingly takes the form of recognizing that some mothers with young children may choose to work outside the home, but that none should be forced by economic necessity to do so. Vatican II's *Gaudium et spes*[14] and John Paul II's *Familiaris consortio*[15] made this argument in summary form, but were soon eclipsed by two Vatican documents which treated this topic at greater length and in even more noteworthy ways.

The first of these two was *Laborem exercens*, the 1981 encyclical of Pope John Paul II. Section 19 treats the topic of women and work in a way which neither simply repeats earlier Church pronouncements on traditional gender and family roles nor makes an abrupt break with the past positions of popes and councils. John Paul recognizes that twentieth-century realities necessitate some updating[16] of the view that "a woman's place is in the home." As he considers the needs of families with young children for both income and the maintenance of a stable home life, the Pope indicates his awareness that conflicting goals confront families (and especially mothers) with difficult choices, and that government policies have the potential to reduce the costs associated with some of these trade-

---

13. QA 71.
14. GS 67.
15. Pope John Paul II, *Familiaris Consortio: Papal Exhortation on the Family* (Washington, D.C.: USCC Office of Publishing and Promoting Services, 1981), pars. 23, 81.
16. LE 19 states: "Experience confirms that there must be a social re-evaluation of the mother's role, of the toil connected with it and of the need that children have for care, love and affection in order that they may develop into responsible, morally and religiously mature and psychologically stable persons." All subsequent citations in this paragraph are from LE 19.

offs. He repeats the traditional call for the "family wage,"[17] but adds a second category of government action to insure the income of families: "through other social measures such as family allowances or grants to mothers devoting themselves exclusively to their families." In the context of U.S. social policy, this is accurately interpreted as a call for a welfare policy which insures a single mother the ability to delay her entry into paid employment until her children are of school age.

Laborem exercens does not represent a break with the Catholic Church's position on gender identities, a stance which feminists term "essentialism"—an approach to gender issues which includes the opinion that there is a natural correlation between biological functions and fixed gender roles. However, it is noteworthy how *Laborem exercens* cites the innate mission of motherhood as a source of women's legitimate claims against social institutions which might threaten their aspirations, not as a reason to subordinate or restrict women in their work and home life options:

> It will redound to the credit of society to make it possible for a mother—without inhibiting her freedom, without psychological or practical discrimination, and without penalizing her as compared with other women—to devote herself to taking care of her children and educating them in accordance with their needs, which vary with age. Having to abandon these tasks in order to take up paid work outside the home is wrong from the point of view of the good of society and of the family when it contradicts or hinders these primary goals of the mission of a mother. . . .
>
> But it is fitting that [women] should be able to fulfill their tasks in accordance with their own nature, without being discriminated against and without being excluded from jobs for which they are capable, but also without lack of respect for their family aspirations and for their specific role in contributing, together with men, to the good of society. The true advancement of women requires that labor should be structured in such a way that women do not have to pay for their advancement by abandoning what is specific to them and at the expense of the family, in which women as mothers have an irreplaceable role.[18]

If public policies based on this moral analysis were implemented, many women would find themselves in an improved economic position. Their desires to pursue the goods of motherhood and professional careers would be better supported by laws (including antidiscrimination measures, provisions for flextime and parental leave, besides welfare laws)

---

17. It is here described as "a single salary, given to the head of the family for his work, sufficient for the needs of the family without the other spouse having to take up gainful employment outside the home. . . ."

18. LE 19.

which recognize the social contributions of both paths and protects the ability of women (whether married or single) to succeed in either or both, according to their wishes. Although they begin from very different perspectives, John Paul's updated version of the Catholic Church's analysis of family life converges somewhat with the position of the mainstream of the feminist movement. These unlikely allies both argue that public policies (such as welfare laws) advance the cause of justice when they support women's aspirations to exercise more choice in such questions as whether to stay home with their young children. This interpretation of justice for low-income single mothers is at odds with the American welfare law of 1996, which enforces work participation quotas, ends the entitlement status of AFDC and gives to the states new freedoms to force single mothers into workfare.[19]

The second document which makes the argument that mothers should not be forced by economic necessity to work outside the home is the Vatican "Charter of the Rights of the Family." It was published in 1983 and is addressed to "all states, international organizations, and all interested institutions and persons"[20] in an attempt to promote respect for family rights. While most of the norms and principles listed herein are mentioned in previous Church documents, the Charter is valuable in that it serves as an orderly "model and a point of reference for the drawing up of legislation and family policy, and guidelines for action programs"[21] to insure that families are strengthened by public policies. Article Ten of the Charter deals with the matters most relevant to social welfare policy; the full text of this article reads as follows:

> Families have a right to a social and economic order in which the organization of work permits the members to live together and does not hinder the unity, well-being, health and the stability of the family, while offering also the possibility of wholesome recreation. a) Remuneration for work must be sufficient for establishing and maintaining a family with dignity, either through a suitable salary, called a "family wage," or through other social measures such as family allowances or the remuneration of the work in the home of one of the parents; it should be such that mothers will not

---

19. This issue accords perhaps the most revealing glimpse into the fundamental differences between how the official Catholic Church, on the one hand, and the "New Religious Right," on the other, use the phrase "family values." Catholic social teaching may be credited with basing its support of certain public policies upon an appeal to enhanced freedom as well as dignity for all family members.

20. "Introduction" to the Vatican's "Charter of the Rights of the Family." Published in *Origins* 13, no. 27 (15 Dec. 1983) 461–4.

21. Ibid., 461.

be obliged to work outside the home to the detriment of family life and especially the education of the children.
b) The work of the mother in the home must be recognized and respected because of its value for the family and for society.[22]

The Charter is even more explicit than previous documents about the importance of the work of the mother within the home in families where children are present. It shares previously expressed concerns about protecting mothers from the necessity of working outside the home, both when an alternate breadwinner is available (thanks to policies which guarantee a "family wage") and when, as in the situation of single welfare mothers, no source of income besides the government is available. It also goes beyond previous Church documents in explicitly stating that the social contribution of homemakers should be "recognized," "respected" and even "remunerated." The Charter thus advances an argument (one which the U.S. bishops would borrow in opposing the welfare proposals of the "Contract with America") for the continuation of a social policy which recognizes a welfare entitlement for mothers of young children— an entitlement free from such conditions as mandatory workfare requirements. Indeed, the Charter invites a re-evaluation of the significance of social provision for such families. Since the efforts of mothers to educate their children have a wider dimension than is generally recognized (they contribute to society as well as the particular family), then welfare benefits may be construed as part of a social obligation to provide single mothers with favorable material conditions to support their work.

The above paragraphs have explored two developments: (1) how the American bishops, in writing *Economic Justice for All*, contributed to the "new welfare consensus" of the 1980s; and (2) how the bishops, drawing upon previous Vatican teachings on family life, demurred from one significant element of that welfare consensus which enjoyed support from both liberals and conservatives, Democrats and Republicans, in recent rounds of the welfare reform debate. A look at one additional document from the U.S. bishops will serve as a transition to the next section of this chapter, which will explore the documents of the U.S. Catholic Church which contributed to welfare reform in the 1990s.

In 1991, three USCC committees (Domestic Social Policy, International Policy, and Marriage and Family Life) co-authored "Putting Children and Families First: A Challenge for Our Church, Nation, and World." This seventeen-page pastoral letter was approved by the assembled bishops near the end of the year and published in 1992. Both chronologically

---

22. Ibid., 463.

and conceptually, it serves as a bridge between two rounds of welfare policy debate: (1) that which produced the FSA of 1988; and (2) that which produced the Personal Responsibility and Work Opportunity Act of 1996. In this document, the bishops focus more intensely on the project they had identified five years earlier in *Economic Justice for All*: subjecting all public policy to a particular form of scrutiny. They call upon readers to view policies through the lens of their effects on family life, especially that of the poorest and most vulnerable in our nation and abroad.

The 1992 letter includes a section which offers policy suggestions for assisting poor children. Two paragraphs reflect the bishops' awareness of the gap between the goals of Catholic social teaching and the actual achievements of the U.S. (in its social policy as well as in common cultural practices) on a key matter which affects the ability of low-income families to live in dignity:

> At a time when most mothers of young children are employed at least part time, our society sometimes loses sight of the value of parental care of young children. As pre-schoolers in day care becomes the norm, we fear the work of mothers in the home is becoming devalued, since it does not offer the economic rewards or recognition of other work.
>
> Our conference strongly supports effective voluntary programs to equip parents with education and job skills. We oppose compulsory and poorly designed efforts to require them to hand over to others the daily care of their preschool children. The fact that children are poor and in need of government aid does not take away their basic human right to be cared for by their parents if that is their family's choice.[23]

This pastoral letter's policy recommendations may be interpreted on two levels. First, the bishops seem to be complaining about the specific ways the policy process had produced unsatisfactory outcomes in the years immediately preceding the publication of this document. The 1988 FSA, while generally reflecting most of the bishops' earlier welfare recommendations, nevertheless had ignored the call (in *Economic Justice for All*) to reject measures which encourage mothers with young children to take paid employment outside the home. The bishops thus express concern that poor mothers will not enjoy the same level of choice in child-rearing arrangements as financially self-sufficient families.

On another level, the document serves as a vehicle for the bishops to register their broader discontent with the general drift of welfare policy

---

23. USCC, "Putting Children and Families First: The Challenge for Our Church, Nation and World" (Washington, D.C.: USCC Office of Publishing and Promotion Services, 1992) 10.

and public sentiment toward a punitive stance vis-à-vis poor families headed by single mothers. The years of the Bush administration witnessed an economic recession which caused welfare rolls to rise sharply and left many states in fiscal crisis, making it more difficult for them to devote to federally mandated welfare-to-work programs the resources necessary to empower single mothers to prepare for employment on reasonable terms. Public frustration with the costly JOBS program grew, as its provision of job training and other services came to be perceived as a luxury which states could not afford. In the years 1990–92, most public discussion about how to improve the program focused on more drastic measures to implement an employment strategy (which would give welfare mothers fewer choices), rather than on an income- and service-based strategy (which would give these women more choices about the terms and timeline for their efforts toward self-sufficiency).[24] The bishops' expression of concern about how such trends would threaten the dignity of family life (of which forced reliance on daycare is emblematic) may indicate that they foresaw how the policy debate would drift even further in subsequent years toward work enforcement (the strategy of the 1996 welfare law) rather than work incentive and preparation (the primary strategy of the 1988 FSA).

Documents of the U.S. Catholic Church, 1994–1996

Candidate Clinton's 1992 promise to "end welfare as we know it" enjoyed broad appeal because it addressed widespread concerns about the cost and seeming ineffectiveness of welfare programs. Clinton's promise also set off an alarm within some prominent sectors of the American Catholic community. This circle of concern included not only the Bishops' Conference, but also the national offices of Catholic Charities USA. Five months before the Clinton administration unveiled its long-delayed proposal for welfare reform in June 1994, Catholic Charities USA released an eighteen-page position paper entitled "Transforming the Welfare System."[25] It was commissioned by the Social Policy

---

24. On these alternative strategies and the history (up to 1994) of the welfare programs which implemented them, see Rebecca M. Blank, "The Employment Strategy: Public Policies to Increase Work and Earnings" in Sheldon Danziger, Gary D. Sandefur and Daniel H. Weinberg, eds., *Confronting Poverty: Prescriptions for Change* (Cambridge, Mass.: Harvard University Press, 1994) 168–204.

25. "Transforming the Welfare System: A Position Paper of Catholic Charities USA" (Alexandria, Va.: Catholic Charities USA, 24 Jan. 1994).

Committee of Catholic Charities USA and written by the dozen members of an ad hoc "AFDC work group."

A word about Catholic Charities USA and its relationship to the Bishops' Conference is necessary. Although Catholic Charities USA is a nonprofit organization which is formally and juridically independent of the Bishops' Conference, it nevertheless maintains a close working relationship with the bishops, since it represents the Catholic Church as its national network of social service agencies.[26] Because of the organizational ties between the Bishops Conference and Catholic Charities USA and, more importantly, the similarity of the policy recommendations of the two groups, we will treat the welfare reform statements of both groups together. Since their documents draw richly from the same tradition of Catholic social teaching, and since their staffs often collaborate on projects, the substance of their policy recommendations is practically identical.

The most substantial document on welfare reform published by the Bishops' Conference is a nine-page statement entitled "Moral Principles and Policy Priorities for Welfare Reform."[27] Because it was approved by the bishops at a meeting of the Administrative Board of the USCC in March 1995, over a full year after the publication of the Catholic Charities USA document, it had the advantage of being able to respond to the events of the intervening months. These included the unveiling of the Clinton welfare reform plan, the writing of the "Contract with America," the electoral success of the Republicans in capturing majorities in Congress, and the early success of The Personal Responsibility Act (the initial version of which had already passed in the House of Representatives).

A number of later documents, briefings and letters from individual bishops, groups of bishops or USCC offices advance the arguments contained in this statement (insofar as they respond to new circumstances such as legislative developments or executive actions), but none substantially deviates from the basic message of "Moral Principles and Policy

26. The organization's recent self-description reads: "Catholic Charities USA is the nation's largest private network of voluntary social service agencies. More than 1,400 local agencies with over 230,000 staff members and volunteers serve more than 14 million people in need—mostly families and children—each year. In 1992, Catholic Charities agencies across the United States spent more than $1.8 billion of combined public, private, and church resources in their efforts to reduce poverty, support families and empower communities."

27. "Moral Principles and Policy Priorities for Welfare Reform: A Statement of the Administrative Board of the United States Catholic Conference" (Washington, D.C.: USCC, 19 March 1995). This statement was published in *Origins* 24, no. 41 (30 March 1995) 673–7.

Priorities for Welfare Reform." Rather, these later documents generally repeat, apply and update the arguments of the major bishops' statement of March 1995. Before undertaking an analysis (in chapter six) of what is distinctive in the moral message of these Catholic documents on welfare reform, we close the present chapter with a brief description of the most important of these documents in which the Bishops' Conference or various bishops speak about welfare reform.[28] These documents fall into three categories.

1. *Letters from bishops.* Perhaps the must visible category of documents from the Bishops' Conference on welfare reform is a series of many letters, public appeals and similar statements written by (1) groups of bishops, (2) individual bishops speaking on their own initiative, or (3) a bishop speaking by virtue of his position in an office within the NCCB. These letters are usually addressed to public officials such as the President, Congress as a whole or various combinations of congressional leaders or committee members. In the first category belongs a 16 February 1995 statement by the bishops of Florida addressed to state and federal officials.[29] Such public actions on this subnational level are emblematic of the increasing importance of the approximately thirty recognized groupings of Catholic bishops, organized along state or regional lines, who cooperate in order to enhance their influence in local public affairs.

In the second category are a number of letters addressed to President Clinton on the three occasions when versions of welfare reform legislation reached his desk. Two typical examples are letters the President received just before he announced he would sign the final bill (one came from Cardinal Roger Mahoney of Los Angeles on 29 July 1996) and just after this announcement (one came from Bishop John Nevins of Venice, Florida, on 1 August 1996). Even in these brief letters which urge the President not to sign the bill, the bishops invoke theological arguments as well as warnings about the legislation's likely consequences which are judged unacceptable from the perspective of Catholic social teaching.

Prominent among documents in the third category are the following: (1) a letter from Bishop John Ricard of Baltimore, in his capacity of chairman of the USCC Domestic Policy Committee, to members of the House Ways and Means Committee, the Senate Finance Committee and the Department of Health and Human Services on 13 January 1995, ex-

---

28. Unless otherwise noted, they are available from the USCC through its Office of Publishing and Promotion Services or through its Office of Domestic Social Development.

29. Published as "Promoting Meaningful Welfare Reform," in *Origins* 24, no. 37 (2 March 1995) 609–12.

pressing objections to the Personal Responsibility Act;[30] (2) a statement from Cardinal William Keeler of Baltimore, in his capacity as president of the NCCB, at the moment of the first of two government shutdowns (15 November 1995) during the 104th Congress, to protest what he called "unacceptable budget priorities . . . that undermine indiscriminately the poorest members of our society;"[31] (3) a letter from Cardinal Bernard Law of Boston, in his capacity as chairman of the USCC Committee for Pro-Life Activities, to President Clinton on 2 August 1996 expressing concern that the new welfare law would increase not only childhood poverty but abortion rates as well.[32]

2. *Occasional statements from the USCC.* An equally visible category of USCC documents which sometimes treats issues related to welfare reform is a series of statements on public affairs which are published on a periodic basis, timed to coincide with national observances. Two such documents are particularly germane to welfare reform. The first is the annual "Labor Day Statement" published each September under the signature of the chairman of the USCC Committee on Domestic Policy. The 1995 version consists of a three-page essay entitled "Renewing the Social Contract, Reclaiming the Dignity of Work and the Rights of Workers" from Bishop John Ricard of Baltimore.[33] This statement has relevance for welfare because it treats not only the situation of workers, but also the various concerns of "the many people [who] do not have the ability to make an effective and dignified contribution" to the present high-tech economy, or to "express their creativity and develop their full potential in this new environment."

The second document in this category is the quadrennial "Statement on Political Responsibility" which the USCC Administrative Board publishes one full year before each presidential election, to orient voters at the start of the campaign season to public issues with moral significance. The 1995 edition is a thirteen-page statement entitled "Political Responsibility: Proclaiming the Gospel of Life, Protecting the Least Among Us

---

30. Published as "Factors of Genuine Welfare Reform" in *Origins* 24, no. 34 (9 Feb. 1995) 564–6.

31. Published under the title "A Catholic Appeal: Leadership for the Common Good" in *Origins* 25, no. 23 (23 Nov. 1995) 393–4.

32. Bishops' statements in all three categories above are occasionally issued as press releases by the USCC Department of Communications.

33. This statement appears, under the alternate title, "A Shifting, Churning Economy," in *Origins* 25, no. 12 (7 Sept. 1995) 199–200.

and Pursuing the Common Good."[34] Besides calling for broad participation in the electoral process, this document devotes several paragraphs to each of twenty key issues, including welfare reform, the economy and "families and children."

3. *USCC memoranda*. This final category consists of USCC documents which are hardly public in nature. In most cases, they are readily available only to "affiliates" of the USCC Office of Domestic Social Development, which include diocesan offices of peace and justice, private Church-based offices of social concern (such as those maintained by Catholic religious orders), and charitable and educational institutions (such as poverty research and advocacy centers) which subscribe to this service. The USCC reaches its social action colleagues through bimonthly mailings which include a broad array of materials on public policy issues. On the issue of welfare reform, four such mailing packages contain especially rich sets of resources: those dated May 1995 and January, March and May 1996. These contain memos (labeled "backgrounders," "policy updates," and "action alerts") which track the status of the welfare legislation, highlight relevant issues of theologically informed moral concern, and develop in considerable detail the USCC position on the welfare law as it emerged amidst congressional deliberations during these months.

Especially informative are two sets of documents which are emblematic of the twin concerns of this USCC office, which maintains one foot in the world of public policy discourse and one foot in the world of moral theology. The first is a six-page chart comparing the provisions of various welfare bills Congress was considering in January 1996 with the USCC position, which expresses reservations about nine aspects of H.R. 4 and associated amendments. The second is a series of regular memos (entitled "Where Are We Now?") written by John Carr, secretary of the USCC Department of Social Development and World Peace. When these memos address welfare reform, they consistently focus on the theological premises of the USCC's stance on welfare reform, sometimes citing papal social encyclicals to ground judgments about policy proposals.

Besides the materials contained in the mailings, the USCC offers to its affiliates an additional service; it sponsors the "Annual Catholic Social Ministries Gathering" in Washington, D.C. The 25–28 February 1996 conference was the occasion for much attention to welfare reform, including the distribution of several new memoranda restating the USCC

---

34. Published as "USCC Statement on Political Responsibility" in *Origins* 25, no. 22 (16 Nov. 1995) 369, 371–83.

position in the context of the (then) most recent legislative developments. The Bishops' Conference took advantage of this annual opportunity (which brings hundreds of local Catholic leaders, both clergy and lay, into close proximity to federal lawmakers) to encourage conference participants to translate their faith-based policy concerns into a united lobbying effort. After a morning of "Domestic Policy Workshops," the USCC scheduled briefing sessions at the Dirksen Senate Office Building on Capitol Hill with four Senators and several media news correspondents, and encouraged conference participants to meet privately with members of their own states' congressional delegations. Willing attendees were supplied with memoranda and "talking points" for meetings with members of Congress and their staffs. These memoranda, like the content of most of the bishops' letters and statements, are clearly derived from the analysis offered in the two most important Catholic documents on welfare reform: "Transforming the Welfare System" from Catholic Charities USA and "Moral Principles and Policy Priorities for Welfare Reform" from the USCC. In several places within the USCC literature surveyed above, the outline of the latter document is presented in this summary form:

> The Bishops' priorities advocated for welfare reform which:
>
> A. Protects Human Life and Human Dignity;
> B. Strengthens Family Life;
> C. Encourages and Rewards Work;
> D. Preserves a Safety Net for the Vulnerable;
> E. Builds Public/Private Partnerships to Overcome Poverty;
> F. Invests in Human Dignity.[35]

The next chapter offers a more detailed and nuanced treatment of the principles which informed all the documents named above. In distilling from the bishops' formal contribution to the welfare reform debate a set of five guidelines for the formation of social policy, my analysis in chapter six builds upon the actual words of the bishops, but seeks to remain faithful to the overall message of the major spokespersons of the U.S. Catholic community.

---

35. The precise wording of this statement is from p. 2 of a "Welfare Reform" memorandum from the Jan. 1996 mailing to affiliates of the USCC.

Chapter 6

Five Guidelines for Social Policy

This chapter's interpretation of the message of the U.S. bishops on welfare reform seeks to highlight the distinctively Catholic contributions to the welfare reform debate. This goal necessitates some selectivity in emphasizing certain parts of the bishops' message and eclipsing others.[1] Some of the five guidelines treated below are barely explicit in the bishops' documents, but rather constitute implicit premises in their arguments. Bringing these to the surface will demonstrate several distinctive features of Catholic social teaching which separate this perspective from the dominant American approaches to issues of distributive justice and social policy.

This chapter also seeks to emphasize the continuity between these five "guidelines for social policy" and the three more general "principles for social policy"[2] identified in chapter two. These five items were selected and formulated as they were so that they could most easily be linked to the three more general principles, of which they are a specification. If the three are viewed as broad "social conditions" which make more likely the realization of human dignity and associated values central to Catholic social teaching, then these five may be termed "governmental strategies" or "policy approaches" which make those social conditions more likely. In Parts Four and Five below, we will consider reasons for the hope that these five guidelines may come to be recognized more widely as an important source of social wisdom in addressing a range of distributive issues besides welfare reform.

---

1. For example, the Catholic documents' advocacy of a better child-support enforcement system need not be developed here, since such measures were almost universally supported by contributors to welfare reform. This chapter develops five guidelines based on theological premises.

2. The three are: (1) Social membership must be universal; (2) No person is to be considered a surplus person; and (3) The preferential option for the poor.

1. Focus on the struggle against poverty itself, not merely against welfare dependency

The Catholic documents on welfare reform repeatedly contend that the proper focus of social policy should be on fighting poverty, not only on reducing the welfare rolls. This claim is sharply at variance with the agenda of federal budget-cutting which prevails in an era where the major parties scramble to portray themselves as supporters of smaller government, wrapping themselves in the mantle of "fiscal responsibility." Since the 1970s, both liberals and conservatives have subscribed to a welfare-to-work agenda which appeals to the desire of the electorate to encourage self-sufficiency among welfare recipients. What separates this dominant American perspective from that of the Catholic bishops is not differing views of the value of work,[3] but rather a fundamental disagreement on how to balance the seemingly conflicting social goods of self-sufficiency and income security (i.e., freedom from the threat and effects of poverty).

This difference affects how the two perspectives target the related problems of dependency and want. It is perhaps most profitably characterized as a matter of "problem definition," an aspect of the American political process upon which the analysis of political scientist John Kingdon[4] sheds much light. Of all the "conditions" which exist in a nation at any given time, only a limited number capture the attention of the public and political leaders, and come to be recognized widely as "problems" which deserve a place on the policy agenda. Once it reaches the necessary threshold of attention, a problem has some chance of being addressed by policy changes.

The related problems of poverty and welfare dependency are two such conditions which have periodically resurfaced on national agendas as high priorities for remedial action. While all observers would like to see both disappear, the national level of commitment to fighting each ebbs and flows. For example, in the mid-1960s, at the height of President Lyndon Johnson's "War on Poverty," a firmer-than-usual commitment to insuring economic security prevailed, especially since the appealing ideal of extending equal opportunity was invoked as the goal and mechanism

---

3. Documents from the Bishops' Conference as well as Catholic Charities USA are unambiguously pro-work; they never deny that the welfare system needs to be reformed so that it better supports employment. They do, however, add the caveat that the terms of that employment must be acceptable, as judged by standards of justice in wages, fair expectations and support for family life.

4. John W. Kingdon, *Agendas, Alternatives, and Public Policies* (N.Y.: HarperCollins Publishers, 1984). Chapter five, entitled "Problems," informs the analysis below.

of the proposed progress against poverty. Since the late 1970s, however, the condition of welfare dependency has been recognized by most American observers as the more salient problem. The shift of emphasis was caused in part by a backlash against the perceived failure (or even counterproductivity) of expensive antipoverty programs.

Although government efforts to fight poverty and to reduce dependency often find themselves in tension with each other, there is no simple inverse relationship between these two social ills nor between policy measures designed to address them. In fact, Charles Murray and others who emphasize intergenerational cycles of dependency argue that, in the long-run, poverty will increase when dependency on government rises. The writers of the "Personal Responsibility Act" claim that, in the long run, the newly adopted welfare reform measures will reduce both dependency and poverty because they will fundamentally alter the social landscape, particularly the prevailing expectations concerning work, welfare and self-sufficiency. The authors of the "Contract with America" subscribe to the premise that only such abrupt policy changes will send the messages which will eventually propel welfare recipients into the responsible work and family behaviors which constitute the only true long-term solution to the plight of America's lowest-income families. They are not unaware of the short-run hardship that will be caused by funding cuts and the ending of welfare's entitlement status, but they nonetheless justify these measures by citing the potential long-run gains in reducing both dependency and poverty.[5]

The Catholic bishops' opposition to the new welfare law is not based on technical arguments about the likelihood that these projected long-term gains will not in fact come to pass, although macroeconomic forecasting could be employed to make this case. Rather, the bishops object to the plan's overall choice of strategy which permits unacceptable short-term consequences. They disapprove of the plan's renunciation of the anti-poverty strategy of previous welfare policy (which included federal income guarantees for low-income families) in favor of a new and almost exclusive reliance on an antidependency, work-based strategy. Even if a more rigorously enforced "employment strategy" proves in the long-run to be the key to alleviating simultaneously both the poverty and depen-

---

5. Said Rep. E. Clay Shaw, Jr. (a Florida Republican): "There will be a certain amount of turmoil in making these changes, and there will be some stories of hardship that tug at all our hearts. But I'm confident that many people will be helped and will take control of their lives, which otherwise would have been destroyed by a corrupt welfare system." Quoted in Robert Pear, "Action by States Hold Keys to Welfare Law's Future," *New York Times*, 1 Oct. 1996, A22.

dency problems, policies which enforce strict time limits and offer former welfare recipients no option for income besides work are sure to cause severe short-term hardship which the bishops deem unacceptable. This is especially true in the absence of a commitment of new resources to job preparation or to job guarantees for those who run up against the newly imposed time limits.

The employment strategy needs to be balanced by the continuation of an income maintenance strategy, something the bishops advocate with their repeated calls for "maintaining a social safety net" and "targeting poverty, not just welfare dependency." Wise social policy, according to the bishops' documents, would continue to strike a careful balance between antipoverty and antidependency goals. Although they are not unaware of the perverse incentives that may accompany income guarantees, the bishops insist that income maintenance continue as a prominent policy goal. To do less would be to abandon our national commitment to the well-being of poor families, allowing those who do not find work to sink into desperation with no reliable source of income. The bishops' reading of Catholic social teaching moves them to protest how the new welfare legislation largely takes poverty off the national agenda and relegates it to a "condition" rather than a true "problem" to which policy must respond.

2. Acknowledge insuperable barriers to employment where they exist

The bishops do send a pro-work message, but unlike the new welfare law, they also recognize that work is not always a possible or desirable solution to a given family's income needs. Two successive paragraphs from "Moral Principles and Policy Priorities for Welfare Reform" illustrate particularly well the dual track the bishops suggest for how social policy should interact with families, depending upon whether these families contain an adult who may reasonably be expected to hold a paid work position:

> Those who can work ought to work. Employment is the expected means to support a family and make a contribution to the common good. . . . Real reform will offer education, training, and transitional help to those who exchange a welfare check for a paycheck. The challenge is to ensure that reform leads to productive work with wages and benefits that permit a family to live in dignity. Rigid rules and arbitrary timelines are no substitute for real jobs at decent wages and the tax policies that can help keep families off welfare. For those who cannot work, or those whose "work" is raising our youngest children, the nation has built a system of income, nutrition, and other supports. Society has a responsibility to help meet the needs of those who cannot care for themselves, especially young children. . . . We can-

not support reform that destroys the structures, ends entitlements and eliminates resources that have provided an essential safety net for vulnerable children or permits states to reduce their commitment in this area. . . .[6]

In drawing a distinction between these two groups, the bishops' analysis begs the question: What are the relevant factors in determining whether (and how much) work should be expected of a given single mother? While the bishops raise the question, only in the longer "Transforming the Welfare System" from Catholic Charities USA is a detailed treatment of the question offered. Here we find an acknowledgment of a crucial but often overlooked aspect of the welfare question, namely that "AFDC recipients can be divided into recognizable groups," one of which consists of the approximately "30% who are chronic or persistent users. Many of these long-term users have severe learning disabilities or serious health problems. Policies or programs of intervention must take into account the differences. . . ."[7]

A major advantage of the welfare reform approach of these Catholic voices is its willingness to consider some welfare recipients as unlikely candidates (at least in the short term) to become independent workers. The bishops and Catholic Charities USA reach this conclusion via two routes. One is through their retrieval of the traditional family life themes found in Catholic social teaching, the documents of which reserve a special place for the role of the mother in the early childhood of her offspring. From this intellectual inheritance the bishops find support for the idea that such mothers ought to enjoy the option of choosing to make their social contribution exclusively in the home (rather than through paid employment) during this period of their lives.[8] Welfare reform, they conclude, should be informed by an awareness that there are other parenting responsibilities besides breadwinning. Legislation which disregards the necessity and value of home-making and child-rearing tasks trivializes this work and dishonors those who contribute to social well-being by performing it.

The second route to this conclusion (that not all welfare mothers are easily converted into job-holders) consists of paying attention to the in-

6. MPP, 6–7.
7. TWS, 7.
8. Although not mentioned in these documents, in the interest of addressing gender asymmetries, it could be the father who chooses to forego paid employment to exercise the function of primary nurturer of the family's children. Unfortunately, since welfare families normally feature nonresident fathers, this is not usually a viable option. Households headed by a single mother generally must rely on daycare for preschoolers if the mother takes on paid employment.

creasingly available data about the phenomenon of "welfare cycling." Careful studies of welfare recidivism and "spell dynamics" conducted by researchers Mary Jo Bane and David T. Ellwood[9] reveal that a substantial percentage of welfare recipients are neither simply "long-termers" or "short-termers." Rather, many single mothers try to make "work exits" from welfare, but despite their best efforts are forced by circumstances back onto the rolls.[10] Because these data demonstrate how hard it is to "make work exits stick," it is not realistic to expect labor markets entirely to replace government programs as a reliable source of income for all single mothers and their children. Even if all such welfare mothers were suddenly fully committed to the goal of maximizing their work earnings, this segment of the population would still face serious disadvantages amidst labor market competition.

Besides the logistical and financial difficulties caused by their child care responsibilities, these single mothers disproportionately experience personal problems, low skill levels, and other difficulties which limit their marketability to employers. In order to succeed in the job market, many welfare recipients would have to overcome a range of disabilities—physical,[11] emotional,[12] and educational[13] in nature—any one of which consti-

---

9. See their co-authored volume *Welfare Realities: From Rhetoric to Reform* (Cambridge, Mass.: Harvard University Press, 1994), esp. chs. 2 ("Understanding Welfare Dynamics") and 3 ("Understanding Dependency").

10. Ellwood estimates that only 40 percent of women leaving welfare actually earn their way off the rolls. Since barriers to work are so prevalent, he reflects, it is "[n]o wonder the most common way to leave welfare permanently is via marriage, not work" (ibid., 152).

11. Besides ordinary physical and medical disabilities, welfare mothers are disproportionately affected by substance abuse and addictions which hinder their employability. Joseph Califano estimates that "at least 20% of women on welfare—as many as one million mothers—have drug or alcohol problems severe enough to require treatment." He claims that because the new welfare legislation "ignores this grim truth . . . it will probably drive thousands of women and children into homelessness . . . ." (Joseph A. Califano, Jr., "Welfare's Drug Connection," *New York Times*, 24 Aug. 1996, 23).

12. A 1996 medical study finds that welfare mothers suffer from debilitating emotional problems (such as posttraumatic stress disorder and major depressive disorder) at much higher rates than the general female population. Regarding major depression, AFDC mothers have a lifetime incidence rate of 40 percent, compared with 21 percent for all women. See Ellen L. Bassuk and others, "The Characteristics and Needs of Sheltered Homeless and Low-Income Housed Mothers," *Journal of the American Medical Association* 276, no. 8 (29 Aug. 1996) 640–6.

13. Based on data collected by the Urban Institute over the period 1979–89, low educational attainment is correlated with welfare recipiency, especially with long spells on the rolls. Thirty-five percent of single mothers receiving welfare for two years or less had not

tutes a significant impediment to holding a job. These barriers to employment render them less likely (1) to be hired initially, (2) to maintain steady employment, and (3) to be promoted into jobs which can support their families without the need for further assistance. The effects of these constraints show up in statistical data which indicate the high likelihood of welfare recipients to "cycle" back into dependency when their attempts to move from welfare to work run into these barriers.

By replacing the former "income maintenance" strategy with a "work strategy" as the answer to the problem of welfare dependency, the new welfare law operates on the questionable assumption that most adult recipients of welfare are potentially able to fend for themselves in labor markets. They merely need to increase their labor effort, which is presumed to be purely a function of moral will rather than one of practical concerns and constraints. Since it commits no new resources to training and education, the terms of the law reveal a further assumption that the nonwork behavior of most members of this group is easily remediable, requiring no more "human capital" than is already possessed by these single mothers. The bishops criticize these aspects of the legislation, pointing out its failure to recognize the many complex factors which account for the great variability of earning potential of welfare mothers. In the place of the law's rigid work requirements, the bishops call for "incentives [which] should be tailored to a particular family's needs and circumstances, not one-size-fits-all requirements."[14] Similarly, Catholic Charities USA affirms the "recognition that AFDC recipients are a heterogeneous population," so it is inevitable that the best approach is one which addresses members of "this population according to their differing needs and focus[es] on investing in families."[15]

The Catholic documents criticize the new welfare law for relying so single-mindedly on the work ethic as a proposed solution to the problems of low-income families. Supporting work is only one of several legitimate goals of social policy. Any welfare arrangement which ignores other social objectives, such as promoting healthy family life and providing income maintenance for those in distress, ignores the distinctive qualities of the welfare population. An adequate consideration of these qualities reveals three truths: (1) for some welfare mothers, work is impossible; (2) for oth-

---

graduated from high school; fully 63 percent of those on the welfare rolls for five years or more were high school dropouts. Few women with any education at all beyond high school were on welfare. Statistics appear in charts accompanying "Spelling the End of Welfare as We Know It," *New York Times*, 4 Aug. 1996, Section 4, p. 3.
14. MPP, 4.
15. TWS, 7.

ers, the costs of work (measured in personal and social terms) outweigh the benefits; and (3) where work is possible, it must be supported by investments in human capital, such as government-sponsored job preparation programs. To overlook these important aspects of the welfare question is to risk punishing poor families for failing to deliver what they cannot deliver, thus turning the "war against poverty" into "a war against the poor."

3. Respect some absolute moral prohibitions for policy

Several phrases the bishops use in "Moral Principles and Policy Priorities for Welfare Reform" suggest the invocation of absolute moral imperatives (especially concerning the policy goal of guaranteeing the well-being of children) as a justification of their policy recommendations. The bishops call for the preservation of "the federal government's role and responsibilities in fighting poverty," which includes "provid[ing] an essential safety net for vulnerable children" and continuing "entitlement programs which provide essential supports for poor children."[16] The document introduces these positions collectively as "a matter of moral consistency."[17]

Similarly, the Catholic Charities USA document alludes to a set of moral imperatives which rightly constrain public policy. It does not hesitate to use the language of "should," "must" and "basic obligations," especially when the welfare of children is at stake. Two statements from "Transforming the Welfare System" typify this approach: (1) "Investing in our children and their families is fundamental to the well-being of society and constitutes a basic obligation of each citizen and the state"; (2) "The purpose of public policy is to enable all people to live with dignity."[18]

Although neither document (nor the other welfare reform statements from official Catholic sources) uses the technical ethical terminology of "deontological constraints" or "absolute prohibitions," it is clear nevertheless that the authors of these documents consider some options for social policy strictly off-limits. For example, on the issue of family caps and teenage mother exclusions (which the new welfare law allows states to adopt), the bishops could not be firmer in their opposition.[19] They cite the

16. MPP, 6–7.
17. Ibid., 5.
18. TWS, 3. 4.
19. "Denying benefits for children born to mothers on welfare can hurt the children and pressure their mothers toward abortion and sterilization . . . . [P]roposals that deny benefits to children because of their mother's age or dependence on welfare . . . ,whatever their intentions, are likely to encourage abortion . . . . In seeking to change the behavior of parents, these provisions hurt children, and some unborn children will pay with their lives" (MPP, 4).

potential harm these measures might cause to innocent children, both those who might be aborted and those whose families will be deprived of welfare benefits because of such policy innovations. The bishops judge these measures intolerable. No attempt to justify them in terms of long-run social benefits (such as fighting the root cause of dependency by "changing the social landscape" of behavioral expectations) could ever override these moral objections to the short-run impact of such policies. Social policy strategies which directly or indirectly cause harm to an already disadvantaged segment of the population are not reconcilable with Catholic social principles such as the preferential option for the poor. Putting children at greater risk of abortion or severe deprivation is simply not allowable no matter what eventual benefits might accrue to taxpayers or members of future generations.

In the eyes of the bishops, then, social policy is constrained by a prohibition against harming poor children, or even serving as an accomplice in situations where innocent children are placed at risk by the irresponsible behavior of their parents. Catholic Charities USA laments the unfortunate fact that, when children "are victims of their parents' choices . . . , all society can do is protect and nurture the children."[20] In the absence of a culturally acceptable and financially feasible way to separate children from their irresponsible parents, the Catholic documents call for the continuation of the principle of categorical entitlement to welfare benefits. While they have sometimes been misused by parents who rely on them as something other than a last resort, federal income maintenance measures are the only way to guarantee protection to all American children, regardless of the conditions (with respect to family situation or geographic jurisdiction) of their birth. Recent U.S. policy debates have emphasized what is wrong with entitlements (especially the risk of introducing perverse incentives and signaling permissiveness). The Catholic documents, conversely, issue a reminder of what is right about them. To compromise the child-protecting role which entitlements have played during six decades of American social policy is to violate a moral prohibition against damaging the life prospects of children in low-income families.

Besides their explicit opposition to removing support for children, the Catholic documents also argue against eliminating welfare entitlements for single mothers. There are more reasons to favor income support for welfare mothers than the truth contained in the maxim "it is impossible to assist children without helping their entire family." Rather, because of their special situation, single mothers should continue to be

20. TWS, 11.

considered the "deserving poor." The bishops recognize that factors other than low motivation prevent welfare mothers from finding jobs which will lift their families to financial independence. Once we acknowledge the considerable barriers to employment and self-sufficiency which welfare mothers face, we immediately judge unacceptable any policy (such as time limitation of welfare benefits) which threatens to take away the vital life-sustaining support offered by government income maintenance programs.

In the absence of job guarantees, the withdrawal of benefits places welfare recipients in the impossible situation of having no dependable source of income whatsoever. Welfare mothers may thus find themselves forced into desperate exchanges, choosing among items on a list of degrading survival options which few would defend. Jason DeParle catalogues some of these:

> No doubt the harsh reality of an empty stomach will cause some people to do better. Some may indeed get jobs and marry. . . . Others may turn to prostitution or the drug trade. Or cling to abusive boyfriends. Or have more abortions. Or abandon their children. Or camp out on the streets and beg.[21]

When people have lost so much control over the circumstances of their lives, to deny then some honorable means of subsistence is to diminish their personal freedom to choose reasonable courses of action. In the absence of a minimal measure of security which acts as a buffer of freedom separating themselves from dire want, people experience markets for goods and services as potentially coercive loci of desperate exchanges. To protect values such as human liberty against the dominance of money, most societies criminalize some activities (prostitution, slavery, abuse of workers) to prohibit "trades of last resort."[22] This same concern to block those exchanges judged exploitative is also part of the rationale for the defense of the "living wage" within the documents of Catholic social teaching.[23]

---

21. Jason DeParle, "The New Contract With America's Poor," *New York Times*, 28 Aug. 1996, Section 4, pp. 1, 14.

22. On "blocked exchanges" and "trades of last resort," see Michael Walzer, *Spheres of Justice* (N.Y., Basic Books, Inc., 1993) 97–103, 120–1.

23. RN 34 claims that when a worker enters into a labor contract through "necessity or fear of a worse evil . . . he is the victim of force and injustice." This principle is also supported by a medieval scholastic maxim about justice in exchange: In order for a contract to be considered just, there must be equity in the bargaining which produced it. Contracts between parties with vastly different levels of power or resources risk becoming veiled instruments of extortion.

The bishops' invocation of the themes of human dignity, common good and preferential option for the poor constitutes a word of judgment against the new welfare law: to rescind the income guarantee[24] from single mothers with poor job prospects is to subject them to intolerable dangers and to render the social environment less humane. Good public policy would heed the moral imperative to prevent such outcomes and would continue providing a floor of income to needy families headed by single mothers.

4. Recognize "carrots and sticks" without subscribing to a reductionistic view of the human person

This guideline illustrates the "both/and" style of thinking which permeates Catholic theology in general, and imbues Catholic social teaching with two poles of concern. On one hand, public policy should be realistic, taking into account the effects of human selfishness and calculating prudential responses to the possibility of abuse. In social policy, this necessitates careful attention to building into public laws acceptable incentive structures which encourage responsible behavior through the operation of rewards and sanctions. On the other hand, good policy respects the complexities of human subjecthood and the transcendent character of human persons, who are free and spiritual beings, never merely objects to be manipulated. Chapter one's investigation of this aspect of Catholic moral anthropology revealed Catholic social teaching's consistent opposition to various versions of reductionism (materialism, scientific behaviorism, "economism"). Each violates human dignity by treating persons in ways which ignore their spiritual dimensions and disregard their aspirations for goods which transcend the material.

The tension between these two poles of policy analysis are readily apparent in the church's statements on federal welfare reform. On one hand, the documents recommend practical measures to alter the structure of welfare program incentives in order to encourage better outcomes. Both of the major documents repeatedly appeal to the principles of "responsibility" and "accountability" which should be more consistently encoded in the structure of program rules. These two words emerge as

---

24. The new welfare law eliminates the income guarantee in a number of ways: (1) freeing states to impose new conditions for eligibility; (2) disqualifying those who have reached time limits; (3) punishing noncompliance with workfare and other new program rules through sanctions. Each of these changes may drive thousands of newly ineligible women into desperate measures, such as entering abusive relationships in order to provide for themselves and their children. Formerly, AFDC provided a more reliable recourse for such women.

shorthand expressions of the bishops' support for a strategy of implementing "carrots and sticks" in a more effective and rational way. The bishops accord a prominent place for incentives in their welfare project, which they describe as one of "proposing alternatives that provide assistance in ways that safeguard children but do not reinforce inappropriate or morally destructive behavior."[25] They also offer an opinion on the relative balance between "carrots and sticks": "Genuine welfare reform should rely on incentives more than harsh penalties."[26] Catholic Charities USA presents a more detailed description of desirable incentive structures in welfare programs. "Transforming the Welfare System" includes several recommendations for changing programs in order to "make work pay," including: (1) revising the formulas for "earnings disregards" and "assets standards" (which help determine eligibility for welfare benefits[27]); and (2) coordinating welfare with an expanded Earned Income Tax Credit. The penultimate paragraph of the document appeals for an improved incentive structure: "We must be willing to build into our welfare system responsibility and accountability on the part of both the recipient and the giver of public assistance."[28]

On the other hand, the Catholic documents nowhere claim that measures to revise program incentives exhaust all the goals of welfare reform or respond to all the needs of America's poor families. Because the participants in the programs are human persons, whose lives are marked by freedom and complexity, no regime of monetary incentives can account for all the values at stake in social assistance. Nor should any attempts at behavior modification be expected to succeed in exerting some crass form of control over the decisions of low-income people. To subscribe uncritically to the maxim that "you get whatever behavior you subsidize" is to demean the aspirations of program recipients for a better life than welfare offers. People generally possess principled, not only self-serving reasons for acting as they do in bearing children, choosing to relocate from one state to another, or deciding how to balance the goods of paid employment and time spent with their children. To focus all our welfare reform energies on revising incentive structures to discourage dependency and encourage work effort is to use a simplistic version of rational-choice theory as a mask for condescending to welfare recipi-

25. MPP, 5.
26. Ibid., 4.
27. TWS, 9.
28. Ibid., 12.

ents.²⁹ Single mothers who rely on public assistance are thus treated as operating according to a different (and far simpler) mode of rationality than other members of society, for whom monetary rewards presumably do not completely determine behavior.

The bishops register their protest against this brand of reductionism in such repeated calls for flexibility in program standards as this:

> Increased accountability and incentives should be tailored to a particular family's needs and circumstances, not "one-size-fits-all" requirements. Top-down reform with rigid national rules cannot meet the needs of a population as diverse as poor families.³⁰

Catholic Charities USA incorporates similar insights into a section of its document labeled "Tailor investments to families":

> A significant shift in the philosophy underlying AFDC is critical. We must move from maintaining families at a subsistence level to tailored investing in families. This means moving from scrutinizing eligibility and qualification requirements to becoming partners with beneficiaries. . . .
> Assistance providers must be retrained to become partners who respond to recipients in culturally appropriate ways. . . . A contract must be forged to specify the responsibilities of both the recipient and the agency providing assistance and make them both accountable for results.³¹

This proposal, in emphasizing direct interpersonal contact and individualized sets of expectations, implicitly passes judgment upon bureaucracies which, without supplementation, are incapable of treating people in ways that respect and enhance their dignity. This does not constitute a reason to abandon all hope, as does Marvin Olasky, that public assistance can play a constructive role in the lives of poor families. Rather, it offers a chastening reminder (one very much in line with the Catholic principle

---

29. One particularly egregious example of such a mechanistic view of human behavior is found in the welfare reform proposal in ch. 4 of Robert Rector and William F. Lauber, *America's Failed $5.4 Trillion War on Poverty* (Washington, D.C.: The Heritage Foundation, 1995). All twelve of the "steps to genuine welfare reform" advocated here consist of thinly veiled attempts at social engineering which proceeds on the assumption that a one-to-one correlation exists between desirable human behavior and financial incentives encoded into public laws. The proposal places heavy reliance on family caps, teenage mother exclusions, strict workfare enforcement and tax breaks for married couples as means to reduce illegitimacy, as if these "additional incentives to encourage constructive behavior" (41) have the potential to serve as a panacea for solving this complex social problem.
30. MPP, 4.
31. TWS, 7.

of subsidiarity) of the limits of rule-bound government bureaucracies. Like any regulations, incentives in welfare programs may be good servants, but are invariably bad masters. Welfare reform should improve the implementation of "carrots and sticks" so that program rules better reflect our shared values of family and work. However, in accord with the Catholic Church's insistence on respecting human transcendence, an overemphasis on tinkering with monetary incentives in social policy must be avoided, for it runs the risk of encoding in law a crass reductionism which ignores such normative values as human dignity and freedom.

5. Avoid fostering the demonization or marginalization of recipients of public assistance

Of the five guidelines, this final one most straightforwardly reflects the content of the three principles discussed in chapter two above. By insisting that U.S. social policy counteract the temptation to exclude welfare recipients from the mainstream of society, the documents from the American Catholic leaders echo the Church's preferential option for the poor and its concern for social cohesion and universal membership. In fact, the bishops' major document makes explicit reference to "an option for the poor," "solidarity with the poor and vulnerable," and the "call to participation."[32] In seeking to dispel the notion that the welfare poor are to be treated as a deviant subpopulation separated from the rest of society by distinctive pathologies, the bishops offer a caveat highlighting the prevalence of deep social problems throughout U.S. society:

> Children thrown from windows, found in dumpsters, and abused in their homes are tragic symptoms of culture in disarray and a welfare system in urgent need of real reform. It is worth noting that it is not just low-income families that sometimes engage in destructive behavior. Personal irresponsibility, family disintegration, and loss of moral values touches not just the "down and out," but also the "rich and famous" and the rest of us.[33]

Of course, the issues pertaining to marginalization and demonization are often quite subtle. A given policy proposal or the social theory behind it seldom explicitly advocates the further stigmatization of recipients.[34] However, in the absence of explicit efforts to foster the inclusion

32. MPP, 2.
33. Ibid., 5.
34. Lawrence Mead's "New Paternalism" explicitly considers the poor to be deviant. Charles Murray and other supporters of drastic reductions in social programs do not necessarily advocate this position as an anthropological claim, but it may be argued that the effects of their proposals (both on the material conditions and public perceptions of the poor) would contribute to further stigmatization and marginalization of low-income persons.

of low-income families in the mainstream of society, social programs tend (even if inadvertently) to isolate recipients. They serve as a wedge dividing a "deserving us" from an "undeserving them." Every child who cringes in fear of peer ridicule when flashing a pass to receive a subsidized school lunch knows the meaning of stigmatization. In measuring means-tested programs in terms of how they contribute to stigma, the "how" of program administration and public perception is often as important as the "what" (i.e., the assistance offered). As the bishops urge: "We must resist the temptation to see poor women, minority families, or immigrants as either passive victims or easy scapegoats for our society's social and economic difficulties."[35]

The Catholic Charities USA statement addresses head-on the question of how much progress can realistically be expected toward the goal of offering a place in the mainstream of society to low-income single mothers and their families. The document lists (1) the numerous barriers to economic success faced by this diverse group and (2) the many social conditions[36] which must be addressed before eventual success could be completed, before identifying this short-term goal for policy: "to help these people obtain an adequate level of financial and social stability in an interdependent society."[37] This modest goal corresponds to the document's earlier description of what constitutes an adequate condition for social life: "Human dignity is reflected in one's ability to live life manifesting a healthy balance between autonomy and interdependence."[38]

Like the bishops, Catholic Charities USA does not imagine that the welfare population will quickly and easily become financially independent. Rather, it recognizes the need for a continuation of substantial assistance to poor families. Along with the bishops, Catholic Charities USA advocates re-envisioning this assistance as "tailored investments in families," not just as means of subsistence which society grudgingly doles out in poor relief efforts which amounts to warehousing people. Both docu-

35. MPP, 8.
36. Ten conditions are listed: (1) "a vibrant economy must provide career opportunities"; (2) "all workers need a level playing field"; (3) "the educational system needs major changes"; (4) "adequate health care must be available"; (5) "the supply of affordable housing must be increased"; (6) "our society must provide greater support for family life"; (7) "quality, affordable child care should be universally available"; (8) "our society must place renewed emphasis on the value of marriage"; (9) "teen-agers and young adults must have attractive life-options"; and (10) "America must address both the societal roots and the individual episodes of domestic violence." Cited phrases are interspersed among several paragraphs in TWS, 4–5.
37. Ibid., 12.
38. Ibid., 4.

ments propose that we think of welfare as part of a "social contract"[39] in which government as well as the private sector become "partners" with recipients.

If complete and immediate financial independence is not to be expected for our poorest families even after the best-imaginable reform of our welfare laws, then these families may at least hope for a diminution of stigma and marginalization. The bishops register their belief that by emphasizing the triad of "hope, opportunity and investment" which "are essential in the transition" from welfare to work,[40] the "othering" of the welfare poor by those who distrust them and their motives may be curtailed. Catholic Charities USA looks forward to a day when a revised message will accompany a welfare check. Instead of being occasions for the communication of stigma-laden distrust, the granting of assistance will be perceived in this way:

> The community makes a fitting investment in a family. This says to a family: "We believe in you. We believe you can succeed and we are here to help you do so." In turn, the recipient says to the community, "Thank you for investing in me and my children. I will do all I can to make sure this investment pays off for us and for the community."[41]

In thus emphasizing mutual gains and increased accountability, this approach to welfare reform reduces stigma by treating recipients in ways more in accordance with the standards of the mainstream of society, although still within the parameters of realistic expectations about the earning potential of single mothers. If welfare is to serve as a "bridge into the social mainstream," a first step must be to alter programs and their perception so that they reduce the "social distance" between recipients and the rest of the population.

* * * *

Part Three of our study has examined a recent episode in the U.S. Catholic Church's efforts to function as a community of conscience, as a "public church." Towards this end, representatives of this ecclesial community retrieved sources of moral wisdom from its tradition of social ethics, interpreting the broad principles found in the documents of papal social teaching in terms of their implications for American social welfare policy. The chief "carrier" of Catholic social thought in this episode was the Bishops' Conference, which acted upon its mandate to establish a Catholic presence in the arena of national policymaking through advo-

39. MPP, 8; TWS, 7–9.
40. MPP, 8.
41. TWS, 8

cacy of measures to advance social justice. The bishops supported a coherent policy perspective which was neither simply liberal nor conservative, but represented a distinctive agenda guided by the Catholic Church's traditional concerns about healthy family life, parenting priorities and abortion.

Obviously, the bishops' recommendations did not carry the day; the new welfare law was enacted over their strenuous objections and despite their vocal support for alternative courses of action. However, in maintaining such a high profile in the welfare reform debate, the Bishops' Conference led the U.S. Catholic Church forward in becoming a more active and responsible "community of moral discourse." James M. Gustafson describes such a community as

> a gathering of people with the explicit intention to survey and critically discuss their personal and social responsibilities in the light of moral convictions about which there is some consensus and to which there is some loyalty.[42]

Some potentially extraordinary features are exhibited by the policy guidelines which the bishops contributed to the welfare reform debate. Although based upon distinctive theological claims and moral traditions not shared by most Americans (and largely unknown even to most Catholics in America), these moral principles and policy guidelines exhibit the potential of serving as a catalyst for the coalescence of a new consensus on distributive justice. Part Four of this study examines the nature of this overlapping consensus, as well as the features and significance of a potentially expanding zone of agreement about social priorities in our nation's welfare policy.

---

42. James M. Gustafson, "The Church: A Community of Moral Discourse," in his *The Church as Moral Decision-Maker* (Philadelphia: Pilgrim Press, 1970) 84.

Part Four

Toward an Overlapping Consensus

Chapter 7

Four Arguments About Practical Issues

Our investigation of the process of welfare reform in Part Two above revealed many areas of contention concerning American social policy. These loci of disagreement include differing theories of poverty, of human motivation, the legitimate role of the federal government in fighting poverty, and the potential of charitable efforts. It is impossible to deny that the American public holds a wide range of viewpoints on these matters, as the political debate which produced the new welfare law demonstrated. Because we do not share a single common perspective on social policy, but rather view social realities through diverse interpretive lenses, we currently cannot even assume unanimity in what counts as gains and losses, successes and failures, costs and benefits of social policy. Because of this pluralism, it is not initially evident that substantial grounds exist for overlapping agreement between the parties to the debate. Consequently, it may appear that ethical advice like that offered by the U.S. Catholic bishops will have no more effect on future rounds of the recurring welfare reform debate than it did in recent years. Is there any basis to hope that those who follow diverse approaches to social policy may nevertheless discover some substantial overlap of conviction, so that a new welfare consensus will emerge in U.S. policy debates?

The purpose of Part Four of our study is to present the case for an affirmative answer to this question. The policy guidelines and analysis presented by the U.S. bishops and Catholic Charities USA may provide precisely the type of policy recommendations around which might coalesce a renewed, broad-based agreement about the purposes and strategies of welfare policy. At the very least, they might inspire a movement to restore the New Deal's protections for low-income families—a system of entitlements in place for the six decades preceding the new welfare law. The optimism of those who look to religious voices to foster such a development must, of course, be tempered by the realization that any new agreement is unlikely to be unanimous. Further, it may turn out that no substantial policy corrections will be possible until the inevitable backlash against the new harsh measures. Tragically, this may come only after our nation witnesses a certain threshold of suffering and hardship endured by the millions of low-income families cut off from assistance when welfare time limits are reached. However, it still appears reasonable to maintain the hopeful expectation that wider agreement may be forged based not solely on the necessity of healing massive social disruptions, but rather primarily on the merits of the arguments for more generous social welfare policies as articulated by "public churches" and other advocates of the poor. If this comes to pass, then welfare policy may be altered even before the feared social upheavals would occur.

Part Four, then, addresses the possibility of agreement amidst pluralism, of forging a consensus on wise social policy where none now exists. Questions about the extent and significance of the proposed new consensus will be deferred until chapters eight and nine. The present chapter presents four potential points of agreement concerning practical issues in welfare policy. Each of these items represents a truth upon which all parties might agree based solely upon criteria regarding what is cost-effective and *feasible*, even prior to consulting more substantive principles regarding what is morally *desirable*. Although the warrants for these four are not primarily moral in nature, each represents an extension of claims made in the documents of Catholic social teaching and the bishops' statements on welfare policy. Each of these four items might be adopted by pluralistic societies like the U.S. on pragmatic grounds which require no prior agreement on deeper normative concerns. Even if our nation remains divided on the meaning of fairness and social responsibility, we may still realistically expect general agreement on these four practical arguments about social policy.

1. Social policy cannot be successful in ushering people to self-sufficiency unless it commits adequate resources to empowering low-income citizens to move into work on reasonable terms

This statement may be called "the preconditions argument." It summarizes the observation that welfare recipients require certain services and resources to make self-sufficiency a realistic possibility in their lives. Even under the unchallenged assumptions (1) that a strictly enforced work strategy is the proper policy stance toward welfare recipients, and (2) that unpaid domestic and childcare work do not count toward fulfilling the terms of work enforcement, certain judgments about low-income single-parent families seem inescapable. Included among these is the admission that the special needs of this segment of the population (mostly less educated single mothers with young children) necessitate some policy flexibility. A work strategy cannot succeed unless it includes provisions for offering such people reasonable access to the goods they require in order to take advantage of work opportunities.

Empowerment must be more than a convenient but empty buzzword. If its meaning is restricted to the negative sense (such as "liberation from the 'poverty trap' built into former welfare regulations"), our understanding of empowerment will overlook the positive task of making work logistically and financially possible for families seeking to leave welfare. The crucial question is whether welfare policy assumes a punitive posture toward poor families or, rather, seeks to "invest" in them. This distinction hinges upon whether policy provides the resources which serve as conditions for the possibility of "earnings exits" from welfare dependency.

If public policy asks welfare families to act more like self-supporting middle-class families, then the success of these policies depends on how consistently they offer welfare families a reasonable share of the same resources which make self-sufficiency through work a possibility for the middle class. In fact, it is the lack of these resources (such as education, job skills, health, and affordable child care) which separates a family from the social mainstream and leads it to seek welfare assistance in the first place. In order to prevent placing welfare recipients in impossible situations, public laws must maintain a delicate balance between what is provided for needy families and what is required from them. Only by implementing reasonable and flexible sets of expectations can policy avoid asking too much or too little from those receiving public assistance. Blanket regulations such as the rigid time limits of the new welfare law run the risk of ignoring the diverse barriers to employment which make individualized attention to the needs and abilities of welfare recipients indispensable to successful policy.

Not surprisingly, the "preconditions argument" has been cited in various forms by participants in many rounds of welfare reform. It arises whenever it becomes necessary to restate the obvious truth that it is not only unfair, but also counterproductive to ask recipients to do what is impossible.[1] Sometimes this occasions a reminder that it is unwise to enforce program rules which punish people for failing to act in ways which may be socially desirable, but which remain logistically impossible without further assistance. One expression of the preconditions argument surfaced during 1994 congressional hearings to evaluate existing welfare-

---

1. Note how this echoes the argument (reviewed in chapter one above) of John Ryan, who frequently invoked the maxim "no one is morally bound to do the impossible."

to-work programs. The Subcommittee on Human Resources of the House Committee on Ways and Means heard much poignant testimony regarding one of the sanctions imposed under the Family Support Act: threats of withholding benefits from program recipients for noncompliance with new work requirements. The consensus of several witnesses representing social service providers was that, in the absence of job preparation resources and realistic work opportunities, such sanctions become irrational policy instruments. They punish behavior (nonwork) over which recipients, in present circumstances, have little control. Commented Larry D. Jackson, commissioner of the Virginia Department of Social Services: "Penalties should not be imposed if [job-preparation] resources aren't available or if jobs do not exist."[2] Subsequent testimony confirmed the unfairness of penalizing welfare recipients for failing to make the transition to work when job opportunities appropriate to their skill levels are not available.

A sober assessment of the preconditions argument invites us to close the gap between political rhetoric about enforcing work obligations among welfare recipients and the perennially underfunded welfare-to-work efforts our government actually undertakes. It reminds politicians to measure policy proposals according to an appropriate yardstick: do they effectively provide the preconditions for true empowerment of recipients? With the passage of the 1996 welfare law, a new layer is added to these concerns. With federal welfare entitlements now replaced by block grants, the states are the new loci where the fate of welfare families will be decided—where they will either find access to the preconditions for empowerment or where they will be asked to do the impossible. Writing in the *New York Times* at the time Congress was hammering out the final details of the new law, David T. Ellwood lamented how the federal failure to provide states funding for job creation and preparation practically dooms the new law to failure. The paucity of new resources makes the law an instrument which the states will likely use to punish rather than to empower program participants, regardless of their work motivation. Ellwood explains:

> States cannot and will not do the impossible. The legislation gives them an out. They may set time limits of any length and simply cut families off welfare regardless of their circumstances. . . .

---

2. U.S. Congress, House of Representatives, Committee on Ways and Means, Subcommittee on Human Resources. *Family Support Act of 1988: Hearing before the Subcommittee on Human Resources*, 103rd Congress, second session, 15 March 1994 (Washington, D.C.: GPO, 1994) 22.

It won't matter if these people want to work. It won't matter if they would happily take workfare jobs so they could provide something for their families. It won't matter if there are no private jobs available.

States may want to offer workfare jobs, but limited Federal grants may preclude that. People who are willing to work but are unable to find a job should not be abandoned.[3]

Part Five of our study will amplify the last sentence of Ellwood's statement, proposing that it serves as a worthy general maxim for how government should protect all members of the population who find themselves unemployed in our postindustrial economy. "Ellwood's maxim" identifies as bad policy any government measure which punishes people for not holding a paying job while simultaneously doing nothing to enhance the employment prospects of these same people. In the limited context of welfare reform, it serves as a general summary of the "preconditions argument" on which widespread agreement seems not only possible but indeed likely. All that is required to agree with Ellwood's assessment is the desire not to place any members of society in an impossible situation, with neither income nor reasonable hope that this situation will change.[4]

In fact, it is not difficult to find in the welfare reform arguments of both conservatives and liberals ready agreement with this basic principle. Testifying before a congressional subcommittee, conservative Lawrence Mead expressed serious reservations about the welfare bill because its work requirements were not matched by a commitment of new resources to make work possible:

> [B]ecause there is now no dedicated money for work enforcement, there is now no assurance that states will spend enough on it to achieve the required work levels. To promote serious reform, it is crucial that Congress manifest that the work requirements are serious, and also that it is possible to meet them. I fear that the new stipulations are not credible as they stand. They call for participation rates never before realized except in a few localities, yet they provide no specific funding or program comparable to JOBS to realize them.[5]

3. David T. Ellwood, "Welfare Reform in Name Only," *New York Times*, 22 July 1996, A19.

4. Of course, reaching a more substantial agreement depends upon a common understanding of how to apply this justification of public assistance to various categories of unemployed people. One key issue is defining what constitutes an insuperable set of barriers to employment. It is notoriously difficult to compare diverse circumstances of geography, job availability, health and family commitments.

5. Lawrence M. Mead, Testimony Before the House of Representatives Committee on Ways and Means, Subcommittee on Human Resources, 104th Congress, First Session,

Robert Rector and William F. Lauber of the conservative Heritage Foundation also argue eloquently against "reforms aimed at enabling single mothers to 'go it alone.'"[6] They cite a number of factors which make a solely work-based strategy not only unrealistic but dangerous for this segment of the population.[7]

On the liberal side, Gary Burtless of the Brookings Institution makes a similar argument. He compiles an impressive set of data on the low earning potential of most welfare recipients in building a strong case against a welfare strategy that does nothing more than enforce work. Burtless cannot recommend the adoption of such an unmitigated work-orientation because "the data . . . suggest that in the short run a large minority of current welfare recipients—and their children—would face extreme hardship if forced to rely solely on earnings for their support."[8] Similarly, the editors of the *New York Times*, commenting on Governor George Pataki's November 1996 proposals for implementing welfare reform in New York, restate the liberal version of the "preconditions argument," nearly paraphrasing Ellwood's earlier expression of concern:

> Mr. Pataki's proposals are puzzling and likely to be self-defeating. Real welfare reform must be accompanied by incentives for people to get jobs, with subsidies for day care, job training and transportation to make it possible for people to work . . . . [T]he arbitrary cutoffs [must] not punish people who have no other recourse to survive.[9]

The overlap of these several assessments of welfare reform, coming as they do from various points on the political spectrum, suggests the possibility of further convergence on what constitutes realistic welfare-to-work

---

6 Dec. 1996 (prepared statement distributed at the Hearing on "The Personal Responsibility and Work Opportunity Act [H.R. 4]") 2.

6. Robert Rector and William F. Lauber, *America's Failed $5.4 Trillion War on Poverty* (Washington, D.C.: The Heritage Foundation, 1995) 40.

7. The factors they mention are "the very low cognitive abilities of welfare mothers, coupled with the impotence of government education and training programs and the cost of child care [which] underscore the futility of reform schemes aimed narrowly at making unwed mothers employed and self-sufficient" (ibid.). They marshal these arguments in order to urge government to use financial and other incentives to reduce illegitimacy and promote stable marriages. Some have dubbed this the "wedfare" strategy to reduce welfare dependency. However, even those who do not share these priorities can readily find in Rector and Lauber's recognition of barriers to employment ample grounds to support a continuation of an "income maintenance" goal of welfare policy alongside the "work strategy."

8. Gary Burtless, "Paychecks or Welfare Checks: Can AFDC Recipients Support Themselves?," *Brookings Review* 12 (fall 1994) 37.

9. "Wrong Way on Welfare," *New York Times*, 13 Nov. 1996, A22.

expectations. Perhaps the future experience of life under the new welfare law—including worsening social conditions and severe hardship faced by poor families regardless of their willingness to work—will convince many others of the irrationality of our nation's new policy directions.

The new welfare law violates "Ellwood's maxim" because of its failure to match its work requirements with a commitment of new federal funds to make work opportunities available to those who run up against the new time limits. In order not to violate "Ellwood's maxim," a reasonable policy regime would have to supplement the new law's restrictions and sanction with a massive infusion of new resources, including some type of public jobs programs which would "make work available" and "make work pay" for former welfare recipients. For public authorities to do less is to require work without enabling work, and to deny recipients the resources which serve as preconditions to actualize their obligation to work.

When the U.S. Catholic bishops call upon social policy to fight poverty, not merely to counteract welfare dependency, they are drawing upon distinctive theological convictions (regarding human dignity and responsible social structures) to reach the same "preconditions argument" others promote on strictly secular grounds. The bishops oppose new work expectations which are not matched by a corresponding increase in work preparation and job opportunities—measures which make it feasible for welfare recipients to meet those expectations. This is not to say that stricter expectations are never appropriate in welfare programs, but rather that changes in program rules are constructive only when they are made in the context of investing in families, so as to make them better able to move toward self-sufficiency on reasonable terms. Otherwise, tougher requirements and the revocation of assistance serve only a punitive function, making the lives of welfare families more difficult and precarious. Such measures threaten to separate these families further from their fellow citizens and to decrease their hope of ever possessing a realistic chance of joining the mainstream of society.

While we should not expect instant unanimity in defining the extent of society's obligation to low-income families, we have reason to hope for a significant sharing of perceptions about what amounts to self-defeating policies—measures which invite public backlash by treating needy citizens in punitive and counterproductive ways. A convergence of opinions about the shortcomings of an exceptionless work strategy for welfare families would allow for a more flexible application of the "personal responsibility" agenda. A wiser welfare policy would emphasize resources for empowerment, allowing families to achieve self-sufficiency on favorable terms and fostering mutual benefits for all members of society.

2. Social policy which invests in improving the lives of recipients will yield cost savings in the long run

Like any investment, resources devoted to improving the well-being and opportunities of vulnerable members of society hold out the promise of deferred returns. We may measure these returns in terms of the decreased future budgetary costs associated with improvements in the prospects of our most disadvantaged citizens. By helping the poor through difficult periods of their lives and allowing them to establish more orderly patterns of work and family behavior, the efforts of public agencies constitute a wager. Not only may present social investment eliminate the need for more costly future interventions, but a successful outcome might transform recipients into taxpayers themselves. If the measuring rod of policy success is even partially a budgetary one, then the list of factors relevant in evaluating social policy must include the opportunity cost of not realizing the fiscal gains which accrue from such "investments."

Public policies which promote the common good, the well-being of the disadvantaged and the goal of social cohesion are to be defended on numerous grounds, of which cost-effectiveness can be only one relevant criterion. In Part One above, we investigated one ethical framework which supports generous social assistance and we discovered that the normative categories (such as the preferential option for the poor) employed in Catholic social teaching defy measurement in pecuniary terms. Consequently, it might seem to be a "category mistake" to leave aside these moral considerations even for a moment in proposing a budget-driven argument for more generous social welfare policies, based on the advantage that such "investments" in people generally return positive dividends. Indeed, Catholic social thought defends such policies and expenditures even if they do not "pay off" this way—even if they entail significant material sacrifice on the part of the more affluent. This is precisely the point suggested by Bishop William F. Murphy when he offers perhaps the most succinct summary of the reasoning behind the U.S. bishops' statements on welfare reform. He insists that social legislation must make more than "economic sense" as measured according to the utilitarian calculus of costs and benefits, but must also "make good human sense" and "minimize any negative human fallout."[10]

However, concessions to the situation of pluralism are necessary and (in the interest of building an eventual consensus reflecting moral as well as strictly economic concerns) even desirable. Because the diverse citizens

---

10. Bishop William F. Murphy, "Helping to Calculate Human Value in the Market," *Boston Pilot*, 7 June 1996, 10.

of modern societies may not agree on a single vision of human dignity, social responsibility or the criteria justifying sacrifice for the less fortunate, arguments must sometimes be advanced which appeal to alternative modes of measuring social benefits—modes upon which all may agree. Budgetary savings are one such yardstick. We defer treating richer elements of an "overlapping consensus" until the next chapter, when we move from practical to more philosophical elements of potential convergence.

Appeals to potential cost savings resulting from investing in needy citizens were frequently heard in the welfare reform debates of recent years. In fact, such appeals represent a common denominator in arguments emanating from all parts of the American political spectrum. The conservative Republican governor of Wisconsin, Tommy Thompson, launched his budgetarily successful "Wisconsin Works" program according to the rationale that upfront investments in the employability of current welfare recipients will pay eventual dividends. The state now spends an annual average of approximately $1400 per recipient (this represents a fivefold increase from previous state policy) for such services as education, job training and child care which are targeted to assist recipients' transitions from welfare to work. Thompson's welfare policy dictum, that "it is necessary to spend now in order to save later," is supported by the finding that "the state now saves $2 in benefits for every $1 it spends making [former recipients] employable."[11] It is possible to object to Wisconsin's policy approach on various grounds, including the difficulties imposed on the lives of vulnerable families by such an exceptionless pro-work strategy,[12] but its demonstrated long-term cost savings have convinced many of the merits of the "human capital investment" strategy it enacts.

Liberals have also cited the cost savings argument as a rationale for their preferred approach to social policy. The liberal tendency to champion increased public expenditures is bolstered by evidence that early interventions are often effective in preventing the long-term family and personal problems which so often plague the lives of low-income Ameri-

11. John McCormick, "Missing the Point on Welfare," *Newsweek*, 14 Aug. 1995, 32.
12. In fact, Milwaukee Archbishop Rembert G. Weakland, O.S.B., was quite outspoken in voicing such objections based on Catholic social teaching, particularly its insistence that the lives of poor children and their parents not be made more difficult because of the effects of changes in welfare policy. See the archbishop's editorial denouncing aspects of Thompson's policy, "'Wisconsin Works': Breaking a Covenant," *Washington Post*, 4 July 1996, A29. For an account of the protracted verbal feud between the archbishop and the governor during July 1996, see Peter Steinfels, "A Healthy Debate on Overhauling the Welfare System Mixes Politics and Principle," *New York Times*, 27 July 1996, 10.

cans. If unaddressed, such problems as illness, learning disabilities and developmental and educational deficits may spiral in intensity and eventually require much more expensive interventions by government or charitable agencies. Liberals frequently argue that social problems such as crime, family instability, urban blight and persistent poverty are the result of neither inevitable social forces nor counterproductive public policy. Rather, they are exacerbated by a failure to launch adequately ambitious social policies to address the root causes of undesirable outcomes, such as inadequate health care and declining educational and community infrastructures. The liberal version of the cost savings argument thus supports government investment in low-income families as not only an exercise of social responsibility, but also as a way of preventing the need for the more expensive future interventions which consist of "picking up the pieces" after burgeoning pathologies have already exploded. Whether the topic is the high cost of foster care placement or the social burdens accompanying each resort to imprisonment or institutionalization, liberals tend to cite the social wisdom that prevention is less costly than the "cure" to many social problems.

Among the most prominent voices in this school of thought are Marian Wright Edelman and Lisbeth B. Schorr. In her longtime capacity as president of the Children's Defense Fund (CDF), Edelman has frequently expressed the rationale behind the various forms of activism in which she has long been engaged:

> CDF came into being in the early 1970s because we recognized that support for whatever was labelled black and poor was shrinking and that new ways had to be found to articulate and respond to the continuing problems of poverty and race, ways that appealed to the self-interest as well as the conscience of the American people. . . . In designing remedies, we also try to keep an eye on building the broadest possible constituency, while ensuring that the least privileged among our children are adequately protected.[13]

During the welfare reform debate of the 104th Congress, Edelman and the CDF[14] frequently repeated a number of arguments which appealed to the self-interest of taxpayers and to the cost savings associated with a continued federal commitment to poor families. Nowhere is this version of the cost savings argument stated more clearly than in Edelman's 1986

---

13. Marian Wright Edelman, *Families in Peril: An Agenda for Social Change*, The 1986 W.E.B. DuBois Lectures (Cambridge, Mass.: Harvard University Press, 1987) ix.

14. Besides conventional forms of advocacy (speeches, press conferences, publications), CDF makes extensive use of internet postings and even staged a massive rally, "Stand for Children," on 1 June 1996 in Washington, D.C. This event, cosponsored by sev-

W.E.B. DuBois Lectures: "We invest in children because the cost to the public of sickness, ignorance, neglect, and unemployment over the long term exceeds the cost of preventive investment in health, education, employed youth, and stable families."[15] Here Edelman cites numerous statistics indicating the wisdom of public investments in such measures as child immunization, prenatal care, Headstart, family planning services, summer jobs programs, nutrition programs such as WIC and income supports for vulnerable families such as AFDC.[16] Each is associated with huge and easily demonstrable dividends measured in cost savings for all Americans, in their capacities as taxpayers, consumers and residents of communities where the quality of life is greatly improved when adequate resources are allocated for crucial social investments.

The writings of social researcher Lisbeth B. Schorr similarly maintain a consistent focus on the overall social ecology in making a case for greater commitment of public resources to low-income families and neighborhoods. In an article published in the early months of the Clinton administration, Schorr seeks to counter the skepticism of the dominant antigovernment attitude which asserts that "nothing works." She issues this reminder: "In the last decade, extensive evidence has shown that the cycle of disadvantage can be broken through systemic societal action"[17] such as the efforts of successful school-based health clinics, intensive family support, progressive child care, and programs which deliver excellent prenatal care and nutrition. The "new knowledge about the details of successful programs"[18] she describes represents an updating of the research presented in her earlier volume, *Within Our Reach: Breaking the Cycle of Disadvantage*,[19] the publication of which had coincided with the previous round of welfare reform and had influenced the adoption of the Family Support Act of 1988. Now that researchers can identify which

---

eral dozen social advocacy groups, served in part as a protest against the soon-to-be-approved welfare law. A CDF press release ("Fourteen Reasons to Vote Against Pending Welfare Bills That Hurt Children," [Washington, D.C.: Children's Defense Fund, July 1996]) issued even closer to the time the welfare bill was finalized, also demonstrates CDF's tendency to appeal to a mix of (1) reasons of conscience and (2) practical reasons (such as long-run cost savings) as warrants for more generous social spending.

15. Edelman, *Families in Peril*, 31.

16. Ibid., 31–2. See also ch. 3 describing the huge cost savings of preventing adolescent pregnancy, which depends on subtle changes in the overall social environment of expectations facing teens as well as some modest, practical programs and initiatives.

17. "What Works: Applying What We Already Know About Successful Social Policy," *The American Prospect*, no. 13 (spring 1993) 43.

18. Ibid., 44.

19. N.Y.: Anchor Books of Doubleday, 1988.

types of childhood interventions are successful in improving the outcomes for individuals and families disadvantaged by poverty, the major remaining roadblock to real social improvement in this area is the inability to muster the political will to commit resources to this ultimately cost-effective enterprise.

Even in isolation from other sets of beliefs about the criteria for wise social policy, the liberal camp's recognition of the huge returns on these types of social spending constitutes sufficient cause for its opposition to the welfare law of 1996. The legislation dramatically reduces the public commitment of resources to low-income groups, in effect turning its back on the "social investment strategy" advocated by Schorr and Edelman. The new law most noticeably repudiates one particular element of such a strategy which virtually every other industrialized democracy in the world provides—a guaranteed floor of income for needy families. Moreover, the welfare law itself is only one part of a larger pattern of recent public policy which, over the objections of most liberals, focuses a disproportionate share of budget cuts (in the interest of deficit reduction) on programs which benefit primarily low-income groups. During the 104th Congress, programs for low-income people absorbed 93 percent of the budget reductions in entitlements ($61 billion out of a total of $65.6 billion in cuts), although these entitlement programs for the poor constitute only 23 percent of all entitlement spending.[20] From the standpoint of the proponents of a "social investment strategy," these measures (ironically proposed in the name of fiscal restraint and cost savings) represent a myopic withdrawal of support which will almost certainly cause higher long-term public costs as well as social distress.

There is considerable evidence that such arguments about the cost savings advantages of social investments have already found a wider audience. We have seen above the example of Wisconsin, where the state's social policy (inaugurated by a very conservative Governor) frankly appeals to the salience of what Schorr calls "pay-some-now-or-pay-more-later arguments."[21] Rudolph Giuliani, Republican Mayor of New York City, cited this same line of reasoning as the basis for his opposition to elements of the new federal welfare law. The mayor argued that the measures cutting assistance to children, legal immigrants and disabled people would not only shift fiscal burdens to local governments, but would result

---

20. Robert Greenstein, Richard Kogan and Marion Nichols, "Bearing Most of the Burden: How Deficit Reduction During the 104th Congress Concentrated on Programs for the Poor" (Washington, D.C.: Center on Budget and Policy Priorities, 26 Nov. 1996) 1.

21. Schorr, "What Works," 53.

in higher eventual aggregate costs to all levels of government. This is so because members of these groups newly denied ordinary income supports and routine health care assistance would soon seek out the more expensive social services associated with emergency relief, acute health problems and inadequate basic nutrition and shelter.[22] When confronted with the prohibitive costs of institutionalization of millions of children living in distressing conditions in welfare households, Newt Gingrich backed away from the "orphanage solution" he had previously proposed. Apparently, what persuaded Speaker Gingrich of the necessity of retaining some elements of the previous welfare system (including Medicaid and certain SSI benefits for poor disabled children) was a cost savings argument; government generally saves money when families are given the means to remain intact.

The salience of the cost savings argument is bolstered by its appeal to pragmatism, consistently a highly valued warrant for decisions in American politics. However, the persuasive power of this line of thinking is limited by several factors which reduce its influence on federal policymaking. Such cost savings do not show up neatly on budget ledgers, as standard accounting procedures place a premium on minimizing upfront expenditures rather than anticipating optimal ways of avoiding long-term costs. Any argument which appeals to gains which are deferred or are difficult to calculate with certainty (such as the eventual cost reductions associated with social investment) is at a marked disadvantage in ordinary budget-writing processes, which exhibit a bias toward "present time horizon." A further complication, to which the frustration experienced by Mayor Giuliani attests, is how the operation of the three levels of American government offers a disincentive for coherent policy strategy. Since states and localities bear most of the costs associated with federal spending reductions for social services, federal policymakers do not feel the full weight of the eventual cost savings incentives as they plan and allocate their present budgets.

Finally, it is important to sound a note of caution concerning reasonable expectations for income support and other social service programs. While there is ample evidence to support optimism that expanding our national commitment of resources for low-income families will bring social as well as budgetary benefits, it would be unwise to portray the gains from such interventions as limitless. In his examination of cost-ef-

---

22. Robert Pear, "Giuliani Battles with Congress on Welfare Bill," *New York Times*, 27 July 1996, 1, 27.

fective public responses to the problems of America's urban underclass, Mickey Kaus offers this balanced assessment:

> Programs like preschool education can make a significant, measurable difference. But even if they are "fully funded" they won't come close to overcoming the multiple pathologies of the underclass. They pass the test of cost-efficiency, but fail the test of sufficiency.[23]

In the Foreword to Schorr's *Within Our Reach*, William Julius Wilson draws the same distinction between the cost-effectiveness of such interventions to improve "the life chances of high-risk children and their families" and their sufficiency ("in a serious attack on persistent poverty and related problems, they are not sufficient"[24]). In the interest of realism, Wilson recommends that the programs Schorr advocates "ought to be combined with a comprehensive economic policy to enhance employment opportunities for disadvantaged Americans and to raise incomes."[25] Wilson elsewhere[26] makes the case that even such ambitious programs may justify themselves to the American public based on their eventual cost savings.

3. The well-being of family life deserves special policy attention because children represent the future of a nation

No one doubts that the future of a nation depends on the health and welfare of its families. The family is the primary social institution entrusted with the vital task of raising the next generation of citizens. However, by underlining the special national stake in the nurturance and well-being of America's children, we call attention to how the goal of healthy family life constitutes a common cause which may unite all Americans in the public purpose of improving the condition of our families. As one commentator says of the task of child-rearing, "society has an interest in having this job done well."[27]

Merely to invoke the commonly shared goal of healthy family life, of course, is not to settle any of the weighty matters of policy priority. As soon as the topic is broached, rival strategies for advancing the well-being of America's families and dealing with their most frequent problems immediately arise and vie for support. Liberals usually favor strategies which offer more resources to families, while conservatives

---

23. Mickey Kaus, *The End of Equality*, second edition (N.Y.: Basic Books, 1995) 123.
24. William Julius Wilson, "Foreword" to Schorr, *Within Our Reach*, xi.
25. Ibid.
26. *When Work Disappears* (N.Y.: Alfred A. Knopf, Inc., 1996), esp. ch. 8.
27. Kaus, *The End of Equality*, 111.

fear that assisting the wrong kinds of families amounts to subsidizing destructive reproductive behavior, so that the problems of poverty and broken families will be exacerbated. We have seen above how the welfare reform debate was often cast as a conflict of such policy approaches—as a battle between pro-income-security and anti-illegitimacy strategies which issued very different recommendations for the proper arrangements for poor relief. No one is against children, but arriving at a precise definition of their interest is a task which often eludes our political leaders.

In order to transform this arena of noticeable disagreement into one of substantial consensus, the challenge is to reframe welfare policy in a more constructive light—one which reveals the presence of mutual gains and common public interests—so that policy may take advantage of convergences of opinion where they are possible. Evidence that this task is achievable appears whenever Americans are polled in opinion surveys which measure support for public assistance to children. When the wording of survey questions allows participants to focus attention on the needs of aid recipients and the ability of public programs to ameliorate social conditions, rather than on the stereotypes of "the lazy poor" and "welfare cheats," Americans' overwhelming support for child assistance programs comes to the fore. The mere omission of the word "welfare" often alters patterns of response markedly.

One illustration of these patterns of opinion is offered in a set of statistics accompanying a June 1996 *Time* magazine feature article on the perceptions of children's issues in the 1996 political campaign.[28] By a margin of 73–22 percent, the sample favored "spending more tax dollars on programs to help children." Responding to another set of questions, only 10 percent of participants favored "cutting back current government programs to help children," while 49 percent preferred that existing programs be expanded, and 37 percent offered the opinion that current programs were "about right." Finally, the survey gauged public support for a list of seven programs for children (immunization, health insurance, nutrition, prenatal care, daycare, preschool education and teen pregnancy prevention). Without exception, by overwhelming margins the sample judged these among "the highest priorities for government." That these patterns of opinion were not generally reflected in the welfare reform debate, which resulted in sharp funding cuts for most of the programs the

28. The polling results appear in sidebars accompanying Elizabeth Gleick, "The Children's Crusade," *Time*, 3 June 1996, 31–5. The survey is described as follows: "From a telephone poll of 1,011 adult Americans taken for *Time*/CNN on May 8 and 9 by Yankelovich Partners, Inc. Sampling error is plus or minus 3.2%. Not sures omitted."

public seems to support, is partially attributable to a discrepancy in perceptions about the meaning and purpose of welfare. Unlike the items in this opinion survey, "welfare reform" was seldom framed as an issue about the well-being of children.

Once we recognize that assisting families with children (even at considerable expense to taxpayers) is a widely popular proposition, we may also acknowledge the variety of reasons which might be invoked by members of the American polity to support this goal as a policy priority. Citizens whose opinions are shaped by more solidaristic worldviews, such as Catholic social teaching, might use the language of "common good" and cite the goal of universal participation to support measures which help realize the social advancement of the most vulnerable persons and families. Others might cite moral reasons expressed in the idiom of rights and duties. Still others might use the language of economic gain, citing the cost savings argument treated above or the need to maintain international competitiveness in an increasingly globalized market—a goal which can only be met by preparing America's children to serve as a first-rate work force for the decades ahead.

Whichever language or combination of idioms is used to frame the national interest in the well-being of our children, the desire to increase the life chances of the next generation potentially leads to a convergence of opinion—if not precisely on policy measures worthy of adoption, then at least on judgments about which types of measures to avoid. Denying necessary goods (education, health care, income support) to poor children because of a desire to punish the actions of their parents or to deter irresponsible behavior on the part of families of the future places children of the present in jeopardy. It punishes them for actions that are beyond their control. The potential harm falls not only upon innocent youngsters, but upon all of us who have a stake in their well-being. Archbishop Rembert Weakland argues that we should not support policies which "hold children hostage" to the failures of their parents.[29] His conclusions may be embraced by many others who do not share the entire moral framework of his arguments, but who nevertheless subscribe to the conviction that our nation cannot afford to cut off this assistance.

None of these arguments amounts to a denial that indiscriminate, open-ended or unconditional assistance to families may have harmful effects. Nor do these arguments suggest an out-of-hand rejection of the proposition that social policy should incorporate elements of an anti-ille-

29. Weakland, "'Wisconsin Works,'" A29. The archbishop explains: "The children of the poor did not choose their families. We should not afflict these children with hunger in order to infuse their parents with virtue."

gitimacy strategy which seeks to create conditions more amenable to the self-help which occurs more readily in intact two-parent families, where children are more likely to thrive. However, these arguments do suggest a set of prudential limits (upon which we hopefully may all agree) for enforcing the goal of fostering intact families. Wise policy must not punish children simply because their families do not conform to a given ideal. The new welfare law violates this admonition by allowing states to impose family caps and teenage mother exclusions. The authors of such policies display a willingness to sacrifice the well-being of the present generation of children in the interest of putative changes in social expectations which might bring about improvements in the lives of some future generation.

The message government sends by "getting tough" with the poor is intended to constitute eventual good news—but only if and when future poverty and dependency rates are reduced. In the short run, however, it certainly constitutes bad news for today's recipients, whose increasing misery is countenanced by public policies insensitive to pressing immediate needs. Practical as well as moral arguments may be marshaled against such a policy strategy—one which runs the risk of so emphasizing what is wrong with welfare (perverse unintended consequences) that it forgets what is right with welfare, the program which represents our nation's major effort to provide material support to children in low-income families.

4. There is no practical substitute for the role of the federal government in serving as the primary conduit of social assistance to low-income families

It is unnecessary to repeat here the evidence from chapter three above which establishes (contra Marvin Olasky) the inability of private charities to substitute for the antipoverty efforts of the federal government. Rather, it will suffice simply to identify, as one of the practical arguments about which all observers might agree, the judgment that the federal government plays an indispensable role in providing income security to low-income U.S. families. It is very much in the common public interest that this role continue.

No matter how attractive is the notion that charitable voluntarism might constitute an adequate response to the unmet needs of our neighbors, it must nevertheless be recognized that the involvement of the national government remains a necessary element of any equitable response to American poverty. Of all the institutions in America, the federal government alone possesses two powers which allow it to exercise essential functions in alleviating dire want: (1) the ability to distribute the burdens of sacrifice nearly universally, according to a rational principle of contributive shares; and (2) a unique ability to provide a reliable flow of resources to those whose very lives depend upon such material assistance. The first item, of course, is attributable to the taxing authority of the federal government. Despite its imperfections, the federal tax system serves as a largely effective mechanism for addressing the problem of "free riders." It functions in a way that protects any segment of the population (e.g., those who live in closer proximity to concentrations of poverty) from having to pay a grossly disproportionate share of the social cost of alleviating poverty. Although the federal bureaucracy is often maligned on numerous grounds, it is only the flow of tax dollars through Washington, D.C., which furnishes some measure of accountability by which states and regions experiencing divergent economic fortunes share resources and bear some of each other's burdens. As such, the federal government is the ultimate guarantor of this element of social cohesion.

The second of these unique federal powers safeguards recipients of assistance against even more serious dangers. The involvement of the federal government in welfare serves as a protection against the racial, geographic and gender biases which may creep into any system of poor relief administered by institutions less committed to the principle of equal regard of persons than the federal government. Interstate differentials in welfare benefit levels supply ample evidence of how arbitrary alternative arrangements may become. Further, the federal government's unmatched capacity to perform means-testing allows it to determine appropriate benefits according to the demonstrated need of applicants—a task which confounds many private philanthropic enterprises.

Including this fourth item on the list of promising points of practical agreement in welfare policy is one way of acknowledging the force of the argument that it is better to plan systematic responses to deep social problems than to rely merely on ad hoc efforts. An organized response to the problem of inadequate income is beneficial for both the recipients and givers of assistance. It eliminates the capriciousness and uncertainty associated with less thoroughly planned arrangements for sharing resources. Because these advantages accrue eventually to all members of society, the continuation of a federal role in welfare constitutes a matter of common public interest.

Chapter 8

Toward a Shared Vision of Fairness: The Contributions of John Rawls and John Courtney Murray

The previous chapter identifies four arguments about practical issues related to welfare. Each points to an area of overlapping public concern and recommends strategies and policies to realize empirical (indeed, often quantifiable) mutual gains. Each of the four appeals to social improvements which almost any policy observer will recognize, so the level of agreement they assume remains quite modest. If our search for a new welfare consensus stops here, it would abandon an important endeavor: the struggle to forge a more substantial social agreement on such normative questions as what low-income families deserve and what social obligations apply to affluent members of society to contribute to the wellbeing of their less fortunate neighbors. In other words, such a modest agenda would exclude from consideration most of the social goods (social unity and cohesion, universal recognition of membership, the common good, the protection of human dignity) recognized by religious social ethics, particularly Catholic social teaching.

If we are to (1) continue the search for more substantial social agreement and (2) still maintain hope that the findings of such a search will be both broadly acceptable in a pluralistic society and effective guides to public policy in a majoritarian democracy, then we must consult available philosophical approaches to the possibility of social consensus. In this endeavor, no social philosophers offer more assistance than John Rawls and John Courtney Murray. Each contributes seminal concepts which are indispensable tools for anyone exploring the possibility of building a shared societal vision of fairness.

Murray, an American Jesuit theologian writing in the middle decades of the twentieth century, was perhaps the most important figure in Catholicism's dialogue with liberalism in America. He articulated numerous pivotal insights about both the content and style of constructive participation of religious voices in the public dialogue of a pluralistic society. Later in this chapter we will consider his assessment of the ability of the "public consensus" to unite a people in the search for a shared vision of fairness, even as they remain divided on "articles of faith." First, we will investigate the contribution of John Rawls in explicating a parallel concept: a "public conception of justice." Among all liberal theorists of justice, it is Rawls who addresses most pertinently the crucial issues involved in defining appropriate standards for a shared vision of social arrangements. By proposing "the idea of an overlapping consensus," Rawls sketches a road map for the type of agreement we might hope and expect to forge in a modern pluralistic society on such issues of economic justice as welfare policy. The contributions of both Rawls and Murray will help us evaluate the prospects of moving beyond a seeming impasse into an initial (and hopefully widening) agreement about wise social policy for the future.

Rawls: An "Overlapping Consensus" Based Upon a "Political Conception of Justice"

Rawls employs the term "overlapping consensus" to describe a specific type of social agreement within societies which form their basic social institutions upon the common (and "liberal," in the classical sense of the term) understanding that personal freedom is a primary value. In order to situate the idea of an overlapping consensus within the author's overall theory of "justice as fairness," we begin with Rawls's summary description of the work done by this concept:

> [G]iven the fact of pluralism, what does the work of reconciliation by free public reason, and thus enables us to avoid reliance on general and comprehensive doctrines, is two things: first, identifying the fundamental role of political values in expressing the terms of fair social cooperation consistent with mutual respect between citizens regarded as free and equal; and second, uncovering a sufficiently inclusive concordant fit among political and other values as displayed in an overlapping consensus.[1]

Even without engaging in a detailed rehearsal of Rawls's entire construct of "justice as fairness," it is evident that "overlapping consensus" constitutes for Rawls (in contrast to its frequent usage in common par-

---

1. John Rawls, "The Idea of an Overlapping Consensus," *Oxford Journal of Legal Studies* 7, no. 1 (Feb. 1987) 17.

lance) a technical term.² It emerges as a central feature of what Rawls calls "a political conception of justice," defined as "the object of consensus . . . [which] includes the conception of society and of citizens as persons, as well as principles of justice. . . ."³ The political conception of justice consists of the basic principles of fairness (including the "difference principle") which Rawls famously describes in part one of *A Theory of Justice*, where he claims that these are the social principles any rational beings would choose under the conditions of the "original position."

This "political conception of justice" is to be distinguished from two other concepts Rawls identifies as its rivals: "comprehensive doctrines"; and a "*modus vivendi*."⁴ A political conception of justice based on an overlapping consensus occupies a middle position between these two extremes, each of which is, Rawls contends, an unacceptable basis for social cooperation within a modern political community. Let us examine each in turn.

In a situation of pluralism (which Rawls considers to be a permanent feature of modern societies⁵), it is unrealistic to expect agreement on comprehensive doctrines of the meaning, value and purpose of human life—including philosophical and theological definitions of "ends," "truth" and "thick conceptions of the good." A central tenet of the liberal project is the necessity that the actions of public authorities be characterized by neutrality among competing conceptions of the good. Rawls's preference for the personal autonomy, individualism and tolerance associated with the neutral state of a liberal order, along with his aversion to metaphysics, teleology, and any brand of perfectionism, problematizes the task of choosing any social goods to pursue in common. One of the key advantages of the strikingly original version of the liberal "method of

   2. The term appears only once (and somewhat off-handedly) in Rawls's 1971 *A Theory of Justice* (Cambridge, Mass.: Harvard University Press, 1971). In the course of clarifying his positions in response to vocal critics over the course of two decades, Rawls amplifies the importance of the idea of overlapping consensus considerably, according it an increasingly prominent role in his social theory. This occurred most notably in the 1987 essay cited above and in Lecture IV (pp. 133–72) of his later volume, *Political Liberalism* (N.Y.: Columbia University Press, 1993), which collects and enlarges several essays Rawls published after 1971. It is this latter version of "overlapping consensus," with its more precise meaning, which is treated here.
   3. Rawls, *Political Liberalism*, 147.
   4. Ibid., 144–50.
   5. In "The Idea of an Overlapping Consensus," Rawls writes: "This diversity of doctrines—the fact of pluralism—is not a mere historical condition that will soon pass away; it is, I believe, a permanent feature of the public culture of modern democracies. . . . [T]he diversity of views will persist and may increase" (4).

conflict avoidance" Rawls adopts is its ability to minimize the type of social conflict which seems unavoidable when any comprehensive doctrine aspires to regulate the social order. As Rawls warns:

> [A] free democratic society well-ordered by any comprehensive doctrine, religious or secular, is surely utopian in a pejorative sense. Achieving it would, in any case, require the oppressive use of state power.[6]

Any attempt to base shared social institutions upon such comprehensive doctrines would sacrifice the neutrality of the state and ultimately betray the cause of fostering social peace and stability. It would necessitate constant and coercive interventions to enforce a unity of opinion that is inconsistent with the existence of the diversity of beliefs in a free society. The modern condition of pluralism practically insures the existence of alternative doctrines—rival systems of thought which would be perceived by adherents of any established doctrine as dangerous rivals, indeed as "heresies" to be snuffed out. This situation (of which the constitutional issue of the establishment of religion is but one example) would be unacceptable for Rawls or for any liberal who champions procedural justice based on the priority of right to good.

Forming a political community based upon comprehensive doctrines is unrealistic and objectionable, then, because it seeks to do too much—assuming and depending upon more social agreement than a situation of pluralism allows. Conversely, the second alternative to a true "political conception of justice," namely the option of a *modus vivendi*, is not desirable because it seeks to accomplish too little. If the members of a political entity resign themselves to treating their political arrangements as a mere *modus vivendi*, they settle for too minimal a set of expectations for their institutions. In effect, parties to so modest an agreement bracket so many of their aspirations that they can hardly be said to have formed a true political community at all.

Rawls illustrates this shortcoming by comparing a *modus vivendi* approach to political order to "a treaty between two states whose national aims and interests put them at odds."[7] Each obeys the terms of the treaty only insofar as it is necessary and advantageous. While they submit grudgingly to the authority of the agreement, "in general both states are ready to pursue their goals at the expense of the other, and should conditions change, they may do so."[8] Political agreements forged on this thin

---

6. John Rawls, "The Domain of the Political and Overlapping Consensus," *New York University Law Review* 64, no. 2 (May 1989) 249.
7. Rawls, "The Idea of an Overlapping Consensus," 10.
8. Ibid., 10–13.

basis are unstable and subject to the vicissitudes of ephemeral power relations. Rawls portrays the *modus vivendi* approach as indicative of "the Hobbesian strand in liberalism."[9]

Rawls offers three reasons why an overlapping consensus allows us to hope for more than this model case of a *modus vivendi*: (1) "the object of consensus, the political conception of justice, is itself a moral conception"; (2) "it is affirmed on moral grounds" since it includes an account of persons, society and cooperative virtues; and (3) an overlapping consensus promises the feature of stability over time, since "the political conception will still be supported regardless of shifts in the distribution of political power."[10] A mere *modus vivendi*, by contrast, includes none of these advantages, since the social unity it features is only superficial, and depends on a precarious convergence of interests where the parties treat the agreement as merely instrumental, not moral in nature.

Rawls's elaboration of this aspect of a "political conception of justice" constitutes his most cogent answer to a vital question which recurs throughout his writings. One appearance of this query surfaces in a 1985 essay: "How is social unity to be understood, given that there can be no public agreement on the one rational good, and a plurality of opposing and incommensurable conceptions must be taken as given?"[11] Rawls rephrases the question in his 1993 volume: "How is it possible for there to exist over time a just and stable society of free and equal citizens, who remain profoundly divided by religious, philosophical and moral doctrines?"[12] Although Rawls poses this question as a general "task for liberalism as a political doctrine . . . to answer,"[13] any adequate response must include reference to Rawls's idea of the overlapping consensus (or some parallel notion). British moral philosopher John Haldane expresses admiration for these accomplishments of Rawls's idea of an overlapping consensus:

> [its] content and justification are independent of any distinctive comprehensive doctrines, but are compatible with many, most, or all such doctrines. Unlike a *modus vivendi*, such a condition does express and sustain genuine social unity, but compatible with Rawls's requirement that liberalism

---

9. Ibid., 23.
10. "The Idea of an Overlapping Consensus," 11. An expanded treatment appears in *Political Liberalism*, 146–9.
11. John Rawls, "Justice as Fairness: Political not Metaphysical," *Philosophy and Public Affairs* 14 (1985) 249.
12. *Political Liberalism*, 4.
13. "Justice as Fairness," 249.

be neutral between competing conceptions of the good, it is not the expression of one, as against another, comprehensive doctrine.[14]

Rawls frequently refers to the general concept of "political values." This invocation of values broadly shared within a common political culture is another strand leading us forward in our investigation of the significance of Rawls's theory for discussions of the American welfare consensus. In labeling his construct "justice as fairness," Rawls explicitly calls attention to the role of political values in shaping the criteria we come to share concerning desirable terms of social cooperation. In other words, "fairness" is always a judgment made by actual people within specific cultural locations, as Rawls relies on social consensus to carry the weight of ethical justification. The ultimate goal of Rawls's political philosophy is not to uncover *a priori* moral truths, but to articulate "those shared notions and principles thought to be already latent in common sense."[15] Rawls's appeal, finally, is to the shared convictions by which humans, necessarily shaped by a political culture, seek the reasonable agreement we call consensus.[16]

It is exactly this point which Rawls reserves for the closing pages of *A Theory of Justice*, in a final section entitled "Concluding Remarks on Justification." Here Rawls contrasts the approach he has adopted (with its reliance on "considered convictions" and "contingent principles" derived from "our considered judgments in reflective equilibrium"[17]) with the approaches he rejected (Cartesian styles of deductive reasoning from first principles which aspire to being self-evident). Rawls's subsequent reminders that the nature of "justice as fairness" is above all political, not metaphysical, underline a point which is instructive in our evaluation of the proper role of religious voices in shaping social welfare laws: public policy must not be based on a comprehensive doctrine held by only a sector of a pluralistic society.

A faithful reading of Rawls, then, recognizes the centrality of the ambient political culture in forming the "political conception of justice" which plays the vital role described above. Since an acceptable political

---

14. John Haldane, "The Individual, the State, and the Common Good," *Social Philosophy and Policy* 13, no. 1 (winter 1996) 64.

15. John Rawls, "Kantian Constructivism in Moral Theory," *The Journal of Philosophy* 77, no. 9 (Sept. 1980) 518.

16. Rawls thus replaces the Kantian notion of objectivity (as something "given by the point of view of the universe") with a new view in which "objectivity is to be understood by reference to a suitably constructed social point of view, an example of which is the framework provided by the procedure of the original position" (ibid., 570).

17. *A Theory of Justice*, 579.

conception of justice cannot consist of a religious or philosophical comprehensive doctrine, Rawls reminds us, it must be formulated "in terms of certain fundamental intuitive ideas viewed as latent in the public political culture of a democratic society. These ideas are used to articulate and order in a principled way its basic political values."[18] Indeed, as Richard Bayer writes, what separates an overlapping consensus from a mere *modus vivendi* is precisely that the latter "depends on a happy coincidence of contingencies and interest" while the former "is based more securely on shared democratic ideals and values that form the political capital of democratic societies."[19]

Rawls acknowledges the likely existence, even given a shared political conception of justice, of "intractable conflicts" which will not "be satisfactorily resolved" by means of universally "generally acceptable answers."[20] Even in admitting that the work of forging political agreement is never completed and that an overlapping consensus will sometimes encounter limits, Rawls nevertheless finds room for optimism about the potential accomplishments of a political community united in a common commitment to deliberation:

> A political conception is at best but a guiding framework of deliberation and reflection which helps us reach political agreement on at least the constitutional essentials. If it seems to have cleared our view and made our considered convictions more coherent; if it has narrowed the gap between the conscientious convictions of those who accept the basic ideals of a constitutional regime, then it has served its practical political purpose. And this remains true even though we can't fully explain our agreement: we know only that citizens who affirm the political conception, and who have been raised in and are familiar with the fundamental ideas of the public political culture, find that, when they adopt its framework of deliberation, their judgments converge sufficiently so that political cooperation on the basis of mutual respect can be maintained.[21]

Rawls's optimism about enduring social agreement based upon an overlapping consensus suggests two propositions about a society fortunate enough to possess a shared conception of justice. First, concerning the features of public debate in such a society, the political conception of justice may acquire a momentum of its own and generate support for itself

---

18. "The Idea of an Overlapping Consensus," 6.
19. Richard C. Bayer, "Christian Ethics and *A Theory of Justice*," *Journal of the American Academy of Religion* 64, no. 1 (spring 1996) 48.
20. "The Idea of an Overlapping Consensus," 16.
21. Ibid.

and its social institutions that amounts to "an allegiance that becomes stronger over time."[22] The process of agreement may feed off its own successes and reach outward to expand the arena of constructive deliberation. Second, concerning the moral development of people inhabiting such a society, an overlapping consensus may actually exert a formational influence upon its adherents, endowing them with the virtues appropriate to members of a society deeply committed to ongoing dialogue. Rawls makes a brief foray into moral psychology[23] to describe these "essential cooperative virtues"[24] ("tolerance and being ready to meet others halfway, and the virtue of reasonableness and the sense of fairness"[25]) and to describe the process by which "citizens come to have increasing trust and confidence in one another."[26] Both these developments are ultimately attributable to the habits, loyalties and affections generated by the adoption and institutionalization of a successful shared political conception of justice. Each bolsters Rawls's original argument that among the achievements of an overlapping consensus is a measure of stability which transcends a mere convergence of interests.

Murray: The "Public Consensus" Based Upon Natural Reason

The parallels between Rawls's analysis of the overlapping consensus and John Courtney Murray's treatment of related topics are quite striking. The two frequently use slightly different terminology to make similar points concerning liberalism's central challenge: the task of promoting social unity amidst irreducible pluralism. This is not to say that the social theories of Rawls and Murray are identical, nor that their positions on the terms of social cooperation are indistinguishable. For example, the two clearly differ on an important aspect of philosophy of government in a liberal order: the degree to which public authorities can and should maintain a stance of neutrality about questions of "the good life." Perhaps because Murray speaks so self-consciously from within the tradition of a particular comprehensive doctrine (the neoscholasticism of Roman Catholicism), he maintains a more robust view of the possible accomplishments of government in identifying and promoting common public interests without engaging in objectionable types of coercion. Despite these differences, Rawls and Murray may be considered together

22. Ibid., 21.
23. "The Idea of an Overlapping Consensus," 22–3; *Political Liberalism*, 158–68.
24. "The Idea of an Overlapping Consensus," 21.
25. Ibid., 17.
26. Ibid., 23.

because each addresses the meaning and possibility of consensus amidst the conflicting viewpoints of a pluralistic society. Each sheds light on the terms of appropriate and constructive religious participation within general public dialogue, especially on the status of policy recommendations advanced from within religious traditions.

John Courtney Murray is perhaps best remembered for the part he played in a crucial *intramural* debate within the Roman Catholic Church: the question of whether the documents of the Second Vatican Council should endorse the principle of religious liberty. In championing the cause of free religious expression, now recognized within the Catholic Church as part of the meaning of freedom of conscience, Murray played a central role[27] in the successful and long-delayed "effort to disentangle Catholicism from its traditional commitment to the altar-and-throne arrangements of the confessional state."[28] Of greater import for the present study, however, are Murray's *extramural* arguments—those which address the broader audience of Americans seeking greater clarity on issues of Church and state. This is where Murray makes his most lasting contribution. He not only calls for a reexamination of the principles by which Americans have patrolled the treacherous border between Church and state, but also recasts this entire set of issues in terms of the broader categories of faith and culture, religion and public life. Murray's lifelong quest was for an adequate response to the pivotal question: what relationship between public and private institutions best serves a free people?

The two keys to Murray's writings on this topic are: (1) his retrieval of "the Gelasian heritage"; and (2) his famous distinction between "articles of peace" and "articles of faith." The first refers to a tradition of reflection on the proper relation of spiritual and temporal authority which dates back to a 494 C.E. letter of Pope Gelasius I outlining the distinction between two spheres: "the sacred authority *[auctoritas]* of the priesthood and the royal power *[potestas]*"[29] of kingship. Murray sees in the

---

27. Murray is generally recognized as the intellectual architect of Vatican II's "Declaration on Religious Freedom" *(Dignitatis humanae)* which represents the Catholic Church's first official recognition of the principle of religious freedom.

28. George Weigel, "The Future of the John Courtney Murray Project," in Robert P. Hunt and Kenneth L. Grasso, eds., *John Courtney Murray and the American Civil Conversation* (Grand Rapids, Mich.: William B. Eerdmans Publishing Co., 1992) 277.

29. The text of this letter appears in Brian Tierney, ed., *The Crisis of Church and State 1050–1300*, Medieval Academy Reprints for Teaching, 21 (Toronto: University of Toronto Press, 1988) 13–4. An excellent treatment of Murray's explication of the "Gelasian thesis" in arguing for the principle of religious liberty is Thomas P. Ferguson, *Catholic and American: The Political Theology of John Courtney Murray* (Kansas City, Mo.: Sheed and Ward, Inc., 1993).

"revolutionary character of the Christian dispensation"[30] a duality of consciousness which, when correctly interpreted, presents numerous advantages to social organization. It simultaneously accords a certain autonomy to the political order and serves as a warrant for the "freedom of the Church." The alternative consists of a monism which endangers human freedom because it risks a totalitarianism of either throne or altar. The laicist state of European liberalism is unacceptable because its orthodoxy of secularism so subordinates the Church to the state that human transcendence is denied and the whole of human life comes to be absorbed in the polis. The confessional state commits an error which is the mirror image; imposing a Christian social order on a pluralistic society enforces a religious orthodoxy which does damage to human dignity because it violates freedom of conscience.

Murray's second essential construct, the distinction between "articles of faith" and "articles of peace," furnishes guidance to those seeking to understand and maintain a healthy balance in their dual loyalties—as adherents of a religious faith and as citizens in a nonconfessional polity. Confronted with the fact of irreducible pluralism in twentieth-century America, Murray undertakes a line of reasoning which anticipates to a remarkable degree Rawls's assessment of the overlapping consensus based on the distinction between a "comprehensive doctrine" and a "public conception of justice." Even though Americans share no theological consensus, Murray observes, they are united by a common profession of certain truths, including the ones introduced by

> the forthright statement of the Declaration of Independence: "We hold these truths. . . ." That is to say, we have a public philosophy; as a people we have come to a consensus. This philosophy is the foundation of our public life; by coming to this consensus we have come to be a people, possessed of an identity.[31]

Murray holds that there is a "three-fold function of the ensemble of truths that make up the public consensus or philosophy." This includes: (1) determining national goals and purposes; (2) providing standards for judging policies, which are means to these goals; and (3) providing "the basis of communication between government and the people . . . furnish[ing] a common universe of discourse in which public issues can be intelligently stated and intelligently argued."[32]

30. John Courtney Murray, *We Hold These Truths: Catholic Reflections on the American Proposition* (N.Y.: Sheed and Ward, 1960) 202.
31. Ibid., 80.
32. Ibid., 80–1.

Murray's primary example of a plank of the public philosophy is the First Amendment to the U.S. Constitution. The "no establishment of religion" and "free exercise of religion" clauses are best viewed as "articles of peace" for they are "restrictions placed upon government [which are] necessary in order to insure freedom."[33] Murray insists that these clauses, which embody "the American proposition" that limited government is possible and desirable, not be interpreted as containing theological content of any sort. Rather, Murray contends, "the American thesis is simply political. It asserts the theory of a free people under a limited government."[34] Constitutions and similar laws within a liberal polity claim only a rather circumscribed authority, deserving status as

> only a law, not a dogma. The constitutional clauses have no religious content. They answer none of the eternal human questions with regard to the nature of truth and freedom. . . .Therefore they are not invested with the sanctity that attaches to dogma, but only with the rationality that attaches to law. . . . It is not necessary to give them a religious assent, but only a rational civil obedience. In a word, they are not articles of faith but articles of peace.[35]

This half of Murray's argument ("civil unity therefore must not hinder the various religious communities in American society in the maintenance of their own distinct identities"[36]) parallels Rawls's insistence that comprehensive doctrines never serve as a basis for a pluralistic society. The remaining part of Murray's message about the American proposition parallels Rawls's description of the unitive power of a political conception of justice, including his disavowal of the proposition that an overlapping consensus is a mere *modus vivendi*. This is the place where Murray balances his reminder that "America is not a church . . . it is simply a civil community whose unity is purely political"[37] with his expressions of confidence in the power of the American consensus to unite its diverse participants into an effective whole ("one civil society"[38]) in a constructive way.

Murray insists that laws promulgated by limited government are more than the terms by which we agree to disagree. Rather, they constitute "moral conceptions"[39] which impose upon us "collective moral obligations,

---

33. Ibid., 69.
34. Ibid.
35. Ibid., 48.
36. Ibid., 45.
37. Ibid., 54.
38. Ibid., 45.
39. Ibid., 108.

binding in conscience"[40] which we must obey as we obey any moral principle. Beyond the instrumental value associated with them as "articles of peace," such civil laws adopted by limited governments can be something good in themselves, especially in light of their proven ability to protect human freedom amidst the challenges of pluralism. The American experience of liberty under law demonstrates the superior advantages of our constitutional arrangements; by foreswearing competence in the field of religion, the American government has engaged in a long experiment in self-restraint which has proven not only possible and stable, but positively desirable.

Murray's analysis of how unity and pluralism are held together in American society is summarized in his explication of the phrase "*E pluribus unum*." Both terms of this seeming paradox are irreducible; "the pluralism remains as real as the unity" because it is a "unity of a limited order."[41] The key remaining question concerns the manner in which the two distinct and subsisting orders, the religious in which we are divided and the civil/political in which we are united, are related. One possible way of relating them looks to Jefferson's phrase "a wall of separation" which putatively must hermetically divide the two spheres. Although such an arrangement might be acceptable to a Rawlsian, it cannot be endorsed by Murray. Although he nowhere denies the existence of a tension between religious and civil spheres and the loyalties operative in each, still Murray proposes that this can be, under proper conditions, a creative tension. The integration implied in the dualism of religious and civic allegiance, despite remaining an "ever precarious synthesis,"[42] may endure with most constructive results.

The key term in Murray's resolution of unity and pluralism is "the public consensus." Murray's understanding of consensus, its origin and its significance differs in noteworthy ways from the Rawlsian version of consensus. Murray's explanation begins:

> The state of civility supposes a consensus that is constitutional. . . . This consensus is come to by the people; they become a people by coming to it. They do not come to it accidentally, without quite knowing how, but deliberatively, by the methods of reason reflecting on experience. . . . It is not simply a set of working hypotheses whose value is pragmatic. It is an ensemble of substantive truths, a structure of basic knowledge, an order of elementary affirmations that reflect realities inherent in the order of existence.[43]

40. Ibid., 63.
41. Ibid., 45.
42. Ibid., 196.
43. Ibid., 9.

Clearly, the public consensus has a higher status and richer possibilities for Murray than it ever could for Rawls. Most of the difference springs from the divergent stances toward the topics of truth, knowledge, and human nature assumed by Murray and Rawls. His location within the Aristotelian-Thomist tradition of natural law theory gives Murray a greater confidence in the human ability to advance propositions on which all can agree. Our common judgments about the efficacy of certain civil laws are based on whether they are "in accord with reason"[44] and correspond appropriately to the subsistent human nature we share. Murray is perfectly aware of the options he has excluded from consideration by adopting this stance. The final chapter of *We Hold These Truths*, entitled "The Doctrine Lives: The Eternal Return of Natural Law," is a spirited defense of the theory of natural law against a catalogue of errors (among them, "rationalism, individualism, and nominalism"[45]) Murray sees as regrettable ramifications of misguided post-Enlightenment social philosophy.

Because Rawls's social theory sidesteps ontological questions (such as whether there exists a common human nature and a universal moral law on which to ground ethical norms for civil law), it is perfectly compatible with the nominalist epistemology Murray rejects. Rawls's understanding of social contract theory postulates an inherent authority for the consensus, thus avoiding Murray's brand of foundationalism altogether. Rawls thus advances a pragmatic theory of truth,[46] an alternative to the correspondence theory of truth which characterizes the natural law approach of Murray. Here Murray stakes out his distinctive position on the warrants for social authority:

> The validity of the consensus is radically independent of its public status as either majority or minority opinion. Moreover, the Declaration of Independence did not hazard the conjecture: "This is the convergent trend of opinion among us. . . ." It made the affirmation: "We hold these truths. . . ." Or in the equivalent formula: "This is the public consensus. . . ."[47]

Murray clarifies what he means by "consensus" in the course of answering the question: "Do the propositions included in the consensus acquire validity through the sheer fact of their general acceptance, or conversely, does the inherent validity of these propositions require that they be generally accepted?"[48] While Rawls would answer yes to the first

44. Ibid., 119.
45. Ibid., 319.
46. On the topic of "truth" in Rawls, see *Political Liberalism*, 150–4.
47. *We Hold These Truths*, 98.
48. Ibid.

part of the question and no to the second, Murray's responses are the opposite, since his natural law approach postulates the existence of eternal truths which are "discovered," not "invented" as are the bases for agreement in the moral world of Rawls.

Murray's statements about the American consensus and its public standards of justice, then, are ultimately colored by his reliance on natural law as the essential bridge between faith and reason. This has advantages as well as disadvantages. On the positive side, it allows Murray to establish that the consensus he refers to is not ephemeral or subject to the temporary errors in judgment which are endemic to majoritarian democracies. Rather, our policies are answerable to a "higher law"[49] which is in accord with the eternal truth of reason. Murray's strongest response to the ethical relativism and legal positivism he feared was his affirmation of the proposition that all people, as possessors of (albeit fallible) consciences capable of connecting "is" and "ought," are living repositories of the natural law. In this sense, we are indeed all "natural-law jurists."[50]

On the negative side, Murray's style of reasoning is often criticized as displaying a certain triumphalism which runs the risk of dividing rather than uniting the polity. This danger is a particular concern when some members of society claim a privileged ability to serve as authentic interpreters of the supposed objective order of reality and morality. To defend Murray against charges of triumphalism, we need only recall one of the central tenets of the natural law approach: the principle that essential truths are knowable to all. This confidence that "the demands of the law are inscribed on [the] hearts" of all (Rom 2:15) leads natural law thinkers to search for nonparticularistic ethical propositions. Perhaps most significantly, in order to deflect charges of triumphalism it suffices merely to take Murray at his word when he professes the belief that pluralism is permanent and irreducible. In light of this enduring feature of the American social context, Murray concludes that the contributions of churches to public debate (such as the Catholic bishops' policy guidelines for social welfare) will be judged in public primarily according to their practical merits. In other words, the worth of the bishops' suggestions is properly measured by the size of the following these policy positions win and the extent of the agreement they inspire. Murray recognizes that, in the context of a pluralistic society, religious contributions to public life are validated by a new kind of authority: not by a traditional authority of office or tradition, but rather by the persuasiveness of the arguments reli-

---

49. Ibid., 325.
50. Ibid., 317.

gious voices advance within a public dialogue. Murray's hopes for social betterment are based not upon a naive utopianism which dreams of the triumph of a forced unity, but rather upon

> modest expectations with regard to the solution of the problem of religious pluralism and civic unity. . . . We cannot hope to make American society the perfect conspiracy based on a unanimous consensus. But we could at least do two things. We could limit the warfare and we could enlarge the dialogue. . . . And amidst the pluralism, a unity would be discernible—the unity of an orderly conversation.[51]

Murray is keenly aware of the fragility of the peace that is democracy as well as the importance of the "social capital" of tolerance and good will that maintain the peace. In his appeal to civility and his high regard for the cooperative virtues of citizenship which make dialogue and public deliberation possible, Murray echoes Rawls's paean to the open deliberation that characterizes the public life of pluralistic societies fortunate enough to enjoy a stable overlapping consensus. Both Rawls and Murray, each on his own terms, thus complete the argument that political stability does not depend on religious unity.

Participating in a Public Dialogue About Economic Fairness

It may seem that our explorations of the social theories of Rawls and Murray have taken us far afield from our topic. However the forgoing analysis allows us now to take full advantage of the insights of these two figures into the meaning and possibilities of a public, overlapping consensus—crucial elements of our investigation of what is desirable and possible concerning distributive justice in general and welfare policy in particular. The process of applying the analysis of Rawls and Murray to the welfare debate proceeds in two steps. The first task is to identify, within the framework supplied by each figure, that part of the content of the consensus which relates to economic justice, especially for the least fortunate members of a society. The second is to describe how religious voices, within a situation of pluralism, may participate in public dialogue on economic and social policy.

First, concerning the content of the consensus as it relates to the economy, we find that the key term for both Murray and Rawls is "fairness."

---

51. Ibid., 23–4. Note Murray's idiosyncratic use of the word "conspiracy" to mean, in a positive sense, a "breathing together," as in a civil dialogue.

Rawls's treatment of the overlapping consensus,[52] although mostly concerned with defining its "depth and breadth" in political terms, does occasionally address the question of economic arrangements. It directs attention to those "principles and values" which must be a part of any "fair system of cooperation"[53] for citizens who are to be considered free and equal. In order to create favorable conditions under which

> a democratic people is sufficiently unified and cohesive . . . there must be fundamental legislation . . . to assure that the basic needs of all citizens can be met so that they can take part in political and social life . . . .
>
> [B]elow a certain level of material and social well-being, and of training and education, people simply cannot take part in society as citizens, much less as equal citizens.[54]

In his original exposition of the overlapping consensus, Rawls notes that "the familiar basic rights" are ineffective without "measures to ensure that all persons in a society have sufficient material means to make effective use of those basic rights."[55] In other words, it is not enough to recognize equal rights and opportunities in the abstract. "A liberal conception of political justice," Rawls insists, is incomplete unless it includes "measures assuring to all citizens adequate, all-purpose means to make effective use of their basic liberties and opportunities."[56] Rawls mentions that this stipulation "can be understood in different ways, and so there are many liberalisms,"[57] but he nevertheless insists that this concern must be part of the content of any liberal order which aspires to protect citizens from unfair or arbitrary treatment.

Like Rawls, Murray rarely explicitly addresses the content of the consensus as it pertains to economic matters; he offers only scattered clues about his judgments on distributive issues. Like Rawls, Murray's chief concern about the economy is that it achieve fairness. Murray takes the position that certain economic practices are unfair and should be checked by governmental interventions to protect victims against abuses. As always, Murray's recommendations are guided by his principle that "constraint must be for the sake of freedom."[58] It is the public consensus

---

52. Recall that Rawls defines overlapping consensus as "a shared idea of citizens' good that is appropriate for political purposes" ("The Priority of Right and the Idea of the Good," *Philosophy and Public Affairs* 17, no. 4 [1988] 258).
53. *Political Liberalism*, 149.
54. Ibid., 166.
55. Rawls, "The Idea of an Overlapping Consensus," 17.
56. Ibid., 18.
57. Ibid.
58. *We Hold These Truths*, 160.

that guides this process, since it "acts as the final arbiter of the legitimacy of economic power and of the rightfulness of its uses."[59] The consensus thus

> recognizes limits on corporate power and submits uses of economic power to public judgment. . . . This is the supreme function of the consensus—to determine the nature of the economy, to specify its style, and thus to insure that the style of the economy accords with the whole larger style of life that the American people has adopted as its own—the democratic style . . . .Thus the consensus furnishes premises that justify governmental intervention in the economy.[60]

Among the issues Murray treats as examples of how the consensus is able to "furnish standards of judgment on economic events"[61] are antitrust violations and corporate abuses which result from great concentrations of economic power. Because Murray does not directly mention poor relief or welfare policy, we can only guess how his concern for freedom and democracy would translate into possible governmental interventions (set in motion by the consensus) to insure that the least advantaged citizens receive fair treatment.

Our second task, which serves as a transition to the next chapter, is a more subtle one. In seeking to outline how Rawls and Murray would characterize the modes of religious participation which are appropriate in the public policy dialogue of a pluralistic society, more is required than a mere consultation of texts. In the case of Murray, we must read between the lines of his distinction between "articles of peace" and "articles of faith" to discern the precise course which prudence dictates to those adherents of a religion who wish to join their voices to public policy debates. Murray offers one clear caveat when he calls attention to "the difference that distinguishes the moral from the legal."[62] Because matters of law and policy are characterized by a "mode of generality,"[63] all participants seeking to contribute to policy discussion would do well to prescind from particularistic and sectarian language in presenting the strongest case for the policy measures they judge to be most prudent.

Murray models this style of participation in chapters six and seven of *We Hold These Truths*.[64] In presenting arguments for government

59. Ibid., 103–4.
60. Ibid., 103–4.
61. Ibid., 108.
62. Ibid., 118.
63. Ibid.
64. Entitled "Is it Justice: The School Question Today" and "Should There Be a Law? The Question of Censorship."

responses to two controversial issues of his time (and ours as well: censorship and public support to Church-affiliated schools), Murray nowhere appeals to specifically religious warrants, such as the ethical ideals associated with the kingdom of God. Rather, he limits his mode of argumentation to what might be called "standards of public reason." This restraint is required and motivated by Murray's view of the purpose of public laws: to reflect the shared public consensus through the adoption of prudent "articles of peace." His very confidence in the abiding wisdom of that consensus limits the scope of his argumentation. His goal is the modest one of contributing to the project of "clarifying the public conscience"[65] so that the eventual legislative process might "make harmonious use of the principles available."[66]

Rawls's most extensive treatment of this question of religiously based contributions to public policy deliberation appears in a section of *Political Liberalism* which seeks to defend his notion of overlapping consensus from charges that it implies indifference or skepticism. Here Rawls acknowledges the necessity for adherents of comprehensive doctrines (such as religious believers) to bracket their claims about ultimate truth when they enter the public arena. He consoles believers with a reminder that such a process of bracketing need not be perceived as doing damage to their system of faith, "since to deny that religious beliefs can be publicly and fully established by reason is not to say that they are not true."[67] His recommendations amount to a call for eschewing sectarian language in the public arena in the interest of wider political goals. Rawls advises: "we do not put forward more of our comprehensive view than we think needed or useful for the political aim of consensus."[68]

While these terms of participation in public life may not seem initially acceptable to all,[69] it is nevertheless noteworthy that Rawls does not mean to imply that believers must sacrifice essential elements of their

65. Ibid., 154.
66. Ibid.
67. *Political Liberalism*, 153. Rawls illustrates this point in his "Introduction to the Paperback Edition" of *Political Liberalism* (N.Y.: Columbia University Press, 1996). Consecutive footnotes (on pp. lxi and lxii) contain remarks expressing appreciation for the nuanced positions staked out by Joseph Cardinal Bernardin (who calls for a "consistent ethic of life" without condoning the use of force against those who disagree with his interpretation of the right to life) and John Courtney Murray (in his careful distinction between public and nonpublic reason—where the latter includes those convictions which lead members of a religious community to adhere to doctrines).
68. Ibid.
69. For a survey of possible objections to the way Rawls limits the public role deemed appropriate for religion, see Richard L. Fern, "Religious Belief in a Rawlsian So-

identity. In accord with his basic distinction between comprehensive doctrines and a public conception of justice, he merely seeks a consistent differentiation of *private* voluntary institutions (where like-minded believers put into practice their particularistic commitments) and the *public* institutions which must remain neutral on doctrinal matters if they are to serve their purpose of enacting a stable overlapping consensus. Further, this "bracketing" of comprehensive doctrines is not only the price of social peace, but may also be an indispensable condition for enhancing the effectiveness and persuasiveness of one's voice, for in public deliberations many participants will turn away from pronouncements that are in too unfamiliar an idiom.

It is not altogether clear that Rawls and Murray have in mind precisely the same advice for holders of religious beliefs seeking to participate in public dialogue. However, the similarity of their positions allows us to consider them together as we seek guidelines for religious participation in public policy debate. A pivotal common element of their recommendations is the importance of keeping the terms and warrants of arguments intended for public audiences as general as possible, eschewing sectarian language that would be unintelligible to many and even potentially offensive to some. As natural law thinkers are fond of repeating, philosophical arguments are preferable to theological ones for the purpose of participating in the public arena. This does not mean that, in the interest of appealing to some least common denominator, we must limit all our arguments to pragmatic warrants (as do the four "practical arguments" explored in the previous chapter). Nor does it necessitate that we reduce our accounting of social costs and benefits associated with policy to consequences measured strictly in quantitative terms. However it does suggest that policy advocacy is most constructive and effective when it is addressed to all, excluding none of the participants in public debate as potential hearers and allies.

When Walter Lippmann (American social critic, journalist and founder of what may be called "the public philosophy movement") sought to articulate the meaning of public philosophy, he arrived at this simple definition: it is "a body of positive principles which a good citizen cannot

---

ciety," *The Journal of Christian Ethics* 15, no. 1 (spring 1987) 33–58. See also three essays on the topic appearing in *The Journal of Religious Ethics*. First is Harlan R. Beckley, "A Christian Affirmation of Rawls's Idea of Justice as Fairness" which appeared in two parts: (1) vol. 13, no. 2 (fall 1985) 210–42; and (2) vol. 14, no. 2 (fall 1986) 229–46. Subsequently, L. Gregory Jones, "Should Christians Affirm Rawls's Justice as Fairness? A Response to Professor Beckley" appeared in vol. 16, no. 2 (fall 1988) 251–71.

deny or ignore."[70] His emphasis, like that of both Rawls and Murray, is on the commonality of the interests and concerns, both practical and ethical in nature, which all responsible members of society are able to discern and share. If we truly seek to formulate the principles of the widest possible consensus, then we need an appropriate language for our exercise in public philosophy—an idiom which eschews particularistic or sectarian elements in the interest of including all citizens in our appeal. This is the case whether we see the consensus (with Murray and natural law thinkers) as something we discover, or (with Rawls and social contract theorists) as something we invent through methods of social agreement. Neither approach guarantees an immediate harmonization of interests, but each suggests a role for a respectful engagement in persuasion that appeals to the reasonableness of other members of society. Our policy recommendations and advocacy are most appropriately expressed, therefore, through arguments in the form of "middle axioms." Because this way of categorizing ethical principles, already encountered and utilized in our study, holds so much promise for forging common public purpose, we shall explore the further possibilities of the concept of middle axioms in the next chapter.

---

70. Walter Lippmann, *Essays in the Public Philosophy* (N.Y.: Mentor Books, 1955) 79.

Chapter 9

Building a Consensus for a Humanized Economy: The Role of Middle Axioms

We return now to a concept introduced in Part One above. Middle axioms are ethical principles which consist of specifications of more general statements of values (such as "human dignity must be protected") but which avoid recommending technical policy actions (such as "justice demands a 15 percent increase in capital gains taxes"). Among the advantages of middle axioms is their ability to offer guidelines for action without explicitly appealing to theological warrants which not all members of the intended audience would share. This advantage is especially salient in areas of public policy (such as social welfare legislation) where agreement on policy goals and standards for determining reasonable expectations for human behavior is so elusive.

When the U.S. Catholic bishops addressed their comments on welfare reform to the general audience of all Americans (rather than just to Catholic or Christian parties to the debate), they followed in the tradition of papal social encyclicals, which in recent decades have been addressed "to all people of good will." Like popes and bishops before them, the U.S. bishops spoke in an idiom accessible to all, proposing for general consideration policy guidelines based on concerns about human dignity, the well-being of the vulnerable and the fulfillment of social obligations. They tended to speak more in terms of justice and prudence than about love or similar standards associated with the Christian symbol of the kingdom of God. The "moral principles and policy priorities for welfare reform" the bishops advocated are readily identifiable as being in the form of middle axioms.

Historically, one of the ethical strengths of Catholic social teaching has been precisely its ability to translate into an agenda for social action (and even for legislation) the timeless concerns it draws from its biblical and theological traditions. In various decades, as Church leaders seek to respond to new social contexts, different aspects of the church's social message come to be emphasized. Ethical responses to such phenomena as large-scale industrialization, the rise of fascism, nuclear proliferation, neocolonialism and postindustrial global capitalism must all be tailored to the special challenges of each era. The translation from general social concern to specific contexts has been facilitated by the use of middle axioms, which have consistently supplied the form in which Catholic social teaching has been enunciated. In a similar way, the concerns relevant to U.S. social policy in the coming decades are only a subset of all the social concerns we might identify. Any association moved to social action by shared humanistic or theological beliefs may turn to middle axioms as an appropriate form for their own policy advocacy. By opening up constructive public dialogue among such parties on those topics with the most direct impact on social policy, it might be possible to identify a common set of middle axioms for guiding future social policy in mutually agreeable directions.

The presumption behind this project is that further dialogue, especially when guided by appropriately formulated middle axioms, is potentially fruitful because of the existence of overlap in the value commitments of most participants in the American policy debate. In other words, more widespread social agreement is possible than the events of the 1994–96 welfare debate would indicate. This is not to suggest that the parties to the welfare dialogue are actually saying the same things—they most assuredly are not. Nevertheless, a carefully structured debate on selected topics of relevance to social policy may reveal that many of the seemingly conflicting opinions are by no means irreconcilable, and that indeed many of the issues invite an unexpected degree of rapprochement of the differing perspectives.

This chapter presents a series of five topics with profound implication for any efforts to "humanize the economy." Each of the five represents an area of potential (though not yet fully existing) normative agreement. Because of the importance of this potential moral consensus, each is a worthy focus of contemporary policy debate. All five constitute aspects of a program of action for shaping economic life so that the distribution of goods better serves the requirements of human life. Each has immediately evident implications for social policy and may be addressed by policy choices ranging from (1) inaction to (2) the commitment of marginally greater resources to (3) major reassessments of social priorities.

The analysis in these five sections is not intended (indeed, it would be quite impossible) to argue definitively for how each of the five should be judged. Rather, the five may be thought of as constituting a partial agenda for future research into the normative bases and empirical consequences of social policy. In that regard, each of the five sections will consider what types of new research would contribute to advancing our knowledge of the given area, helping us to form adequate middle axioms based upon this knowledge and potentially leading us to a higher level of healthy social agreement—indeed to a growing consensus on U.S. social policy.

1. Recognizing human dependency

Social policy becomes more rational and effective when its operations are based on a more accurate picture of the lives of actual people. This is especially true in the determination of work expectations for welfare recipients. Before we make policy judgments about the practicality and desirability of requiring poor single mothers with young children to work outside the home, we need to clarify two items: (1) our understanding of the facts of their lives; and (2) our set of common values pertaining to the meaning and desirability of self-sufficiency. The first item calls for the gathering of empirical data about the disabilities, work histories, job prospects and family responsibilities of women in this group (as individuals and in the aggregate). A realistic assessment of the actual situation may produce a more commonly shared answer to the question: Is this a population likely to be jolted into self-sufficiency by the threat of withdrawing welfare benefits?

This initial clarification may prevent the debate about welfare dependency from degenerating into a relentless clash of abstract worldviews. Since it will not wholly suffice, we turn to the second item: clarifications about dependency which proceed on more normative terms, pertaining to the justifiability of some economic dependency. Here lies a potential stumbling block for our hopes for consensus around policies which permit the continued reliance on public assistance for some low-income families. Defenders of social entitlements must grapple with the arguments of a school of social thought which celebrates and seeks to enforce the principle that all families should be self-sufficient. The 1994–96 round of welfare reform coincided with the ascendancy of an approach to social policy which seeks to discourage reliance on public assistance because dependence entails a putative diminishment of "personal responsibility." This school of thought is exemplified by Speaker Newt Gingrich who frequently lauds the principles of risk and entrepreneurship within a productive capitalist system which transforms "anxiety into energy"[1] for economic achievement and inventiveness.

1. Newt Gingrich, *To Renew America* (N.Y.: HarperCollins Publishers, Inc., 1995) 246.

A constructive approach to this seeming impasse requires a "sorting out" of those questions which need to be settled and those philosophical differences which are destined to remain unresolved. There is no need for the social policy debate to become an arena for evaluating the global claims of Gingrich and those who share his high esteem for the value of individual responsibility. While needless dependency constitutes an affront to their brand of individualism, a disciplined debate strictly about policies designed to address the social distress caused by unavoidable dependency may still conceivably proceed on terms acceptable to such parties. Nor is it necessary to recapitulate the arguments of the entire post-Enlightenment era concerning the desirability of autonomy over centralized authority, of personal freedom over social control, or the "unencumbered selves" of liberalism over the more thoroughly "socialized selves" of more communitarian worldviews. In the context of social policy discussions, the trading of charges and countercharges about the relative merits of such systems of philosophical thought shed more heat than light and should therefore be eschewed in favor of the more pragmatic considerations which shape good policy.

Even aside from such areas where we may agree to disagree, there are some areas where we may probe the terms of our initial agreement in order to discover further overlap of common prudential judgments. From an initial agreement that economic self-sufficiency is a suitable ideal for which all families should strive, we may concur further on the desirability of reliable relief arrangements to provide for the needs of families which cannot immediately meet the ideal. Welfare should be judged consistently as what it essentially is: a "second best solution" to the income needs of a small percentage of the U.S. population, not as a full-blown ideological rival to the work ethic or family values. Our attention should remain squarely focused on the practicalities of the struggles of our society's poorest families to secure a reliable and adequate income in the face of multiple barriers to "earnings exits" from poverty.

Even the most enthusiastic supporters of the principle of personal responsibility may reconsider their stance on ending welfare entitlements when confronted with data (such as those gathered by economists in the "structuralist" school) about environmental factors which block opportunity for residents of inner-city America. In the face of evidence such as that compiled by William Julius Wilson,[2] it is possible that we may reach

---

2. See esp. *When Work Disappears: The World of the New Urban Poor* (N.Y.: Alfred A. Knopf, Inc., 1996). Of course, these claims beg the question of whether alternative interpretations of the same data may be found equally convincing. Even if the holders of the most extreme forms of libertarianism and "boot-strap individualism" do not find struc-

a consensus on a middle axiom such as this: since no amount of individual willpower can compensate for deep structural disadvantages, good social policy will not require the immediate self-sufficiency of families for whom this is impossible. Such an axiom does not abandon the goal of self-sufficiency, but it does acknowledge the dangers associated with raising the ideal of independence to a universal norm for all families. Policy which treats poor families in such an inflexible manner runs the risk of asking the impossible of some families.

A good example of the type of practical agreement which can be forged as a result of such circumscribed debate concerns the matter of time limitation of benefits. Even those who support time limits in the abstract (as a means of encouraging self-reliance through work effort) may find amidst the public debate reasons to nuance their views about the human reality of independence. Carefully articulated contributions to the debate may underline how the human life cycle includes times (infancy, childhood, old age, illness) when all humans are not only quite dependent, but often require care which renders our caregivers (most often women) unable to achieve financial independence as well. To be human means to experience alternating periods of dependence and interdependence as well as self-reliance. Because the events which touch off periods of dependence are often unpredictable and uncontrollable, rigid time limits for public assistance are too blunt an instrument for good social policy.

Coming to terms with these realities which touch all human lives, especially the lives of those people affected most directly by social policy, may clarify our shared perceptions of the issue of self-sufficiency. Ultimately, it may foster wider agreement on criteria for appropriate social assistance. Opening up a dialogue on such matters may eventually make the reality of economic dependency less objectionable to those initially disposed to cut social spending, and it may help forge wider agreement on what constitutes reasonable expectations for welfare recipients.

2. Fulfilling social obligations

This point of discussion, like the previous one, could easily be construed in such a broad sense that it divides opinion more sharply rather than uniting it in a general consensus on social policy. It could expose deep divisions in the fundamental way social life is interpreted—including the questions of whether humans are essentially social beings and whether membership in entities larger than the family are central or merely

---

turalist analysis convincing, policy debates may nevertheless take advantage of such insights into the nature of economic opportunity in contemporary American society.

peripheral to human existence. In keeping the focus where it will be most helpful for the purposes of the welfare debate (i.e., limiting the topic to deciding proper terms for spending a small percentage of public budgets on poor relief), we need only reach the thinnest of agreements on these larger questions. It might suffice to say no more than seems obvious: to affirm the importance of both individual freedom and a sense of belonging to a community, since it would be a half-truth to claim either individuals or society as prior to the other.

Any dialogue which considers human loyalties to groups and concerns beyond the selfishly acquisitive soon asks about obligations—first to those we know, then to strangers, perhaps eventually to "distant strangers." There are numerous familiar secular as well as religiously grounded rationales for considering the needs of distant strangers as a morally relevant criterion for the economic activities of all. Many of these seek to justify redistribution, the pooling of resources and various types of material sacrifices; indeed, the affirmation of such sharing of economic destiny is enshrined in the historical project of the modern welfare state. Humans in every age have experienced distress at the coexistence of extreme poverty alongside great wealth. Ethical theories (such as "moral sense theory") have sought to understand more fully this "tug of conscience" in terms of human reason and the emotions. A promising part of a research project aimed at exploring the grounds for wider consensus on distributive issues would include further efforts to develop moral theories to understand the basis for this uneasiness.

Even if we agree to define the well-being of others as a legitimate concern for oneself, intentions to assist those in need are fruitless in the absence of the power to command and allocate material resources. The control of property thus becomes an important issue in the dialogue. Of most relevance to the quest for wider agreement on social policy is the term "social responsibility." This term is usually employed to capture the idea that those members of society who are in a position to share from their abundance of resources are rightly considered potential contributors to a process of redistribution (through the payment of taxes upon wealth or income) which benefits those who are materially needy. Not coincidentally, talk of "social responsibility" serves as a counterweight to the rhetoric of "personal responsibility"—a term often cited in recent policy discussions to support enhanced expectations upon recipients of public assistance. To speak of social responsibility is most fundamentally to posit an obligation (i.e., a matter of justice, beyond the "random acts of kindness" of voluntary charity) to engage in systematic efforts to address unmet human needs, so that no group or category of needy persons is overlooked.

These statements are deliberately very general, since part of their purpose is to assume no level of agreement beyond that which participants in a debate over social policy are likely to come to the table already possessing. Attempts to specify the magnitude or features of social obligations raise many controversial issues concerning at least two items: (1) the bases for entitlement to goods (i.e., by merit, contribution, need or right); and (2) the wisdom of altering present patterns of distribution (including the potential danger of the loss of incentive and productivity). Potentially helpful in the search for an overlapping consensus is any research which sheds light on how societies, past or present, have attempted to balance attention to the parts (individuals) and to the whole (through notions of social obligation) in determining questions of distributive equity.

One particularly well-positioned example of such a study is Barry Alan Shain's *The Myth of American Individualism: The Protestant Origins of American Political Thought*.[3] This work contributes to ongoing scholarly debates surrounding the era of the founding of the United States by reexamining the intellectual legacy of America's founders. In analyzing numerous texts from colonial and early federal history, Shain finds not the expected "monolithic commitment to classical liberal ideas,"[4] including an unmitigated social atomism and rugged individualism, but rather a careful balancing of "individual rights with the social responsibilities on which families and communities depend."[5] That this unrelenting commitment to communal well-being was enacted under the rubrics of "ordered liberty" and "public good" from the very beginning of our nation is instructive in reassessing this aspect of our cultural inheritance.

It would be possible to cite numerous other works which illuminate how the notion of social obligation has been understood in various historical moments. What is most helpful in the contemporary debate on social policy is the realization of the universality of the notion of social obligation. As Michael Walzer has aptly pointed out, "every political community is in principle a 'welfare state' . . . committed to the provision of security and welfare."[6] Our task in building an overlapping consensus on social provision is to recover those elements of this common social wisdom which are most constructive in the contemporary economic context.

---

3. Princeton: Princeton University Press, 1994.
4. Ibid., xvi.
5. Ibid., xiv.
6. *Spheres of Justice* (N.Y.: Basic Books, Inc., 1983) 68.

3. Extending the practice of decommodification

The term decommodification refers to measures which allocate resources according to criteria that prescind from pure market determination of outcomes. Because of concerns that transcend ordinary property relations within capitalist economies, the political system sometimes intervenes in markets to insure that certain types of goods are allocated to intended recipients. In most cases, the goods in question are the essentials of life: food, housing, medical care. They are provided for those who would otherwise be denied access to them because, for a variety of reasons,[7] a society adopts the view that certain categories of goods should be within the reach of all, regardless of ability to pay.

Even in a society such as the United States, where free economic markets are generally recognized as the dominant legitimate means for the distribution of goods, members of society may cite a number of reasons for supporting an agenda of decommodification. Religious themes such as human dignity and the universal destination of material goods may be invoked as a rationale for social provision. Many secular humanitarian arguments likewise point to human rights to justify economic practices which insure that people are treated in ways which recognize them as transcendent centers of value—a value which goes beyond their productivity, acquired wealth, or other quantifiable indicators of social contribution. Some of these arguments are enshrined in the form of the principles of social democracy, an historical movement which posits the existence of economic rights to certain goods—claims based on the political status of citizenship, rather than solely upon one's financial status as a paying customer.

If a consensus supporting a broader agenda of decommodification is to develop in the United States, it will probably not depend upon the bases mentioned above, which seem to entail the adoption of ideologies, or what Rawls calls "comprehensive doctrines." More likely to win general support amidst the pluralism of the American social context is a rationale for social provision based on pragmatic considerations. Such rationales may be somewhat more robust in nature than the four "arguments about practical issues" in welfare policy treated in chapter seven. In fact, the U.S. political system has already witnessed the adoption of several major programs of decommodification (Medicaid, Food Stamps,

---

7. A frequently invoked rationale is to prevent "desperate exchanges." In providing a safety net so that a person's very life is not at stake in the course of economic transactions, many societies provide an alternative to morally objectionable market interactions (prostitution, selling oneself into slavery) which are outlawed as "blocked exchanges."

AFDC, and other programs which prescind from purely contributory bases for social benefits).

For the most part, these government efforts to decommodify the essentials of life take the form of categorical (as opposed to universal) means-tested programs. Political support for these is generated not solely by pragmatic arguments but also by common elements in American political culture which perceive such assistance to those otherwise unable to pay for the essentials of life as a demand of fairness. Even within a system where work earnings are judged to be the ordinary source of legitimate income, history demonstrates that there is still room for a modest agenda of decommodification and redistribution, justified by a general desire not to expose the most disadvantaged members of society to the moral arbitrariness of market forces. Indeed, attacks upon these U.S. social programs have mostly focused on the extent and details of coverage, not on the basic principle of providing some public assistance to needy and eligible members of society.

A strong case (one potentially acceptable to nearly all parties to the debate on U.S. social policy) may be made that the continuation of a welfare entitlement for single-parent families is among the elements of a desirable program of decommodification. This is not to deny the likely continuation of strong opposition to any proposal which, as Charles Murray phrases it, "takes the trouble out of things"[8] and therefore introduces the moral hazards of perverse incentives and the "helping conundrums." While it is wise to take seriously Murray's argument against overgenerous assistance which risks relegating some people to a condition of permanent passivity, it is nevertheless possible to defend a carefully structured program of decommodification as a moral desiderata, at least as a second-best solution to the plight of families for whom earnings do not or cannot provide the basics of life.

The passage of the 1996 welfare law and the earlier defeat of President Clinton's health care reform proposal certainly represent setbacks, but need not be perceived as permanent repudiations of government involvement in this area. In future public policy deliberations, various participants will no doubt continue to take turns defending or attacking decommodification measures for various and shifting reasons. An important potential contribution of social ethicists is to engage in the constructive task of identifying the major idioms (or at least family groupings of languages) amidst this cacophony. A serious effort to translate rival

---

8. Charles Murray, *In Pursuit of Happiness and Good Government* (N.Y.: Simon and Schuster, 1988) 267.

claims about distributive justice into a smaller set of common terms (such as rights, needs and duties) may well facilitate a crystallization of more consistent support for a prudent agenda of further decommodification.

4. Advancing the health of family life

Unlike the previous topics, the search for consensus here is almost completely a matter of deciding on optimal strategy, rather than one of choosing goals. While Americans mostly agree on the contours of what constitutes a stable home environment in which children can flourish, the challenge is to forge further agreement on how public policy might effectively encourage healthy family life. What strategy should we adopt to help families provide a secure environment for the development of their children?

One school of thought emphasizes family self-reliance. If government policies toward families headed by single parents and adults with low attachment to labor markets are too generous, the argument runs, these policies encourage dependency and discourage the formation of two-parent families. The maxim "you get more of what you subsidize" summarizes the case for guarding against such perverse policy incentives. A second school of thought advocates more activist governmental interventions to assist struggling families. Under the rubric of "family policy" comes support for income maintenance and similar measures which create a sphere shielded from the strict logic of exchange which dominates economic markets, including labor markets. Interventions such as the provision of means-tested welfare, in-kind benefits, and social services may be justified on the basis of an appeal to either need or rights. Families are judged to be entitled to assistance because the ordinary *quid pro quo* of economic life does not provide them with enough resources to meet their basic needs or to satisfy their claims to the goods to which all members of society are entitled by right.

The claims of these two schools of thought are not permanently irreconcilable, as they may at first appear. Most other advanced industrial societies have reached a stable consensus on family policy—a consensus which includes a recognition of certain claims families legitimately make upon the wealth generated by a nation's economy. We have already noted that most affluent societies do set a minimum level of social provision for their members. Although the U.S. has consistently been a "welfare state laggard" compared with other industrialized societies, there is no unimpeachable reason why a constructive dialogue on how best to assist families in need cannot succeed in producing a more coherent family policy. The major challenge is to find practical ways to translate the universal

American concern for healthy family life into a serious commitment of public resources.

The successes of other nations demonstrate that prudent means of administering assistance to families, even income guarantees such as the "family allowances" adopted by many Western European nations, may prevent what many American observers most fear about social policy: that offers of public assistance necessarily discourage self-help. Further research into how families actually make decisions about the trade-off between work and family obligations may allow us to move beyond stereotypes (such as those portraying welfare mothers as lazy shirkers of work) and toward a consensus concerning how policy may foster a healthy balance of the roles of parents as breadwinners and caregivers. Eventually, the search for public policies to assist contemporary family life may move beyond such narrow questions as what constitutes reasonable expectations for welfare mothers, to include broader issues which link family life to the wider arena of the communities where families live. We might ultimately hope for a more satisfactory debate which considers such questions as: How may public policy foster a healthier social ecology? How may government encourage the development of the kind of communities where social responsibility toward families in need receives more sustained attention?

5. Preserving a social safety net through public action

A major objection to public provision of an adequate social safety net for needy Americans is that the cost of such generosity is prohibitively high in an era requiring budgetary restraint. Differing interpretations of the current fiscal capacity of government divide opinions about what is possible and what is prudent in social policy.

The initial impasse has been characterized as a conflict between "angels" (those whose primary concern is immediate assistance for the poor) and "accountants" (those more inclined to focus on the costs) where "angels question the motives of the accountants and accountants question the understanding of the angels."[9] What is needed, of course, is a combination of good intentions and compassion for the poor, on one hand, and a realistic assessment of the costs and limits of government activism, on the other. The common realization that both elements are indispensable for future welfare policy is one possible catalyst for widening the zone of agreement.

---

9. D. Eric Schansberg, *Poor Policy: How Government Harms the Poor* (Boulder, Colo.: Westview Press, Inc., 1996) 162.

A dialogue aimed at defining a desirable welfare role for government makes progress when it builds upon the existing American consensus supporting the mixed capitalist economy we already have. It is counterproductive continually to revisit past debates over the relative merits and dangers of extreme models of economic arrangements (unrestricted, libertarian-style free markets as opposed to centrally controlled collectivism) which have already been repudiated by the mainstream of American political thought. Contemporary policy deliberations serve us best when they are confined in scope and focused on practical decisions—in this case, on determining precisely what level of government intervention in the economy will respond appropriately to social concerns (such as the well-being of low-income families) without imposing an unbearable cost upon taxpayers and the system of public finance.

From time to time, helpful benchmarks for these judgments are offered by insightful leaders whose articulation of the goals of public action serve to coalesce support for appropriate policies. President Franklin D. Roosevelt's "Four Freedoms" (which included freedom from material want) and President Lyndon B. Johnson's goal of an "equal opportunity society" each served in its own time as an emblem of our general national commitment to guarantee, even at considerable expense, that everyone has a reasonable chance for a good life. This commitment is, perhaps paradoxically, easier to sustain when dramatic challenges (a severe depression, the practice of blatant racial discrimination) draw attention to the plight of the vulnerable than when the ordinary workings of a capitalist industrial order account for the factors which limit the economic attainments of disadvantaged groups.

Constructive debates over safety net measures such as welfare, then, are mostly about the wisdom of making marginal adjustments in the level and type of economic interventions government makes in order to promote goals upon which we can generally agree. Those who defend a continuation of our sixty-year national commitment to providing a social safety net may thus have room for optimism. They have the advantage of building their case upon a set of prevalent American beliefs that seem to form the core of a preexisting consensus—one reflected in U.S. social policy, at least until the passage of the welfare law of 1996. If we can speak of this core of beliefs as a "consensus," then the content of this consensus may be summarized by a few key propositions which capture the generally shared interpretations of what is true and what is desirable concerning the reality of low-income American families. These propositions include: (1) no members of American society should be completely excluded from the means to full social participation; (2) the attainment of a secure livelihood is something which does not occur automatically within the structures of the contemporary capitalist economy, even for those willing to work to support their families; and (3) furnishing a modicum of security for those unable to earn their way out of poverty is a proper concern of government and a legitimate objective of public action.

Naturally, a range of opinions persists about each of these propositions. In Part Two above, we encountered the diversity of views regarding, for example, how deeply entrenched are the structural causes of unfair income inequality, and how much government activism is justified in pursuit of the goals of security, equal opportunity and distributive equity. Nevertheless, these three propositions constitute elements of a general consensus supporting the continuation of at least some social provision. The basic principle that government acts legitimately when it provides a safety net of security for the most vulnerable among us thus forms a baseline for U.S. welfare policy debates. We should not allow policy discussions to be sidetracked by false claims of unacceptable trade-offs in the goals we adopt, whether those goals are equity and efficiency, security and economic progress,[10] or prosperity and social justice.[11]

If the existing agreement is to be expanded, it will be necessary to confront a number of potential stumbling blocks. Chief among these is the pervasive skepticism about government's ability to be an effective instrument of our national desire for fairness without intruding unnecessarily into our lives. This is a constant challenge in a nation which traces its founding to a tax rebellion against a despotic regime. For encouragement in the belief that a narrowing of differences of opinion on social provision is possible, we might look to episodes in recent American history when the moment seemed ripe for cooperation across the political spectrum in order to fortify the safety net.

In this endeavor, the passage of the Social Security Act of 1935 and the "War on Poverty" in the 1960s naturally draw the most attention, but often overlooked is the nearly successful movement for a guaranteed annual income (GAI) for all American families during the presidency of Richard M. Nixon. What is remarkable about GAI is not just that it came within a few votes in the U.S. Senate of becoming law,[12] but that it received

---

10. In *The Zero-Sum Society: Distribution and the Possibilities for Economic Change* (N.Y.: Basic Books, 1980), economist Lester C. Thurow, argues persuasively that a constructive government role in the economy is not only possible but necessary. He refutes the conventional wisdom that economic security and productivity are somehow incompatible.

11. See Robert Kuttner, *The Economic Illusion: False Choices Between Prosperity and Social Justice* (Boston: Houghton Mifflin Co., 1984).

12. For an account of the legislative history of this measure, called the "Family Assistance Plan" by the Nixon administration which sponsored it, see Daniel P. Moynihan,

substantial backing from advocates of so many political stripes. Particularly celebrated was the support it garnered from Milton Friedman,[13] a right-wing advocate of monetarist policies, who made common cause with unlikely allies on the left (e.g., economist Robert Theobald[14]) and center (including the officials of the Nixon administration) who supported GAI for a variety of reasons. The mere fact that these prominent figures with such diverse ideological commitments reached the same policy conclusions does not necessarily mean that a Rawlsian-style "overlapping consensus" had been attained. Indeed, the coincidence of support for GAI bears many of the marks of what Rawls would call a *modus vivendi*, since it represents a convergence of opinion around a specific policy, not around a foundational principle directing societal action. Nevertheless, we can find in this episode some illuminating lessons about how numerous unlikely partners may reach the same conclusion on social policy: that the national interest (however defined) would be advanced if a floor of income were available to all citizens. Further research on these historical moments which witnessed a surge of support for safety net measures might reveal much about the conditions conducive to the formation of broad coalitions advocating public action on behalf of the most vulnerable members of society.

* * * *

The lasting contribution of Catholic social teaching to debates about U.S. social policy involves its form as much as its content. Catholic social teaching consistently advances its arguments in the form of middle axioms—moral principles which frequently find resonance with the numerous ethical inheritances represented in American society. Other traditions of ethical thought have produced equally cogent arguments and even strikingly similar conclusions about human dignity, social responsibility and other moral reasons why the poor should not be considered merely as a burden to others. However, Catholic social teaching may play a special role in a new American welfare consensus because of its com-

---

The Politics of a Guaranteed Income: The Nixon Administration and the Family Assistance Plan (N.Y.: Random House, 1973).

13. Milton Friedman, *Capitalism and Freedom*, second edition (Chicago: University of Chicago Press, 1982) 192–5. In this work, originally published in 1962, Friedman argues for the "negative income tax" (his preferred name for GAI).

14. Theobald's most important contributions to the GAI movement were two volumes he edited: *The Guaranteed Income: Next Step in Socioeconomic Evolution?* (Garden City, N.Y.: Anchor Books of Doubleday and Co., Inc., 1966); and *Committed Spending: A Route to Economic Security* (Garden City, N.Y.: Doubleday and Co., Inc, 1968).

mitment to articulating policy principles in an idiom which invites the growth of an overlapping consensus.

The U.S. Catholic bishops' contribution to the welfare reform debate is just the latest example of how Catholic social teaching utilizes middle axioms in articulating moral concerns. Although Catholic voices did not in the end prove to be very influential in shaping the 1996 welfare law, the bishops and their supporters may take heart that the recent welfare debate will likely be revisited in the coming years. The focus of future policy deliberations may well be expanded to include not only the income needs of single-parent families with young children (the "welfare population"), but also the severe economic insecurity potentially to be experienced by millions of families currently enjoying the advantages of regular paid employment. This foreboding note is sounded because so many currently well-off families may soon become victims of declining wages, constricted job opportunities and corporate downsizing—the features of a postindustrial economy. The implication for social policy of this dawning postindustrial challenge is the topic of Part Five.

Part Five

Guidelines and Prospects for the Postindustrial Era

Chapter 10

Postindustrial Social Policy

The welfare law of 1996 represents a retreat from the federal government's previous commitment to providing a measure of income security for certain categories of the able-bodied poor. The rationale behind the new law seems to reflect George Gilder's contention that, since "endless injustices and anomalies are absolutely unavoidable in any means-tested system, . . . [t]here is no such thing as a good method of artificial income maintenance."[1] Supporters of the new welfare law defend its "work strategy" as preferable to the "income maintenance strategy" of AFDC on the same grounds Gilder proposed during the Reagan administration: that removing the floor of income for welfare families is a necessary step in encouraging self-sufficiency through work.

Even if we grant that a "work solution" is generally preferable (or even morally superior) to an "entitlement solution" to the income needs of poor families, there may still exist extenuating reasons to continue some income guarantees. The reasons to be considered in this chapter concern the availability of work opportunities in a postindustrial society. Ethical reflection on postindustrialism begins with the observation that the contemporary economy seems to require fewer workers (at least of the well-paid variety), and proceeds to ask how the burdens of this situation may be justly distributed to prevent disproportionate sacrifices from falling upon blameless victims of the job shortage. If we are indeed entering an era characterized by a permanently sub-full-employment economy, then the very survival of many millions of people in all demographic groups—not just single mothers and their young children—depends squarely upon reliable social provision. When non-work can no longer be attributed to the moral failings of culpable individuals, but rather stems from structural dimensions of the economy which restrict the availability

---

1. George Gilder, *Wealth and Poverty* (N.Y.: Basic Books, Inc., Publishers, 1981) 117.

of jobs capable of supporting a family, then society must rethink its distributive arrangements. Contra Gilder, we need a way for individuals to be out of work and still retain access to adequate resources for material sustenance as well as the social goods of recognition and participation.

In light of the challenge of postindustrialism, the new welfare law's elimination of income entitlements appears objectionable on two grounds: (1) practical necessity; and (2) moral desirability. On the first count, the unmet physical needs of a significant sector of an affluent society may soon become a source of social division and instability. Americans will not tolerate severe, even life-threatening material deprivation of millions in our midst. We will recognize profound, arbitrary and unevenly distributed economic insecurity as a danger to our social cohesiveness. Such a situation threatens to separate us further into a sharply divided two-tier society—an outcome no one favors. On the second count, that of moral desirability, most serious moral conceptions of human life would recognize some obligation to prevent massive suffering. Few in the mainstream of American life would disagree with the principle that those denied a reasonable opportunity to earn their livelihood through work should enjoy some alternative to total destitution. Income entitlements seem to be the only feasible way to guarantee access to crucial social goods in a postindustrial age.

The hypothesis that our economy is entering a postindustrial era in which work opportunities will become significantly more scarce has not, of course, been demonstrated to the satisfaction of all observers. In fact, the performance of the American economy in recent years, especially the low unemployment statistics of the mid-1990s, may cast significant doubt on the claims of the vocal prophets of the "end of work" scenario.[2] In order to affirm the postindustrialism hypothesis, we must posit massive future technological changes and troubling developments in labor markets which are more than simple extrapolations from current economic experience. If work remains generally available to succeeding generations, then the inquiry of this chapter into the ethical challenges of a postindustrial age will remain merely a "thought experiment" concerning the requirements of distributive justice in the hypothetical situation of widespread joblessness in an affluent society.

However, if currently burgeoning economic insecurities associated with corporate downsizing, cybernation and the globalization of capital-

2. See Jeremy Rifkin, *The End of Work: The Decline of the Global Labor Force and the Dawn of the Post-Market Era* (N.Y.: G. P. Putnam's Sons, 1995); Stanley Aronowitz and William DiFazio, *The Jobless Future: Sci-Tech and the Dogma of Work* (Minneapolis: University of Minnesota Press, 1994).

ist production do prefigure a massive restructuring of labor markets as some predict, then efforts to come to grips with the ethical challenges of a postindustrial scenario entail more than idle speculation. In this case, an entirely new consciousness of many issues is required. One immediate implication for American social policy is that "work solutions" to poverty lose their salience once we consider jobs to be scarce goods. Unless government steps forward in a nearly unprecedented way to become "the employer of last resort"[3] to create a situation of artificial full employment[4] when the private sector proves unable to employ most of those seeking jobs, there will arise new urgency to sever the ties between work and income and to expand our nation's arrangements for social provision.

It is practically a reflex for American politicians and policy analysts to tout job creation as the solution to economic and social problems. Indeed, one of the most cogent criticisms of the new welfare law is that it reflects the emptiness of the pro-work rhetoric of the debate which produced it; the law mandates a "work solution" without providing resources for a real "jobs solution" to the income needs of poor families. A central challenge of the postindustrial scenario is precisely that jobs alone may no longer provide an adequate income for a huge part of the population. The preferred solution of American economic thought on the topic of poverty is simply not available to a discussion of postindustrial social policy.

When sociologist Herbert Gans turns his attention to the topic of "joblessness and antipoverty policy in the twenty-first century,"[5] he comments that the trends associated with postindustrialism can be either very good or very bad omens for economically vulnerable people. If we can find ways equitably to spread the benefits of unprecedented and increasingly drudgery-free production, then even members of the underclass may share "a glorious future in which people would only have to work a

---

3. Except for emergency employment programs instituted during the Great Depression, American government has generally not played this role. Full employment remains an important policy goal—one pursued by macroeconomic measures such as the techniques of Keynesian demand management—but rarely a rationale for direct allocation of resources. Even periodic declarations of the intention of government to foster higher employment (such as the Full Employment Act of 1946 and the Humphrey-Hawkins Act during the 1970s) have shied away from committing public resources to direct jobs programs. William Julius Wilson is exceptional in his support for direct public sector job creation.

4. The term "full employment" is of course subject to diverse interpretations. Over time, unemployment rates of anywhere from three to eight per cent have been judged acceptable and consistent with a healthy economy.

5. *The War Against the Poor: The Underclass and Antipoverty Policy* (N.Y.: HarperCollins Publishers, Inc.) 133.

few hours a day, spending the rest of their time in educational and constructive leisure activities."[6] However, Gans notes, a massive reduction in the need for work could also have the effect of creating a dystopia, especially if we find no mechanism for reaching agreement on how to distribute the gains and burdens associated with this restructuring of work. Gans warns: "As long as people must live from what they earn, poverty would not only be at least as widespread and severe as during the Great Depression, but it might also become permanent."[7]

This chapter sketches out the ethical concerns that arise in postindustrialism and suggests some general guidelines for social policy in an era of restricted work opportunities. First, we will explore how a postindustrial order challenges us to grapple with the plight of potentially "surplus people." Second, we investigate how the resources of Catholic social teaching may be invoked to address the problems likely to be encountered by postindustrial social policy. The worldview of Catholic theology supports the principle of income guarantees for those whose labor is displaced by economic forces, for the same reasons it supports public policies providing income maintenance for welfare families. Finally, this chapter places the challenge of postindustrial social policy within a context it shares with the welfare reform debate: American political culture and its dominant value-orientations. We will consider the prospects for "social learning" which results from the process in which religious voices contribute to public debates over social policy.

The Postindustrial Challenge

We have already noted some of the central features of the postindustrial condition: a sharply diminished need for labor in the production process, the possibility of a massive crisis of unemployment, and the need for new ways of thinking about the income needs of those whose work roles are displaced. The awareness of these possibilities is not new. At least as early as 1888, when Edward Bellamy published *Looking Backward*,[8] a novel in the tradition of utopian literature, observers of technological progress speculated on the social ramifications of future changes in work arrangements. Gradually, concern about the people whose labor would be displaced and whose livelihoods would thus be endangered crept into writings about the future of work. In 1934, Lewis Mumford mused:

    6. Ibid., 134.
    7. Ibid., 135.
    8. Edward Bellamy, *Looking Backward, 2000–1887* (Boston: Houghton Mifflin, 1888).

> As more and more work is transferred to automatic machines, the process of displacing workers from industry under this system is the equivalent of disenfranchising them as consumers . . . . Lacking the power to buy the necessities of life for themselves, the plight of the displaced workers reacts upon those who remain at work. . . .[9]

While not as sanguine as Bellamy about the ability of an enlightened technocratic elite to look after the interests of all, Mumford nevertheless calls for some form of economic planning "to take advantage by adequate social provision of the new processes of mechanized production."[10]

Despite the generally strong economic performance enjoyed by Western industrialized economies after the Second World War, several observers of American society continued to call attention to ominous signs of a future convulsion we would today describe as part of the challenge of postindustrialism. In 1962 Swedish economist Gunnar Myrdal warned that mechanization would exacerbate "rising unemployment levels" and "that the surplus of manual labor released by technical developments in agriculture and manufacturing industry" would have destabilizing economic effects on the American economy.[11] The influential research of Michael Harrington into the condition of chronically poor groups within our society corroborated Myrdal's observation "that unemployment and underemployment in America are increasingly becoming structural,"[12] as opposed to cyclical or merely frictional. Harrington's prescription for addressing the poverty caused by the systemic effects of structural economic factors (as opposed to the random effects of bad luck or moral failings of individuals) includes a program of conscious and democratic economic planning on the national level.[13]

The writings of both Harrington and Myrdal echo John Kenneth Galbraith's earlier disavowal of the conventional wisdom that causes economic policy to be preoccupied with sustaining increases in productivity. In the "affluent society" Galbraith has described since the 1950s, production is no longer the central economic objective.[14] In one sense, "production is

9. Lewis Mumford, *Technics and Civilization* (N.Y.: Harcourt, Brace and Co., 1934) 401–2.

10. Ibid., 402.

11. *Challenge to Affluence* (N.Y.: Pantheon Books, 1962) 67.

12. Ibid., 66.

13. Michael Harrington, *The Accidental Century* (Baltimore: Penguin Books, 1965), esp. 275–306; see also his *The Other America: Poverty in the United States* (N.Y.: Macmillan Publishers, 1962) and *The New American Poverty* (N.Y.: Penguin Books, 1984).

14. John Kenneth Galbraith, *The Affluent Society* (Boston: Houghton Mifflin Co., 1958) esp. 270–91, 332–5.

now more necessary for the employment it provides than for the goods and services it supplies."[15] Because new economic realities call for a new consciousness, Galbraith appeals to policymakers to shift priorities and place more emphasis upon the goals of maintaining income and personal security.

The early prophets of postindustrialism focused primarily on the *availability* of work and the possible obsolescence of many workers in advanced industrial societies. More recent commentators supplement these concerns by addressing the *structure* of work arrangements, particularly how class position and educational attainment determine the differential effects of technological unemployment on various segments of the population. Whereas technological advances formerly served to make labor more productive and to increase job opportunities for all categories of workers, recent developments such as cybernation tend increasingly to render some types of workers altogether redundant and largely to eliminate certain categories of jobs.[16]

The control of technology falls to a "new class"[17] or a "fortunate fifth"[18] of the workforce—individuals whose credentials as educated professionals open for them doors permanently closed to others who occupy lower positions in the meritocracy of intelligence and training. These elite professionals direct the use of capital (whether or not they own it) through the possession of information and expertise. The globalization of production, accelerated by the transportation and communication revolutions as well as by trade agreements which expedite the flow of goods and capital across borders, has magnified the leverage of this class of professionals vis-à-vis the rest of the population. Many of the same developments which decrease job security for the majority of industrial workers actually increase the advantages and privileges enjoyed by this "knowledge class."

This last term was employed by Daniel Bell, whose 1973 work *The Coming of Postindustrial Society: A Venture in Social Forecasting*[19] brought

15. John Kenneth Galbraith, *The Good Society: The Humane Agenda* (N.Y.: Houghton Mifflin Co., 1996) 3.

16. For an early assessment of these effects of cybernation see Robert Theobald, "The Background to the Guaranteed Income Concept," in Theobald, ed., *The Guaranteed Income: Next Step in Socioeconomic Evolution* (Garden City, N.Y.: Anchor Books of Doubleday and Co., Inc., 1966) 93–106.

17. Galbraith used this phrase as early as 1958. See *The Affluent Society*, 340.

18. Robert Reich (*The Work of Nations* [N.Y.: Alfred A. Knopf, Inc., 1991] 179) calls them "symbolic analysts" and estimates that they comprise 20 percent of the contemporary work force.

19. N.Y.: Basic Books, 1976 [1973].

the concept of postindustrialism into common parlance. Bell contends that postindustrial society could just as easily be called the "information society" or the "knowledge society"[20] because these elements are at the very core of the phenomena he forecasts:

> Postindustrial society is organized around knowledge, for the purpose of social control and the directing of innovation and change; and this in turn gives rise to new social relationships and new structures which have to be managed politically.[21]

Because postindustrial society is increasingly interdependent (Bell favors the term "communal society"[22]), public policies become increasingly important (and markets less so) as brokers of resource allocation. Bell insists that, in the interest of establishing fair practices of reward and distribution in this new context, the role of politics as a mediator of claims and of government as an ordering mechanism must be expanded.[23] This is especially so regarding the pursuit of such social goals as "the inclusion of disadvantaged groups into society" and the general task of coping with "the strains of change."[24]

Among the most influential recent attempts to build upon Bell's seminal work is Jeremy Rifkin's 1995 volume, *The End of Work: The Decline of the Global Labor Force and the Dawn of the Post-Market Era*. Rifkin combines both strands of the postindustrialism hypothesis. He invokes the hope-laden prospect of a utopia of improved modes of living ushered in by unprecedented technology-driven gains in productivity. He also considers the possible dawn of a nightmarish dystopia if these gains cannot be divided equitably, so as somehow to provide for those whose labor is no longer marketable.[25] Reconfigurations in the pattern of work have the potential to produce great good or evil, depending upon how political arrangements manage their effects and distribute burdens and gains.

Everything Bell and Rifkin say about the threat of new social division depends upon the premise that economic and technological change are ushering in a new era of restricted work opportunities. This heightens the importance of the question: Are we indeed entering a permanently

20. Ibid., 37.
21. Ibid., 20.
22. Ibid., 160.
23. See esp. ch. 6 ("'Who Will Rule?' Politicians and Technocrats in the Postindustrial Society") in ibid.
24. Ibid., 264–5.
25. See the extensive description of the promises and dangers of technological change in Part One (entitled "The Two Faces of Technology") of Rifkin, *The End of Work*.

sub-full-employment economy? The search for reliable evidence of the definitive displacement of human labor by technology is a problematic one, for it must account simultaneously for many complex factors (such as demographic changes, the movement of labor to alternative employment, and fluctuating rates of capital accumulation and technological innovation across the business cycle) which economists find notoriously difficult to isolate. However, one revealing piece of recent economic evidence warrants investigation: the disturbing phenomenon described as "jobless growth."

The United Nations Development Program's *Human Development Report 1993* highlighted an ominous trend affecting the economies of industrialized nations. During the generally prosperous years 1973–87, a huge gap opened up between productivity (which skyrocketed) and employment (which stagnated and, in the case of certain nations, including Germany and France, actually fell). The economic recovery of the U.S. during the late 1980s fits this pattern, as statistics reveal that it was largely a "jobless recovery."[26] Even while industrialized economies were experiencing prosperous years,

> three-quarters of the rise in output in these countries came from increases in total productivity, with the rest from increased capital investment—without creating new jobs. The developing countries have had a similar problem, though they have experienced at least some employment growth. . . . Less than a third of the increase in outputs in developing countries between 1960 and 1987 came from increased labor, more than two-thirds from increases in capital investment.[27]

The report attributes the phenomenon of jobless growth largely to technological change. It interprets "the search for labor-saving technology" as an attempt on the part of elite capitalists and managers to keep labor costs as low as possible, and reaches the conclusion: "Clearly, technology will cater to the preferences of the richer members of the international society."[28] Conversely, the report predicts that employment prospects for poor workers worldwide will decline dramatically, especially in light of population increases and the entrance of more women into labor markets. The data above remind us that economic growth is a necessary, but by no means a sufficient condition for improvement in the standard of living of the economically marginalized. With one billion

---

26. United Nations Development Program, *Human Development Report 1993* (N.Y.: Oxford University Press, 1993) 36.
27. Ibid., 35.
28. Ibid., 37.

new jobs required each decade just to maintain current levels of global underemployment, there is no way to escape the grim conclusion: "Without substantial policy changes, the employment outlook for these people is bleak."[29]

The well-documented trend of jobless growth lends considerable support to the postindustrialism hypothesis. If technological advances permit economic growth to occur without corresponding increases in employment, then the social and political changes predicted by Rifkin and Bell may well be more than hypothetical possibilities. The case that technology is beginning to have the effects on employment predicted by theorists of postindustrialism is bolstered by additional, perhaps more subtle evidence from the economic arena. Here we note the current climate of job insecurity, in which employees are gradually coming to be seen as liabilities rather than as vital assets to the corporations employing them. The practices of drastic corporate downsizing and frequent rounds of layoffs are becoming commonplace.[30] Attention to the bottom line increasingly leads to the perception of a sharp dichotomy between the economic health of a business enterprise and the well-being of its workers. The resulting antagonism in labor-management relations is perhaps one of the already visible faces of the postindustrial order.

The transition in the material conditions of life as we move from an industrial to a postindustrial age calls for a simultaneous transition in consciousness. The major focus of our economic activity shifts from (1) the allocation of scarce material resources so as to maximize increases in production to (2) the proper management of the relative abundance we already experience so that all members of society benefit in an equitable manner. The special ethical challenge of this dawning age is to reach agreement on some methods to prevent a disproportionate share of sacrifice and insecurity from falling upon any sector of the population. Of greatest concern, of course, are those who suffer from a sharp constriction of work opportunities in this new era. They are the members of society who risk becoming "surplus people" because their potential contributions through labor are becoming devalued.

Unless it is supplemented with prudent public interventions in the form of tax and social policy, the mechanism of the market alone will not address the needs of such people for income security and the social goods

29. Ibid.
30. See *The New York Times, The Downsizing of America* (N.Y.: Times Books of Random House, Inc., 1996). This volume collects and expands the text of a six-part series on the effects of corporate downsizing which appeared in *The New York Times* 3–9 March 1996.

of membership and participation. Indeed, a strict adherence to the *quid pro quo* of market logic and an exceptionless application of the principles of the work ethic are perfectly compatible with a caste system which locks a large percentage of the population out of any reasonable hopes for a decent life. Some alternative logic of distribution is required to protect the "losers" in postindustrial labor markets from falling into the desperate situation of having no reliable sources of income at all. The next section of this chapter will consider resources within the tradition of Catholic social teaching which may contribute to the public adoption of a cogent rationale for preventing this nightmarish postindustrial scenario.

Toward a New Logic of Distribution

It is possible to imagine many different reasons why a society may commit itself to spreading the benefits of automated production even to those whose labor is not required in the production process. Many industrialized nations around the world have cited diverse reasons in justifying their generous programs of social provision for the needs of displaced laborers and other nonworkers. Concern for the plight of the most vulnerable members of society may be expressed in various moral idioms, including the theological language of love and dignity, the humanitarian language of need and decency, and the liberal discourse of rights and justice. Any of these may be invoked in support of economic arrangements which do not reserve all material and social benefits for paying customers alone.

We focus here on how four key concepts from Catholic social teaching may be interpreted as supporting extramarket rationales for distribution in a postindustrial age. The purpose of this exploration is not to propose Catholic positions as suitable for adoption *in toto* by our entire pluralistic society. Rather, the intention is to illustrate how one set of religious voices may offer its contribution in the modest hope that a careful articulation of the wisdom contained in their traditions of ethical reflection might help others to clarify their own value commitments and apply them to matters of public policy in a more informed way. Obvious connections may be drawn between (1) how Catholic social teaching defends adequate social provision to protect casualties of a postindustrial order from becoming "surplus people" and (2) how the U.S. bishops utilized these same resources in advocating for the needs of low-income families in the welfare reform debate.

When the documents of modern Catholic social teaching address questions of poverty and the role of public authorities in alleviating economic insecurity, they generally consider the type of poverty associated with industrialized society as experienced by the West in the past century.

In this context, work opportunities have generally been available as potential sources of income, but access to employment earnings may have become blocked for a certain time for a particular family. It is therefore necessary to extrapolate from the actual texts of this tradition of thought in order to apply its ethical analysis to the new realities of postindustrial society, where the very possibility of work-based independence is systematically compromised. As Daniel Patrick Moynihan contends in his 1989 call for a postindustrial social policy, there is a serious need to update former patterns of thinking to deal with "a new form of social distress" and "an emergent form of dependency, the kind associated with postindustrial society."[31]

The papal social encyclicals do not directly address the phenomenon of postindustrialism. In this entire literature, only a few passages reflect even a germinal awareness of the challenges of postindustrial social policy. One is contained in *Octogesima adveniens*, where Paul VI calls for the defense of the dignity of all who are disadvantaged or displaced by "industrial change."[32] *Sollicitudo rei socialis* expresses alarm that, in both the developed and developing nations, "the sources of work seem to be shrinking, and thus the opportunities for employment are decreasing rather than increasing" even in times of prosperity.[33] Even more recently, *Centesimus annus* calls for reforms by which "society and the state will both assume responsibility, especially for protecting the worker from the nightmare of unemployment." This may require such measures as "economic policies aimed at insuring balanced growth and full employment, or through unemployment insurance and re-training programs."[34] Indeed, when this document reaffirms the necessity of public interventions in markets to protect human dignity, it emphasizes the "right to work"[35] without considering the possibility that contemporary life unfolds in an era of permanently sub-full-employment economies where the labor of all is no longer required. Statements of the U.S. bishops occasionally mention the problems faced by workers in low-wage sectors of our increasingly service-dominated economy,[36] but do not directly address the social challenges associated with the qualitatively new features of postin-

---

31. Daniel Patrick Moynihan, "Toward a Postindustrial Social Policy," *The Public Interest*, no. 96 (summer 1989) 17.
32. OA 15.
33. SRS, 18.
34. CA 15.
35. Ibid., 43.
36. See for example EJA, 144–50. This section, entitled "Unemployment in a Changing Economy," lists a number of trends (the displacement of workers, shifts in occupa-

dustrialism. In order to discern what Catholic social thought would recommend concerning appropriate social policy responses to the postindustrial challenge, we must perform the work of reinterpreting the principles and positions of this tradition in light of a new social context.

Recall the three Catholic social principles identified in chapter two above: (1) social membership must be universal; (2) no person is to be considered a surplus person; and (3) the preferential option for the poor. Informed by the desire to realize the goods[37] identified by the Catholic tradition of ethical reflection, these three general principles motivate us to discover practical ways (including the formation of public policies) to advance social cohesion and the well-being of the disadvantaged. Four concepts introduced in chapter one (in its consideration of private property and the role of the state in Catholic thought) are especially instructive for recommending an ethical postindustrial social policy.

First, the notion of the "social mortgage on property"[38] serves as a reminder that the coexistence of great wealth alongside life-threatening deprivation cannot be justified. Because God intends the material goods of creation to serve the sustenance and development of all humans, a postindustrial order which denies the basics of life to any segment of the population in an affluent society is unacceptable. The criterion of need thus emerges as a legitimate claim of the desperately poor upon the superfluous goods of the affluent. As we noted in chapter one, the criterion of need is defended explicitly by Aquinas as a legitimate basis for distribution in certain cases; it is also prominent in patristic social thought. In modern Catholic social teaching, need is frequently invoked as an important criterion for just allocative decisions.[39] *Gaudium et spes* issues a reminder that this attention to human need is justified by the notion of the universal destination of the created world—a fundamental theme within Christian social thought which demands that "there must be made available to all men everything necessary for leading a life truly human."[40]

---

tional structure toward low-wage jobs, increased international competition and trade, the globalization of capital flows) associated with postindustrialism, without mentioning that term.

37. Including the three treated in ch. 1 above: human dignity, solidarity and the common good.

38. This phrase appears in SRS, 42.

39. For example, John Paul II asserts: "It is a strict duty of justice and truth not to allow fundamental human needs to remain unsatisfied, and not to allow those burdened by such needs to perish" (CA 34).

40. GS 26.

Second, the ethical concept of the "living wage" constitutes an important application to the institutions of an industrial order of the imperative to provide for the legitimate needs of the most vulnerable members of society. Both Leo XIII and John Ryan championed the living wage as a guideline for providing a decent standard of living for families' breadwinners who depend upon wage earnings for access to the essential goods of life. In updating the notion of the living wage so that it applies to the postindustrial condition, a helpful guide to our efforts is Ryan's consistent concern to hold together moral requirements and practical possibilities—that is, the "ought" and the "can." The obligation to provide for one's family (ordinarily through wage earnings) is conditioned on the enjoyment of reasonable access to work opportunities, because "no one is morally bound to do the impossible."[41] Since a postindustrial social order denies this possibility to a significant sector of the potential workforce, alternative arrangements must be found to provide for the unmet needs of the affected families. The perspective of Catholic social teaching does not tolerate abandoning these vulnerable unemployed members of society to the vicissitudes of market forces which, if unchecked, would lock them out of the goods required for a decent life.[42] Even though need is notoriously difficult to define and delimit, and is rarely recognized in societies as the primary criterion for allocating distributive shares,[43] it is imperative that a family's reasonable needs somehow enter the equation by which each family is given its due.

Third, Catholic social teaching has for decades called attention to the ever-increasing trend toward economic interdependence. The technical term "socialization" captures this awareness of the ethical obligations created by the "multiplication in social relationships."[44] Since the social responsibilities incumbent upon holders of property and employers require coordination and enforcement, public authorities emerge as irreplaceable agents of accountability. The postindustrial condition presents a new urgency and a new rationale for such governmental interventions

---

41. *A Living Wage* (N.Y.: The Macmillan Co., 1912) 249.

42. Note that John Paul II conditions his endorsement of markets upon the adoption of provisions to make up for market defects, since "there are many human needs which find no place in the market" (CA 34).

43. More commonly recognized primary claims to goods are merit, contribution, effort, and inheritance. However, Ryan (see *Distributive Justice* [N.Y.: The Macmillan Co., 1925] 357) stakes out a finely nuanced position on how needs constitute a subsidiary title claim to goods, not replacing but rightly constraining the operation of other titles.

44. See the section of ch. 1 above entitled "The Role of the State" for an analysis of the texts (MM 59–60; GS 70) which introduce this term.

in economic relations. The purpose of these actions is not crassly to centralize economic authority—a project which would endanger local autonomy and other values invoked in the Catholic concept of subsidiarity. Rather, it is to oversee society's efforts adequately to respond to what Paul VI called the "need to establish a greater justice in the sharing of goods, both within national communities and on the international level."[45] Postindustrial social policy is one area in which government is called upon to protect those whose very livelihood depends upon greater accountability in the sharing of resources in an increasingly interdependent world.

Fourth, Catholic social teaching brings an additional resource to the search for methods of insuring social responsibility in a postindustrial world: the concept of the "indirect employer." Since *Laborem exercens*[46] introduced this term in 1981, it has served to call attention to the existence of an entire network of institutional influences which affect the well-being of workers, both employed and unemployed. Labor contracts which set the terms of employment are more than merely private documents involving the contracting parties. Likewise, the plight of the unemployed is a matter of concern for all members of society, necessitating public as well as private charitable responses. In both cases, it is legitimate to look to government as a source of enlightened labor policies which insure adequate wage levels and protect the unemployed. To portray government as the indirect employer is to recognize a legitimate role for public authorities in intervening in labor relations to protect the well-being of vulnerable citizens. It is not to absolve direct employers of all responsibility, just as it does not entail the unnecessary abrogation of the freedom of private enterprises. The awareness of the public significance of work arrangements which informs the concept of the indirect employer is another potential contribution of Catholic social teaching toward a responsible postindustrial social policy.

Other themes and categories from the tradition of Catholic social teaching could be added to these four. However, further analysis would only reconfirm the two major ethical insights which this tradition offers to contemporary reflection on the challenge of postindustrialism. First, in the face of a growing gap between the affluent and the disadvantaged, a new priority must be placed upon meeting human needs. Second, since dependency is a permanent and unavoidable condition in a sub-full-employment

---

45. OA 43.
46. The principal text is LE 17–18. See the section entitled "The Role of the State" in ch. 1 above for an analysis of the text.

society, an enhanced role for public authorities in coordinating social provision seems unavoidable. Of course, on both these items, weighty objections could be raised concerning the practicality and moral desirability of whatever programs of action we might design as a response to the moral imperatives identified by Catholic social teaching. For example, on the second item above, fears that Catholic social thought risks a drift into statism have often been expressed. On the first item, it is possible to object that any criterion which refers to needs immediately becomes too subjective to serve as a useful guide for policy. Since the category of needs is notoriously open-ended, further specification is clearly required.

If the criterion of need is to play a prominent role in postindustrial social policy, a carefully articulated rationale for state-directed distribution according to need must be advanced. It may be that a discourse of need will remain forever prohibitively problematic, but a promising place to look for incipient approaches to solving this problem is in the body of literature which treats "basic human needs." This concept has served primarily as a resource for economists considering government-sponsored strategies for international development programs, but its potential application to domestic social policies in a postindustrial age should not be overlooked. It provides an alternative to responses to persistent poverty of the trickle-down variety, and is especially helpful as a guide to addressing dire deprivation which is impervious to amelioration through economic growth—precisely the most distinctive feature of the postindustrial era.

In evaluating the ethical dimensions of development programs which utilize the basic human needs approach, Drew Christiansen assesses the strategy of attending first to survival needs:

> This approach to the promotion of economic and social progress aims at eliminating the worst aspects of poverty by providing the necessities of life to families at the bottom of the economic ladder. . . .
>
> [T]he strategy reasserts human welfare as a normative criterion justifying all development, for needs are only the most urgent aspects of personal welfare.[47]

Although he is aware of the difficulty of reaching agreement on standards which specify the meaning of "welfare" and "the necessities of life," Christiansen counts as one of the advantages of a basic needs criterion its

---

47. Drew Christiansen, S.J., "Basic Needs: Criterion for the Legitimacy of Development," in Alfred Hennelly, S.J. and John Langan, S.J., eds., *Human Rights in the Americas: The Struggle for Consensus* (Washington, D.C.: Georgetown University Press, 1982) 245.

ability to sidestep the even more intractable questions of how and whether public policy should pursue equality of opportunity or even equality of result. A basic needs strategy embarks on the modest endeavor of "setting a moral minimum"[48] rather than "establishing a leveling sort of equality."[49]

In *The End of Equality*, Mickey Kaus proposes a strikingly original version of a basic needs strategy as a program of public action tailored to fit the condition of contemporary American society. Kaus begins with the judgment that the several liberal attempts in recent decades to use government power (through such strategies as enhancing labor unions, training programs, tax and transfer, protectionism) to counteract the trends toward income inequality and meritocracy have been discredited. Ultimately, all such efforts will fail because Americans by and large do not favor the imposition of "money equality" through state coercion. What our political culture does support is the struggle for "social equality," a condition "where nobody starves or goes homeless, where everybody can get ahead without bumping up against arbitrary barriers, where nobody has to hang their heads or fawn or toady to anybody else."[50]

The "Civic Liberalism" Kaus proposes (as an alternative to the failed "Money Liberalism") seeks to limit the use of government power, employing it only where it is most appropriate and likely to be effective in enhancing social equality, rather than material equality. Kaus targets two related goals: (1) establishing fairness in public institutions (the electoral process, the military); and (2) decommodifying some essential goods (health care, education). "Civic Liberalism" would try to "restrict the sphere of life in which money matters, and enlarge the sphere in which money doesn't matter."[51] Without explicitly mentioning postindustrialism, Kaus takes on the ethical challenges raised by its distributive effects. He does so by distinguishing between those features of the postindustrial condition which seem inevitable and those which public authorities might reasonably hope to correct. His strategy for avoiding the nightmarish scenario of a caste society is to tap government's power to build an "egalitarian public sphere"[52] where the postindustrial trend toward sharp differentials in income will constitute less of a threat to the social equality that the majority of Americans most fundamentally desire.

---

48. Ibid., 259. Notice that this moral minimum is not necessarily restricted to providing mere subsistence. Christiansen notes that most writers on this topic consider "survival plus" options, providing for additional goods such as "dignity" and "decency."
49. Ibid., 276.
50. Mickey Kaus, *The End of Equality*, second edition (N.Y.: Basic Books, 1995) 16.
51. Ibid., 18.
52. Ibid., 24.

Kaus's proposal leaves many questions unanswered. Among its problematic aspects is the positing of an impermeable boundary between public and private spheres of life—domains where money does and alternately does not determine one's status and life chances. However, Kaus does at least provide an example of how liberalism may adapt its distinctive value commitments to the ethical challenges presented by postindustrialism. The type of compromise Kaus envisions is not unusual in the history of liberal political orders. As Michael Ignatieff notes,[53] in the many different cultural contexts where it has exerted influence, liberalism has displayed a proclivity to recognize a few basic needs as entitlements and relegate other needs to the domain of private choices. Postindustrialism leads Kaus to settle for half a loaf. He favors a compromise which preserves at least some level of participation for the newly vulnerable:

> Equality isn't the gut issue here; starvation is—the availability of some basic minimum necessary to allow a person to participate in society. We can argue about what that minimum is . . . . But it's still a minimum we're talking about.[54]

Interesting parallels might be drawn between the ways in which liberalism (as represented by Kaus or others) and Catholic social teaching (at least the interpretation above) respond to the ethical challenges of postindustrialism. The most obvious area of overlap is in the renewed importance of the call to augment the functioning of markets with mechanisms to insure equity in distribution. Without some economic intervention, whether by government or another institution capable of providing for the survival needs of the newly marginalized, severe deprivation will spread in unacceptable ways. Both Catholic social teaching and liberalism can be interpreted as offering support for the adoption of a new logic of distribution appropriate for a postindustrial era. In an age when work opportunities are evaporating for many, each advocates an expanded recognition of the legitimacy of nonwork criteria for distribution.

In the present market-dominated system, the incomes of most people are determined by the value which labor markets place upon their contribution to the production process. To break the work-income nexus is to recognize factors other than work effort and productivity as morally relevant in determining the income of an individual or family. The major alternatives to the distributive criteria of an uncompromising work ethic are distribution according to: (1) need for income; and (2) right to in-

---

53. *The Needs of Strangers* (N.Y.: Viking Penguin, Inc., 1984) 135.
54. Kaus, *The End of Equality*, 15.

come. Each of these options introduces "status" as a consideration for determining desert; individuals are owed some things by virtue of their standing as citizens or human persons. While the work ethic favors a conception of merit which generally reserves goods for those who perform remunerated labor, the idioms of "right" and "need" both support programs of distributing some goods on a more universal and unconditional basis. Various traditions of ethical reflection offer distinctive reasons to justify such universal claims. Our examination of Catholic social teaching demonstrates, for example, how a doctrine of transcendent human personhood may be invoked to support certain positions on what is owed to human persons on the basis of their inherent dignity.

Among the pioneers in this approach to distribution is the movement for "social democracy," which has long championed measures to institutionalize "income by right" and has engaged existing democratic political processes to enact guaranteed income policies in many countries.[55] But even beyond the existence of such organized movements and circles of ethical reflection (whether religious or political in nature), it is possible to detect in contemporary society a new consciousness supporting a non-work-based logic of distribution. We might identify (or, at the very least, imagine) several possible touchstones of support for change, each suggesting a potentially burgeoning awareness that the adoption of a new logic of distribution is desirable on normative grounds and perhaps even necessary on practical grounds.

One such touchstone would be a rejection of the quasi-theological belief that work forms the core of personal identity. This development would allow a post-full-employment society to begin regarding people in terms of bases of selfhood (such as rights and dignity) which prescind from work-related identities. To continue to define people primarily by their work is to guarantee the increased marginalization of those who will soon find themselves with sharply diminished prospects of paid employment.

A second touchstone would be an increased proclivity to view the productive achievement of a society (and perhaps of all humankind) as the common possession of all its members. The notion that there is a "national wealth" to which all citizens have some type of claim forms the basis of some of the more communitarian approaches to the idea of a guaranteed annual income.[56] According to this warrant for redistribution, even those who are not employed in the productive economy deserve

---

55 .For a description of the history, strategies and principles of the international social democratic movement, see Gosta Esping-Andersen, *Politics Against Markets: The Social Democratic Road to Power* (Princeton: Princeton University Press, 1985).

56. One example is Robert Theobald, *The Guaranteed Income*, esp. 15–37, 231–7.

some share of what is produced from the collective resources of society. Of course, this idea contradicts many of the fundamental tenets of liberal individualism, for it relativizes the institution of private property and challenges the perception that a person deserves the entirety of what is produced through the application of his or her talent and effort. However, in a postindustrial era when only a fraction of the population will have the opportunity to convert its talent into material production, many will possess nothing unless they are accorded a type of recognition which includes a claim to a share of national wealth.

We might perceive numerous other marks of this new consciousness by extrapolating from current expressions of concern about a number of issues relating to economic justice. A recent upsurge of attention to the topic of greater corporate responsibility,[57] for example, indicates an increased willingness to hold possessors of capital and other resources more accountable to the common good of all members of society. Distress at rising levels of income inequality has attracted attention in popular media as well as scholarly works which document the growing trend toward the advent of a two-tier society and offer prescriptions to address this ominous development.[58] This is not to say that all parties voicing objections to these obstacles to the establishment of a more humanized economy find themselves in instant agreement. Differing ethical assessments of economic practices will continue to be expressed in various idioms. However, it is at least possible to interpret these many expressions as part of an incipient common awareness of the need to adjust our thinking about distributive issues to the challenges of a postindustrial age.

Prospects for the Future: Political Culture, Religious Values and Social Learning

We conclude our investigation of postindustrial possibilities by considering how political culture forms the context in which the above moral analysis of distributive concerns is situated. Clearly, a comprehensive inventory of the numerous elements of the American cultural inheritance and its operative social mores is beyond the scope of this brief section. It

---

57. Compelling evidence that corporate responsibility has indeed risen to the top of the agenda of concern for many Americans is presented in the report "Corporate Irresponsibility: A Study of the Political and Policy Implications of Public Attitudes Toward Corporate America" (Washington, D.C.: The Preamble Center for Public Policy, 29 July 1996).

58. See Robert H. Frank and Philip J. Cook, *The Winner-Take-All Society* (N.Y.: The Free Press, 1995); Sheldon Danziger and Peter Gottschalk, *America Unequal* (Cambridge, Mass.: Harvard University Press, 1995).

will be instructive, however, to consider how arguments supporting a new logic of distribution might intersect with the sphere of values (including values rooted in religious beliefs) which give shape to American political discourse, set the terms of potential social learning, and exert influence upon public policy.

Although any responsible statement about American political culture[59] must acknowledge the irreducible plurality of intellectual strands present in the discourse of our public life, it is nevertheless true that most participants in U.S. politics share a common first language. This fact lends to the American political scene a marked homogeneity which many other nations do not experience. The perspective of what Louis Hartz famously calls "the liberal tradition"[60] exerts a considerable level of hegemony over American politics, narrowing the spectrum of opinions which have significant influence on policy decisions. This American brand of liberalism emphasizes a bundle of values familiar to us all: individual liberty, political equality, constitutional democracy, the opportunity for unlimited mobility, an aversion to authority, an affinity for the operations of competitive market capitalism and a work ethic which allows individuals to succeed or fail according to personal abilities and efforts. These features of American liberalism have frequently been praised for their merits as well as excoriated for their failings, but they must be recognized as inescapable features of the American political landscape.

If the American intellectual inheritance were limited to Lockean liberalism and post-Enlightenment individualism, we would rarely turn to public authorities to perform needed tasks. The influence of other strands of thought, such as pragmatism and even occasionally communitarianism, lead the U.S. to turn to government as the agent of collective action for commonly desired ends. The American cultural repertoire also includes value commitments and other behavioral motivations which are religious in origin, even if they are not always consciously associated with organized religion.[61] Religion plays an irreplaceable role in foster-

---

59. See two excellent recent examples: Richard J. Ellis, *American Political Cultures* (N.Y.: Oxford University Press, 1993); Seymour Martin Lipset, *American Exceptionalism: A Double-Edged Sword* (N.Y.: W. W. Norton and Co., 1996).

60. Louis Hartz, *The Liberal Tradition in America: An Interpretation of American Political Thought Since the Revolution* (N.Y.: Harcourt, Brace and Co., 1991 [1955]).

61. A phenomenological description of the influence of religious ideas on the social thinking of most Americans (the study is limited to self-identified Christians) appears in Stephen Hart, *What Does the Lord Require? How American Christians Think About Economic Justice* (N.Y.: Oxford University Press, 1992). Hart lists a number of elements of Christianity (the love command, universalism, voluntarism), some of them operating in

ing "community, commitment and citizenship"—a trilogy invoked by the authors of *Habits of the Heart* "as useful terms to contrast to an alienating individualism."[62] The ability of religious organizations to serve as mobilizers of political participation and as loci of alternative practices and ideas is well documented.[63]

We have already considered the discourse of principles, and especially those in the form of middle axioms, as one of the ways in which the voices of organized religion exert an influence upon public life. In serving as markers of religiously motivated values, such middle axioms may offset the influence of other ideas within the inherited political culture. An example of great relevance to our investigation of postindustrialism concerns the work ethic and associated attitudes toward the poor. The package of liberal political ideas to which contemporary Americans are heirs views poverty primarily as a personal failure. Because of the cultural hegemony of the work ethic (the origin of which is, ironically, closely associated with Christian ideas), our society generally stigmatizes nonworkers and others who are poor. This is not likely to change in the near future, regardless of an increased consciousness of postindustrial realities. The *long-range* challenge for voices of religion seeking to contribute to the formation of a more humanized economy is to find an effective way to articulate values and principles so that society as a whole may reconsider how it regards the misfortunes of those who do not earn enough to support themselves. The *short-range* challenge is to serve as effective advocates for the continuation of social provision (including welfare and other means-tested programs) for the survival needs of the poorest. Even if we continue to withhold approval from nonworkers, new economic conditions make it imperative that society not withhold basic sustenance from those who are poor and unemployed.

Because of deeply held cultural convictions about the meaning of fairness and a preference for relationships of reciprocity, Americans gen-

---

polar tension (individualism and corporatism, inner- and other-worldliness), which affect how faith influences perceptions of economic justice in the American context.

62. Robert Bellah and others, "Introduction to the Updated Edition: The House Divided" in *Habits of the Heart: Individualism and Commitment in American Life*, updated edition (Berkeley: University of California Press, 1996 [1985]) xi.

63. This function is referred to as the building up of "social capital." In the description of Bellah and others, it includes "associational membership and public trust" (ibid., xvi). Research by Sydney Verba and Gary R. Orren (*Equality in America: The View from the Top* [Cambridge, Mass.: Harvard University Press, 1985], ch. 11) portrays religion as an important source of ideas and values supporting the notion of equality. Such religious ideas (as well as institutional practices fostering political participation) challenge the dis-

erally are not enthusiastic about programs of material redistribution. Research demonstrates that Americans tend to favor using government power to extend political equality, but not economic equality.[64] Recognizing this state of affairs supplies further impetus for religious voices concerned about the fate of the victims of postindustrialism to adopt a "basic human needs" strategy rather than a more ambitious program of egalitarianism as a response to the postindustrial challenge. Drew Christiansen reflects an awareness of the necessity of operating within the constraints of present political culture when he writes: "The moral appeal of a basic needs strategy can be traced to the popular belief that serious deprivation is qualitatively a graver offense than simple inequality, and therefore practically never justifiable."[65]

In an even more poignant fashion, political scientist Hugh Heclo characterizes the entire U.S. pattern of poor relief programs (which consists of a patchwork of categorical means-tested programs rather than universal entitlements) as a huge national compromise justifying the adoption of a minimalist strategy regarding social provision. On one hand, because we generally favor smaller government and do not support egalitarianism in the economic sphere, "Americans do not endorse a publicly guaranteed right to income as such."[66] On the other hand, Americans are a decent and compassionate people:

> Across the spectrum of political opinion there is a strong residual concern that as we grow economically we should not shrivel socially. Few Americans wish to live amid two nations of children, or two nations of the elderly, or in a society that is willing to ignore some fraction of its inhabitants because they can be regarded as economically superfluous.[67]

Given the terms of this compromise, our nation's arrangements for assisting the poor are perennially politically vulnerable and dependent upon the delicate balance of concerns described by Heclo. This underlines the important function performed by religious voices in issuing much-needed

---

tortions of ideologies (on the right as well as the left) which posit a world driven solely by interest, to the exclusion of normative values.

64. See Jennifer Hochschild, *What's Fair? American Beliefs About Distributive Justice* (Cambridge, Mass.: Harvard University Press, 1981). Key to Hochschild's analysis is the observation that Americans consistently distinguish between criteria of distribution appropriate in the economic, political and social spheres of life.

65. Christiansen, "Basic Needs," 250.

66. Hugh Heclo, "The Political Foundations of Antipoverty Policy," in Sheldon H. Danziger and Daniel H. Weinberg, eds., *Fighting Poverty: What Works and What Doesn't* (Cambridge, Mass.: Harvard University Press, 1986) 338.

67. Ibid., 340.

reminders (often in the form of principles and middle axioms) of values such as generosity and compassion—values which justify making sacrifices for our fellow citizens whose very survival depends upon the sharing of resources.

Religious voices are often the primary "carriers" of these values, but they are not exclusively so. In chapter seven above, we identified one appealing formulation (expressed in terms which prescind from religious language) of a guideline for social welfare policy which enacts these values. This policy principle is David Ellwood's maxim which states that "people who are willing to work but who are unable to find a job should not be abandoned."[68] As it pertains to welfare policy, this maxim is a summary of the "preconditions argument" which recommends the continuation of income maintenance measures until a strategy of empowerment (through job training, education, etc.) can lead welfare recipients into self-sufficiency. "Ellwood's maxim" may be applied to the postindustrial economy as well. In a situation where the economy requires many fewer workers, it is unrealistic to expect involuntary unemployment to be remedied in all cases by an empowerment strategy of job preparation. In order to avoid placing unemployed people and their families in impossible situations, it falls to social policy to provide them with income security. This assistance may have to be offered on an open-ended (as opposed to time-limited) basis, as these families face a crisis situation not of their making and beyond their control.

If principles such as "Ellwood's maxim" come to be incorporated into social policies appropriate for a postindustrial situation, it would indicate that our nation has undergone a process of what is perhaps best labeled "social learning."[69] The content of this social learning may be described succinctly: The social good of income security for vulnerable families requires increased protection by public authorities in a postindustrial era. Even though it leads to the heretofore unpopular conclusion that an unprecedented commitment to providing income by right or need is desirable, the appropriation of this lesson does not require the acceptance of a set of values utterly alien to the American political culture. It merely depends upon the consistent application of familiar values (such as social cohesion and mutual responsibility for all citizens) to the new

68. "Welfare Reform in Name Only," *New York Times*, 22 July 1996, A19. This principle is treated in detail in ch. 7.

69. This term here refers to changes in broadly shared cultural perceptions of the desirable mix of values and of strategies for pursuing normative concerns. It assumes the possibility of transforming the discourse regarding values, beyond the mere comprehension and internalization of received norms.

context of a postindustrial economy, where millions of families may no longer have the opportunity to achieve self-sufficiency. In this new environment, safeguarding the welfare of many members of society will require more ambitious programs of collective action.

One optimistic observer of the process of social learning is Robert Reich. His sanguine assessment of the possibilities of ongoing and cooperative social learning makes frequent use of phrases (such as "civic discovery" and "public deliberation") which indicate his confidence that deliberation presided over by prudent "public managers . . . provides an opportunity for people to discover shared values about what is good for the community."[70] Reich expresses optimism that "through such deliberations opinions can be revised, premises altered, and common interests discovered,"[71] although even he concedes that "there is no guarantee that the resulting social learning will yield a clear consensus at the end."[72]

Other observers portray social learning (whether or not precisely this phrase is invoked) as proceeding in less linear, sometimes more conflictual modes. Samuel Huntington interprets American history as a series of thirty-year cycles which witness the ebb and flow of commitment to enacting the "American creed" of "national political values and beliefs."[73] Huntington describes a fitful process whereby our nation's institutional practices periodically drift away from the espoused values upon which they are based. This opens up an "IvI gap"[74]—a "cognitive dissonance"[75] between our institutions and our shared political ideals—which recurringly inspires "a politics of creedal passion" demanding change. Periodic reform movements seek to reestablish the legitimacy of our political system by struggling to narrow the gap between our commonly professed ideals and our actual institutions.

Social commentator Kevin Phillips also sees evidence within American history of cyclic reactions inspired by the need for social learning (or relearning of forgotten value orientations). He portrays upsurges of egalitarian populism as needed corrections after periods of "capitalist over-

---

70. Robert B. Reich, "Policy Making in a Democracy," in Reich, ed., *The Power of Public Ideas* (Cambridge, Mass.: Harvard University Press, 1988) 146.

71. Ibid., 144.

72. Ibid., 154.

73. Samuel P. Huntington, *American Politics: The Promise of Disharmony* (Cambridge, Mass.: Harvard University Press, 1981) 13. Huntington lists five core elements of this creed: "ideas of constitutionalism, individualism, liberalism, democracy and egalitarianism" (15).

74. Ibid., 39. The abbreviation stands for "ideals versus institutions."

75. Ibid., 61.

drive"[76] which cause "excessive stratification" and which "eventually incite political upheaval."[77] Needless to say, Phillips's view that muscular displays of popular backlash are signs of social advancement is not shared by all theorists of social learning.

Whatever version of the process of social learning we enlist, it is clear that some discomfort and displacement is involved as a population adjusts its understanding of inherited elements of its political culture to new social conditions. Pollster Daniel Yankelovich refers to this phenomenon as "lurch and learn"[78] and, alternatively, as "working through." He notes that "people need impressive moral, cognitive and emotional resources to succeed in working through,"[79] as when ethical blind spots are exposed and corrected. In considering issues of distributive justice, the central challenge for members of a society is to adjust the social priorities governing their joint endeavors so that they bring into balance such competing values as independence and cohesion, individuality and social responsibility. The expectation is not that social learning will result in a unanimity of opinion on how to put into practice a specific set of shared values, but merely that a revised consciousness of central social priorities will lift up certain important items as concerns worthy of continued attention.

The advent of a postindustrial era confronts us with a number of economic conditions which threaten fundamental human values: the superfluousness of much of the workforce, massive income insecurity, and new patterns in the distribution of wealth which undermine the achievement of egalitarian democracy. Each of these "conditions" deserves to be defined as a "problem,"[80] and thus to find its way onto the policy agenda in the coming years. In previous eras, social progress was achieved when reform movements sped the pace of social learning by (1) exposing what they perceived to be ethical inadequacies in social practices, and (2) by presenting proposals for policy improvement as reasonable measures to advance the common good. Examples from U.S. history include the movement for regulating business practices and instituting Mothers'

---

76. Kevin Phillips, *The Politics of Rich and Poor: Wealth and the American Electorate in the Reagan Aftermath* (N.Y.: HarperCollins Publishers, 1990) 35.

77. Ibid., 208.

78. Daniel Yankelovich, "Current Trends in American Cultural Values" (paper presented at the conference, "Religion and the American Family Debate: Deeper Understandings, New Directions," sponsored by the Religion, Culture and Family Project at the Divinity School of the University of Chicago, Chicago, Illinois, 10 Sept. 1996).

79. Daniel Yankelovich, *Coming to Public Judgment: Making Democracy Work in a Complex World* (Syracuse, N.Y.: Syracuse University Press, 1991) 137.

80. John Kingdon's use of these categories is explained in ch. 5 above.

Pensions in the Progressive era, the establishment of the Social Security Act during the Great Depression, and the War on Poverty in the 1960s. Each of these represents a clarification and defense of the human values perceived to be at risk in unsatisfactory economic arrangements.

It is impossible to predict the precise form social learning will assume in the future of American economic policy. In the *long run*, the advent of conditions such as postindustrialism and ascendant ideologies such as neoliberalism[81] may be met by social movements seeking to offset the working of harsh economic laws and the effects of ruthless forces of global competition. If the postindustrialism hypothesis is true, then we might expect significant grassroots responses to economic developments which relegate millions worldwide to the status of "throwaway workers," squeezing them out of labor markets and exerting downward pressure on the wages of those who do find employment. In the *short run*, the evidence of social learning might include a gathering momentum of support for a reassessment of the new American welfare law—legislation which drastically reduces the incomes and prospects of millions of our most vulnerable citizens. Several provisions of the new law practically invite popular backlash, especially those measures which in effect punish millions (children, legal immigrants and the elderly poor) for reasons and circumstances clearly beyond their control. The willingness of American political leaders to admit mistakes will be tested by well-founded calls for prudent corrections and for restoration of funding and entitlements.

In both the long and short run, adequate policy responses to concerns about distributive justice will be guided by statements of principle (such as "Ellwood's maxim" or the middle axioms offered by the U.S. Catholic bishops) which measure public policies according to their advancement of values such as fairness and security. Religious voices contribute to policy debates by offering their own distinctive interpretations, from within their own traditions of ethical reflection, of the values that inform constructive policy. Catholic social teaching seeks to contribute to policy debates, as well as to the formation of an overlapping consensus on the meaning and practice of social justice, by articulating the ethical ideals it draws from the Christian gospel in a way that attempts to appeal to all.

---

81. This term refers to policies which encourage the globalization of free trade and the internationalization of capital. For an analysis which raises up many concerns germane to distributive justice in a postindustrial era, see ch. 5 "Neo-liberal Policies and Their Rationale," in Gary Teeple, *Globalization and the Decline of Social Reform* (Toronto: Garamond Press, 1995) 75–127.

Like any responsible social ethic, Catholic social teaching must respect the tension between ideals (such as the Christian proclamation of universal, unconditional love) and the actualities of power relations in the political order. Yet even as it acknowledges the necessity of pragmatic compromise in a pluralistic world where politics remains the "art of the possible," the Church seeks to remain faithful to its task of evangelizing culture. The mission of a "public church" includes pursuing the highest attainable degree of justice in a troubled world—not hesitating to stand in solidarity with the most vulnerable members of society and to speak out in defense of the well-being of the poorest families. For the contemporary U.S. Catholic Church, this includes an agenda of advocating principled policy positions on public issues such as social welfare policy.

Epilogue

The twelve months which followed President Clinton's signing of the 1996 welfare law have witnessed a number of developments relevant to our study. Although it is too soon to assess the final significance of these events, two sets of observations (regarding implementation of the new law and potential policy correction) seem inescapable.

First, even though its measures take effect with staggered deadlines and gradual phasing in over many months, the various provisions of the new welfare law have set off a scramble for affected demographic groups and jurisdictions to adjust to a changed policy environment. A flurry of media attention to looming personal hardships has accompanied several of the benefit cutoff dates, starting with the September 1996 termination of food stamps for needy immigrants and proceeding through the discontinuation of SSI benefits for nearly one hundred thousand disabled poor children in the summer of 1997. Garnering particular public notice have been the desperate efforts by millions of immigrants to complete the process of procuring citizenship status before deadlines which would leave them without a safety net. Political firestorms erupted in many state capitals as legislators engaged in a yearlong process of establishing local program standards such as new criteria for determining eligibility for benefits. Indeed, many state budgets were delayed for months by heated deliberations over allocating local resources to fill part of the gap left by the federal retreat from assistance to the poorest families.

It is hazardous to make even preliminary generalizations about the outcome of these state-level debates. The devolution of welfare through the mechanism of block grants means that the safety net formerly built around federal income entitlements has been replaced by a crazy quilt of policies which vary from state to state. Even our tentative judgments are complicated by the fact that over forty states hold HHS waivers allowing them partial exemptions from the timeline and provisions of the federal measures. There are now in place fifty different systems featuring various combinations of policies on time limits, work requirements, family caps, interstate migration, and subsidized employment. Some states have opted to provide for a "softer welfare landing" by extending deadlines, offering vouchers and non-cash assistance for needy families, and even finding legal loopholes that allow them to interpret the new law in the most generous way. For example, at least ten states are feeding needy immigrants out of their own pockets; dozens are invoking clauses permitting hardship exemptions for areas with high unemployment in order to continue food stamp coverage to inner-city residents for whom workfare slots are unavailable. Some states have passed major responsibilities for social program design and implementation on to the county level. What seems safe to say, in sum, is that all jurisdictions have adopted new combinations of "carrots" and "sticks" which have sharply altered the social policy landscape since the enactment of the 1996 welfare law.

Second, even beyond these observations about the implementation of the 1996 welfare law, recent months have witnessed significant efforts at policy correction. At first, even proponents of the new law admitted the need for some technical corrections which would adjust the terms of the welfare law to updated information and unanticipated exigencies. Subsequently, the negotiations over the 1998 federal budget revealed unexpected support in Congress for a substantial restoration of funding to certain of the affected social programs—something President Clinton had proposed even before signing the bill. The preliminary budget agreement approved by Congress in July 1997 reverses a few of the harshest aspects of the 1996 legislation. It restores eligibility for social assistance to many immigrants (especially those who arrived before 1996), creates tax incentives for businesses to hire former welfare recipients, and mandates that minimum wage and other labor protections apply to workfare participants. Perhaps most significantly, it extends Medicaid protection to half the nation's ten million uninsured children; this measure's five-year price tag of $24 billion will be funded partially through increased cigarette taxes.

These changes certainly represent a remarkable turnaround since the events of the previous summer in the political fortunes of low-income Americans. While it is encouraging to think that these measures represent a full-blown return to the New Deal's ethos of social responsibility, or at least to the pragmatic center of opinion about effective social policy, it is also possible to interpret them as holding little ultimate significance. These changes may be construed as nothing more than small bargaining concessions traded for other prominent elements of a budget deal that includes large tax cuts for the wealthiest Americans. After all, even with the expensive child health care initiative, the 1998 budget accord restores far less than half of the 1996 welfare law's funding cuts in social programs.

The new budget accord overturns none of the major principles of the Personal Responsibility and Work Opportunity Act: its work requirements, time limitation on benefits or its substitution of block grants for the former income entitlement to single parents of young children.

More substantial policy correction (and perhaps even reversal) will come only after a true transformation on the level of cultural awareness and political will. This can happen only when a broad national dialogue brings about a new consensus on distributive justice—a convergence of opinion demanding the reconsideration of our national responsibility to improve the life prospects of our low-income neighbors. This includes those who apply for social benefits like welfare as well as the working poor who struggle to make ends meet through jobs in the low end of the labor market. Are we willing to invest national resources to make work more widely available, to make work pay for all, and to preserve the human dignity of those who cannot immediately overcome barriers to employment? Will we measure the success of welfare reform by the raw statistics of declining rolls and budget expenses, or in terms of the actual well-being of families forced off the welfare rolls by the time limits which many will "hit" starting in 1998?

The effects of the 1996 welfare reform law are still largely unknown. While welfare rolls are down by 25 percent from their peak of fourteen million in the early 1990s, most of these gains may be attributed to general economic prosperity, not to the effects of policy innovation. No one has calculated the human toll that would accompany a severe recession in which millions of families, unable to make the shift to work and self-reliance mandated by the 1996 welfare law, are stripped of the income protections formerly available under AFDC. The very least we may hope for is a growing sensitivity throughout society to the suffering of those who do become casualties of the federal retreat from income assistance. If the next round in our nation's recurring episodes of welfare reform is to produce a more adequate response to the needs of America's families, then we will have to make space in our policy deliberations for appeals to conscience such as those offered by the U.S. bishops. Such religious voices play a crucial and constructive role when they enter the national dialogue with a call to focus on the human dimensions of policy as we reassess the American welfare system.

Bibliography

Abbott, Walter, ed. *The Documents of Vatican II*. N.Y.: Guild Press, 1966.

Abramovitz, Mimi. *Regulating the Lives of Women: Social Welfare Policy from Colonial Times to the Present*. Boston: South End Press, 1988.

Apple, R. W. "His Battle Now Lost, Moynihan Still Cries Out." *New York Times*, 2 August 1996, A16.

Aquinas, St. Thomas. *Summa Theologica*, English Blackfriars edition, 60 vols. N.Y.: McGraw-Hill Book Co., 1966.

_____. "On Kingship." In *Saint Thomas Aquinas: On Law, Morality and Politics*, eds. William P. Baumgarth and Richard J. Regan. Indianapolis: Hacket Publishing Company, 1988.

Aristotle. *Nicomachean Ethics*. Trans. J.A.K. Thompson. London: George Allen and Unwin, Ltd., 1953.

_____. *Politics*, Book I. In *Basic Works of Aristotle*, edited and with an introduction by Richard McKeon, 1127–46. N.Y.: Random House, 1941.

Aronowitz, Stanley, and William DiFazio. *The Jobless Future: Sci-Tech and the Dogma of Work*. Minneapolis: University of Minnesota Press, 1994.

Association of the Bar of the City of New York. "Report and Recommendations on H.R. 4, 'The Personal Responsibility Act of 1995." *Record of the Association of the Bar of the City of New York* 50 (June 1995) 493–521.

Atherton, John. *Christian Social Ethics: A Reader*. Cleveland: The Pilgrim Press, 1994.

Avila, Charles. *Ownership: Early Christian Teaching*. Maryknoll, N.Y.: Orbis Books, 1983.

Baker, Peter. "Virginia Targets Welfare Moms in Effort to Track Down Absentee Dads." *Washington Post*, 31 July 1995, A1.

Bane, Mary Jo, and David T. Ellwood. *Welfare Realities: From Rhetoric to Reform*. Cambridge, Mass.: Harvard University Press, 1994.

Banfield, Edward. *The Unheavenly City Revisited*. Boston: Little, Brown and Co., 1974.

Bassuk, Ellen L., and others. "The Characteristics and Needs of Sheltered Homeless and Low-Income Housed Mothers." *Journal of the American Medical Association* 276, no. 8 (29 August 1996) 640–6.

Bayer, Richard C. "Christian Ethics and *A Theory of Justice*." *Journal of the American Academy of Religion* 64, no. 1 (spring 1996) 45–60.

Beckley, Harlan R. "A Christian Affirmation of Rawls's Idea of Justice as Fairness—Part I." *Journal of Religious Ethics* 13, no. 2 (fall 1985) 210–42.

———, "A Christian Affirmation of Rawls's Idea of Justice as Fairness—Part II." *Journal of Religious Ethics* 14, no. 2 (fall 1986) 229–46.

Bell, Daniel. *The Coming of Post-Industrial Society: A Venture in Social Forecasting.* N.Y.: Basic Books, Inc., Publishers, 1976 (1973).

Bellah, Robert, and others. *Habits of the Heart: Individualism and Commitment in American Life*, updated edition with a new introduction. Berkeley: University of California Press, 1996.

Bellamy, Edward. *Looking Backward, 2000–1887.* Boston: Houghton Mifflin, 1888.

Bernardin, Joseph Cardinal. *Consistent Ethic of Life.* Ed. Thomas G. Fuechtmann. Kansas City, Mo.: Sheed and Ward, 1988.

Bernstein, Nina. "Do Plans to Restructure the Welfare System Pose a Burden for Foster Care?" *New York Times*, 19 Nov. 1995, 1.

Berrick, Jill Duerr. *Faces of Poverty: Portraits of Women and Children on Welfare.* N.Y.: Oxford University Press, 1995.

Blank, Rebecca M. "The Employment Strategy: Public Policies to Increase Work and Savings." In *Confronting Poverty: Prescriptions for Change*, eds. Sheldon H. Danziger, Gary D. Sandefur and Daniel H. Weinberg, 168–204. Cambridge, Mass.: Harvard University Press, 1994.

Bottomore, Tom, ed. *Citizenship and Social Class.* London: Pluto Press, 1992.

Boulding, Kenneth E. "The Boundaries of Social Policy." *Social Work* 12, no. 1 (Jan. 1967) 3–11.

Boyer, Paul. *Urban Masses and Moral Order in America, 1820–1920.* Cambridge, Mass.: Harvard University Press, 1978.

Bread for the World Institute. *Let's Get Real About Welfare*, Occasional Paper No. 5. Silver Spring, Md.: Bread for the World Institute, 1995.

Burns, Gene. *The Frontiers of Catholicism: The Politics of Ideology in a Liberal World.* Berkeley: University of California Press, 1992.

Burtless, Gary. "The Effect of Reform on Employment, Earnings and Income." In *Welfare Policy for the 1990s*, eds. Phoebe H. Cottingham and David T. Ellwood, 103–45. Cambridge, Mass.: Harvard University Press, 1989.

———. "Paychecks or Welfare Checks: Can AFDC Recipients Support Themselves?" *Brookings Review* 12 (fall 1994) 35–7.

Califano, Joseph A., Jr. "Welfare's Drug Connection." *New York Times*, 24 August 1996, 23.

Carlson-Thies, Stanley W., and James W. Skillen, eds. *Welfare in America: Christian Perspectives on a Policy in Crisis.* Grand Rapids, Mich.: William B. Eerdmans Publishing Co., 1996.

Catholic Charities USA. "Transforming the Welfare System: A Position Paper of Catholic Charities USA." Alexandria, Va.: Catholic Charities USA, 24 Jan. 1994.

Center on Budget and Policy Priorities. "Urban Institute Study Confirms that Welfare Bills Would Increase Child Poverty." Washington, D.C.: Center on Budget and Policy Priorities, 26 July 1996.
Children's Defense Fund. "Fourteen Reasons to Vote Against Pending Welfare Bills That Hurt Children." Press Release. Washington, D.C.: Children's Defense Fund, July 1996.
Christiansen, Drew, S.J. "Basic Needs: Criterion for the Legitimacy of Development." In *Human Rights in the Americas: The Struggle for Consensus*, eds. Alfred Hennelly, S.J. and John Langan, S.J., 245–88. Washington, D.C.: Georgetown University Press, 1982.
Coleman, John, S.J. "Development of Church Social Teaching." In *Readings in Moral Theology No. 5: Official Catholic Social Teaching*, eds. Charles E. Curran and Richard A. McCormick, S.J., 169–87. N.Y.: Paulist Press, 1986.
_____, ed. *One Hundred Years of Catholic Social Thought: Celebration and Challenge*. Maryknoll, N.Y.: Orbis Books, 1991.
Conlon, Timothy. *New Federalism: Intergovernmental Reform from Nixon to Reagan*. Washington, D.C.: The Brookings Institution, 1988.
Coston, Carol, O.P. "Women's Ways of Working." In *One Hundred Years of Catholic Social Thought: Celebration and Challenge*, ed. John A. Coleman, S.J., 256–69. Maryknoll, N.Y.: Orbis Books, 1991.
Cunniff, Ruth. "Big Bad Welfare." *The Progressive* 58 (August 1994) 18–21.
Curran, Charles E. *Directions in Catholic Social Ethics*. Notre Dame, Ind.: University of Notre Dame Press, 1985.
Danziger, Sheldon H., and Peter Gottschalk. *America Unequal*. Cambridge, Mass.: Harvard University Press, 1995.
Danziger, Sheldon H., Gary D. Sandefur, and Daniel H. Weinberg, eds. *Confronting Poverty: Prescriptions for Change*. Cambridge, Mass.: Harvard University Press, 1994.
Danziger, Sheldon H., and Daniel H. Weinberg, eds. *Fighting Poverty: What Works and What Doesn't*. Cambridge, Mass.: Harvard University Press, 1986.
DeParle, Jason. "Aid from an Enemy of the Welfare State." *New York Times*, 28 Jan. 1996, Section 4, p. 4.
_____. "The New Contract With America's Poor." *New York Times*, 28 August 1996, Section 4, p. 1.
Dorr, Donal. *Option for the Poor: A Hundred Years of Catholic Social Teaching*. Maryknoll, N.Y.: Orbis Books, 1992.
Edelman, Marian Wright. *Families in Peril: An Agenda for Social Change*. The 1986 W.E.B. DuBois Lectures. Cambridge, Mass.: Harvard University Press, 1987.
Ellis, Richard J. *American Political Cultures*. N.Y.: Oxford University Press, 1993.
Ellwood, David T. *Poor Support: Poverty in the American Family*. N.Y.: Basic Books, 1988.

———. "Welfare Reform in Name Only." *New York Times*, 22 July 1996, A19.
Elshtain, Jean Bethke. "Single Motherhood: Response to Iris Marion Young." *Dissent* (spring 1994) 267–9.
Esping-Andersen, Gosta. *Politics Against Markets: The Social Democratic Road to Power*. Princeton: Princeton University Press, 1985.
———. *The Three Worlds of Welfare Capitalism*. Princeton: Princeton University Press, 1990.
Ferguson, Thomas P. *Catholic and American: The Political Theology of John Courtney Murray*. Kansas City, Mo.: Sheed and Ward, 1993.
Fern, Richard L. "Religious Belief in a Rawlsian Society." *The Journal of Christian Ethics* 15, no. 1 (spring 1987) 33–58.
Finn, Peter. "Welfare Shifts Tax Child-Care Funds: Area's Working Poor Caught in Child-Care Bind." *Washington Post*, 7 Oct. 1996, B1.
Florida Conference of Catholic Bishops. "Promoting Meaningful Welfare Reform." *Origins* 24, no. 37 (2 March 1995) 609–12.
Frank, Robert H., and Philip J. Cook. *The Winner-Take-All Society*. N.Y.: The Free Press, 1995.
Fraser, Nancy. "Women, Welfare and the Politics of Need Interpretation." In her *Unruly Practices: Power, Discourse and Gender in Contemporary Social Theory*, 144–60. Minneapolis: University of Minnesota Press, 1989.
Freudenheim, Milt. "Charities Say Government Cuts Would Jeopardize Their Ability to Help the Needy." *New York Times*, 5 Feb. 1996, B8.
Friedman, Milton. *Capitalism and Freedom*, second edition. Chicago: University of Chicago Press, 1982 (1962).
Galbraith, John Kenneth. *The Affluent Society*. Boston: Houghton Mifflin Co., 1958.
———. *The Good Society: The Humane Agenda*. N.Y.: Houghton Mifflin Co., 1996.
Gans, Herbert. *The War Against the Poor: The Underclass and Antipoverty Policy*. N.Y.: HarperCollins Publishers, Inc., 1995.
Gilder, George. "End Welfare Reform as We Know It." *The American Spectator* (June 1995) 24–7.
———. *Wealth and Poverty*. N.Y.: Basic Books, Inc., Publishers, 1981.
Gillespie, Ed, and Bob Schellhas, eds. *Contract With America: The Bold Plan by Rep. Newt Gingrich, Rep. Dick Armey and the House Republicans to Change the Nation*. N.Y.: Times Books of Random House, Inc., 1994.
Gingrich, Newt. *To Renew America*. N.Y.: HarperCollins Publishers, Inc., 1995.
Gleick, Elizabeth. "The Children's Crusade." *Time*, 3 June 1996, 31–5.
Golden, Tim. "If Immigrants Lose U.S. Aid, Local Budgets May Feel Pain." *New York Times*, 29 July 1996, A1.
Goodman, John C. "Welfare Privatization." *Wall Street Journal*, 28 May 1996, A18.
———. "Why Not Abolish the Welfare State?" *Common Sense* 2 (winter 1995) 63–72.

Gordon, Linda. *Pitied But Not Entitled: Single Mothers and the History of Welfare 1890–1935*. N.Y.: The Free Press, 1994.

Greenhouse, Steven. "New York Union Leader Urges Halt to Broadening Workfare." *New York Times*, 23 Sept. 1996, A1.

Greenstein, Robert, Richard Kogan, and Marion Nichols. "Bearing Most of the Burden: How Deficit Reduction During the 104th Congress Concentrated on Programs for the Poor." Washington, D.C.: Center on Budget and Policy Priorities, 26 Nov. 1996.

Gueron, Judith M., and Edward Pauly (with Cameron M. Lougy). *From Welfare to Work*, A Manpower Demonstration Research Study. N.Y.: Russell Sage Foundation, 1991.

Gustafson, James M. "The Church: A Community of Moral Discourse." In his *The Church as Moral Decision-Maker*, 83–95. Philadelphia: Pilgrim Press, 1970.

Gutmann, Amy, ed. *Democracy and the Welfare State*. Princeton: Princeton University Press, 1988.

Haldane, John. "The Individual, the State, and the Common Good." *Social Philosophy and Policy* 13, no. 1 (winter 1996) 59–79.

Handler, Joel F. *The Poverty of Welfare Reform*. New Haven: Yale University Press, 1995.

Harrington, Michael. *The Accidental Century*. Baltimore: Penguin Books, 1965.

_____. *The New American Poverty*. N.Y.: Penguin Books, 1984.

_____. *The Other America: Poverty in the United States*. N.Y.: Macmillan Publishers, 1962.

Hart, Stephen. *What Does the Lord Require? How American Christians Think About Economic Justice*. N.Y.: Oxford University Press, 1992.

Hartz, Louis. *The Liberal Tradition in America: An Interpretation of American Political Thought Since the Revolution*. N.Y.: Harcourt, Brace and Co., 1991 (1955).

Heclo, Hugh. "The Political Foundations of Antipoverty Policy." In *Fighting Poverty: What Works and What Doesn't*, eds. Sheldon H. Danziger and Daniel H. Weinberg, 312–40. Cambridge, Mass.: Harvard University Press, 1986.

Hehir, J. Brian. "The Consistent Ethic: Public Policy Implications." In *Consistent Ethic of Life*, ed. Thomas G. Fuechtmann, 218–36. Kansas City, Mo.: Sheed and Ward, 1988.

Herbert, Bob. "Welfare Hysteria." *New York Times*, 5 August 1995, A17.

Himmelfarb, Gertrude. *The De-Moralization of Society: From Victorian Virtues to Modern Values*. N.Y.: Alfred A. Knopf, 1995.

Hochschild, Jennifer. *What's Fair? American Beliefs About Distributive Justice*. Cambridge, Mass.: Harvard University Press, 1981.

Hollenbach, David. *Justice, Peace, and Human Rights: American Catholic Social Ethics in a Pluralistic Context*. N.Y.: The Crossroad Publishing Co., 1988.

Holmes, Steven A. "Public Cost of Teen-Age Pregnancy Is Put at $7 Billion This Year." *New York Times*, 13 June 1996, A19.

Holy See of the Roman Catholic Church. "Charter of the Rights of the Family," Vatican document released 24 Nov. 1983. *Origins* 13, no. 27 (15 Dec. 1983) 461–4.

Hughes, Mark Alan. "Welfare Dust Bowl." *Washington Post*, 25 Sept. 1995, A23.

Hunt, Robert P., and Kenneth L. Grasso. *John Courtney Murray and the American Civil Conversation*. Grand Rapids, Mich.: William B. Eerdmans Publishing Co., 1992.

Huntington, Samuel P. *American Politics: The Promise of Disharmony*. Cambridge, Mass.: Harvard University Press, 1981.

Ignatieff, Michael. *The Needs of Strangers*. N.Y.: Viking Penguin Inc., 1984.

Institute for Family Studies at Marquette University. *The New Consensus on Family and Welfare*. Washington, D.C.: American Enterprise Institute for Public Policy Research, 1987.

Jencks, Christopher, and Kathryn Edin. "Do Poor Women Have a Right to Bear Children?" *American Prospect*, no. 20 (winter 1995) 43–52.

Jencks, Christopher, and Paul E. Peterson, eds. *The Urban Underclass*. Washington, D.C.: The Brookings Institution, 1991.

Jeter, Jon, and Judith Havemann. "Rural Poor May Seek Greener Pastures: Welfare Recipients Face Relocation As a Result of Work Rules." *Washington Post*, 14 Oct. 1996, A1.

"John Engler, Welfare Maverick." *New York Times*, 21 March 1996, A24.

Johnson, Dirk. "Wisconsin Welfare Effort on School Is a Failure, Study Says." *New York Times*, 19 May 1996, 20.

Jones, L. Gregory. "Should Christians Affirm Rawls's Justice as Fairness? A Response to Professor Beckley." *Journal of Religious Ethics* 16, no. 2 (fall 1988) 251–71.

Kamerman, Sheila B., and Alfred J. Kahn, eds. *Family Policy: Government and Families in Fourteen Countries*. N.Y.: Columbia University Press, 1987.

Katz, Jeffrey L. "Provisions of the Welfare Bill." *Congressional Quarterly Weekly Report*, 3 August 1996, 2192–4.

_____. "Welfare: After 60 Years, Most Control Is Passing to the States." *Congressional Quarterly Weekly Report*, 3 August 1996, 2196.

_____. "Welfare Overhaul Law." *Congressional Quarterly Weekly Report*, 21 Sept. 1996, 2696–705.

Katz, Michael B. *The Undeserving Poor: From the War on Poverty to the War on Welfare*. N.Y.: Pantheon Books, 1989.

Kaus, Mickey. *The End of Equality*, second edition. N.Y.: Basic Books, 1995.

Keeler, William Cardinal. "A Catholic Appeal: Leadership for the Common Good." *Origins* 25, no. 23 (23 Nov. 1995) 393–4.

Kilborn, Peter. "Little-Noticed Cut Imperils Safety Net for the Poor." *New York Times*, 22 Sept. 1996, 1.

Kingdon, John H. *Agendas, Alternatives, and Public Policies*. N.Y.: Harper-Collins Publishers, 1984.
Kuttner, Robert. *The Economic Illusion: False Choices Between Prosperity and Social Justice*. Boston: Houghton Mifflin Co., 1984.
Land, Philip S., s.j. *Shaping Welfare Consensus: U.S. Catholic Bishops' Contribution*. Washington, D.C.: Center of Concern, 1988.
Lerman, Robert I. "Child-Support Policies." In *Welfare Policies for the 1990s*, eds. Phoebe H. Cottingham and David T. Ellwood, 219–46. Cambridge, Mass.: Harvard University Press, 1989.
Levitan, Sar A., and Isaac Shapiro. "What's Missing in Welfare Reform." *Challenge* 30 (July–August 1987) 41–8.
Lippmann, Walter. *Essays in the Public Philosophy*. N.Y.: Mentor Books, 1955.
_____. *The Public Philosophy*. Boston: Little, Brown and Co., 1955.
Lipset, Seymour Martin. *American Exceptionalism: A Double-Edged Sword*. N.Y.: W. W. Norton and Co., 1996.
"The Long-Term Recipients of Welfare." *New York Times*, 1 August 1996, A23.
Mann, Judy. "Welfare Cuts: Making Children Pay." *Washington Post*, 6 Dec. 1995, C26.
Mare, Robert D., and Christopher Winship. "Socioeconomic Change and the Decline of Marriage for Blacks and Whites." In *The Urban Underclass*, eds. Christopher Jencks and Paul E. Peterson, 175–202. Washington, D.C.: The Brookings Institution, 1991.
Maritain, Jacques. *Man and the State*. Chicago: University of Chicago Press, 1951.
_____. *The Person and the Common Good*. Trans. John J. Fitzgerald. N.Y.: Charles Scribner's Sons, 1947.
Marshall, T. H. "Citizenship and Social Class." In *Citizenship and Social Class*, ed. Tom Bottomore, 3–51. London: Pluto Press, 1992.
_____. *Social Policy in the Twentieth Century*, third revised edition. London: Hutchinson and Co., Ltd. 1970.
McCormick, John. "Missing the Point on Welfare." *Newsweek*, 14 August 1995, 32.
McFate, Katherine. *Making Welfare Work: The Principles of Constructive Welfare Reform*. Washington, D.C.: Joint Center for Political and Economic Studies, 1995.
McGrory, Mary. "Welfare Checkmate." *Washington Post*, 23 May 1996, A2.
Mead, Lawrence M. *Beyond Entitlement: The Social Obligations of Citizenship*. N.Y.: The Free Press, 1986.
_____. *The New Politics of Poverty: The Nonworking Poor in America*. N.Y.: BasicBooks, A Division of HarperCollins Publishers, 1992.
_____. "The Personal Responsibility and Work Opportunity Act (H.R. 4): Testimony before the Subcommittee on Human Resources, Committee on Ways and Means, U.S. House of Representatives, 104th Congress, First Session." Unpublished summary of testimony distributed at hearing, 6 Dec. 1995.

———. "The Poverty Debate and Human Nature." In *Welfare in America: Christian Perspectives on a Policy in Crisis*, eds. Stanley W. Carlson-Theis and James W. Skillen, 209–42. Grand Rapids, Mich.: William B. Eerdmans Publishing Co., 1996.

Mitchell, Alison. "Greater Poverty Toll Is Seen in Welfare Bill." *New York Times*, 10 Nov. 1995, A27.

Moffitt, Robert A. "The Effect of Employment and Training Programs on Entry and Exit from the Welfare Caseload." *Journal of Policy Analysis and Management* 15 (winter 1996) 32–50.

Moore, Stephen, ed. *Restoring the Dream: The Bold New Plan by House Republicans*. N.Y.: Times Books of Random House, Inc., 1995.

"More Voices on Welfare." *Congressional Quarterly Weekly Report*, 27 July 1996, 2118.

Moynihan, Daniel Patrick. *The Politics of a Guaranteed Income: The Nixon Administration and the Family Assistance Plan*. N.Y.: Random House, 1973.

———. "Toward a Post-Industrial Social Policy." *The Public Interest*, no. 96 (summer 1989) 16–27.

———. "Welfare Reform: Serving America's Children." *Teachers College Record* 90 (spring 1989) 337–41.

Mumford, Lewis. *Technics and Civilization*. N.Y.: Harcourt, Brace and Co., 1934.

Murphy, Bishop William F. "Helping to Calculate Human Value in the Market." *Boston Pilot*, 7 June 1996, 10.

Murray, Charles. *In Pursuit of Happiness and Good Government*. N.Y.: Simon and Schuster, 1988.

———. *Losing Ground: American Social Policy 1950–1980*. N.Y.: Basic Books, 1984.

———, "What to Do About Welfare." *Commentary* 98 (Dec. 1994) 26–34.

Murray, John Courtney, S.J. "Leo XIII: Two Concepts of Government." *Theological Studies* 14 (1953) 551–63.

———. *We Hold These Truths: Catholic Reflections on the American Proposition*. N.Y.: Sheed and Ward, 1960.

Myrdal, Gunnar. *Challenge to Affluence*. N.Y.: Pantheon Books, 1962.

———. *The Challenge of World Poverty*. N.Y.: Random House, 1970.

Nakashima, Ellen. "Learnfare Starts off Slowly in Virginia." *Washington Post*, 12 Feb. 1996, D1.

Nash, James A. "On the Goodness of Government." *Theology and Public Policy* VII, no. 2 (winter 1995) 3–25.

Nash, James L. "The Distinction Between Public Order and the Common Good in Roman Catholic Social Teaching." Unpublished paper presented at the annual meeting of the Society of Christian Ethics, Savannah, Georgia, 7 Jan. 1993.

Nathan, Richard P. "Will the Underclass Always Be with Us?" *Society* 24, no. 3 (March/April 1987) 57–62.

National Conference of Catholic Bishops. *Economic Justice for All: Pastoral Letter on Catholic Social Teaching and the U.S. Economy.* Washington, D.C.: National Conference of Catholic Bishops, 1986.

Neuhaus, Richard John. *Doing Well and Doing Good: The Challenge to the Christian Capitalist.* N.Y.: Doubleday, 1992.

The New York Times. The Downsizing of America. N.Y.: Times Books of Random House, 1996.

Novak, Michael. *The Catholic Ethic and the Spirit of Capitalism.* N.Y.: The Free Press, 1993.

Novak, Michael, and others. "Towards the Future: Catholic Social Teaching and the U.S. Economy, A Lay Letter." *Catholicism in Crisis* 2, no. 12 (Nov. 1984) 1–53.

Novarro, Mireya. "Teen-age Mothers Viewed as Abused Prey of Older Men." *New York Times*, 19 May 1996, 1.

O'Brien, David J., and Thomas A. Shannon. *Catholic Social Teaching: The Documentary Heritage.* Maryknoll, N.Y.: Orbis Books, 1992.

Olasky, Marvin. *Renewing American Compassion: How Compassion for the Needy Can Turn Ordinary Citizens into Heroes.* N.Y.: The Free Press, 1996.

_____. *The Tragedy of American Compassion.* Washington, D.C.: Regnery Gateway, 1992.

Ostrower, Francie. "The Rich Don't Give Block Grants." *New York Times*, 11 Jan. 1996, A25.

Parrott, Sharon. "How Much Do We Spend on Welfare?" Washington, D.C.: Center on Budget and Policy Priorities, 4 August 1995.

Patterson, James T. *America's Struggle Against Poverty 1900–1980.* Cambridge, Mass.: Harvard University Press, 1981.

Pear, Robert. "Actions by States Hold Keys to Welfare Law's Future." *New York Times*, 1 Oct. 1996, A22.

_____. "Giuliani Battles with Congress on Welfare Bill." *New York Times*, 27 July 1996, 1.

_____. "Senate Votes to Deny Most Federal Benefits to Legal Immigrants Who Are Not Citizens." *New York Times*, 20 July 1996, 9.

_____. "Welfare Provisions of Clinton's 1998 Budget Plan." *New York Times*, 7 Feb. 1997, A25.

Peterson, Paul E. *The Price of Federalism*, A Twentieth Century Fund Book. Washington, D.C.: The Brookings Institution, 1995.

Phillips, Kevin. *The Politics of Rich and Poor: Wealth and the American Electorate in the Reagan Aftermath.* N.Y.: HarperCollins Publishers, 1990.

Piven, Frances Fox, and Richard Cloward. *Regulating the Poor: The Functions of Public Welfare*, updated edition. N.Y.: Vintage Books of Random House, Inc., 1993 (1971).

Polanyi, Karl. *The Great Transformation: The Political and Economic Origins of Our Time.* Boston: Beacon Press, 1944.

Pope John Paul II. *Familiaris Consortio: Papal Exhortation on the Family*. Washington, D.C.: USCC Office of Publishing and Promoting Services, 1981.

The Preamble Center for Public Policy. "Corporate Responsibility: A Study of the Political and Policy Implications of Public Attitudes Toward Corporate America." Washington, D.C.: The Preamble Center for Public Policy, 29 July 1996.

Preston, Ronald H. "Middle Axioms in Christian Social Ethics." Reprinted in *Christian Social Ethics: A Reader*, ed. John Atherton, 144–53. Cleveland: The Pilgrim Press, 1994.

Quadagno, Jill. *The Color of Welfare: How Racism Undermined the War on Poverty*. N.Y.: Oxford University Press, 1994.

Rabinovitz, Jonathan. "Welfare Cuts for Truancy Are Stalled: Task Force in Hartford Finds Problems in Plan." *New York Times*, 7 May 1996, B1.

Rawls, John. "The Domain of the Political and Overlapping Consensus." *New York University Law Review* 64, no. 2 (1989) 233–55.

———. "The Idea of an Overlapping Consensus." *Oxford Journal of Legal Studies* 7, no. 1 (Feb. 1987) 1–25.

———. "Justice as Fairness: Political not Metaphysical." *Philosophy and Public Affairs* 14 (1985) 223–51.

———. "Kantian Constructivism in Moral Theory." *The Journal of Philosophy* 77, no. 9 (Sept. 1980) 515–72.

———. *Political Liberalism*. N.Y.: Columbia University Press, 1993.

———. *Political Liberalism*, paperback edition with a new introduction. N.Y.: Columbia University Press, 1996.

———. "The Priority of Right and the Idea of the Good." *Philosophy and Public Affairs* 17, no. 4 (1988) 251–76.

———. *A Theory of Justice*. Cambridge, Mass.: The Belknap Press of Harvard University Press, 1971.

Rector, Robert, and William F. Lauber. *America's Failed $5.4 Trillion War on Poverty*. Washington, D.C.: The Heritage Foundation, 1995.

Reich, Robert B. *The Work of Nations: Preparing Ourselves for 21st-Century Capitalism*. N.Y.: Alfred A. Knopf, Inc., 1991.

———, ed. *The Power of Public Ideas*. Cambridge, Mass.: Harvard University Press, 1988.

Reischauer, Robert D. "The Welfare Reform Legislation: Directions for the Future." In *Welfare Policy for the 1990s*, eds. Phoebe H. Cottingham and David T. Ellwood, 10–40. Cambridge, Mass.: Harvard University Press, 1989.

———. "Welfare Reform: Will Consensus Be Enough?" *Brookings Review* 5 (summer 1987) 3–8.

Reischauer, Robert D., and R. Kent Weaver. "Financing Welfare: Are Block Grants the Answer?" In *Looking Before We Leap: Social Science and Welfare Reform*, eds. R. Kent Weaver and William T. Dickens, 13–36. Washington, D.C.: The Brookings Institution, 1995.

Ricard, Bishop John. "Factors of Genuine Welfare Reform." *Origins* 24, no. 34 (9 Feb. 1995) 564–6.
_____. "A Shifting, Churning Economy." *Origins* 25, no. 12 (7 Sept. 1995) 199–200.
Rich, Michael J. *Federal Policymaking and the Poor: National Goals, Local Choices and Distributive Outcomes*. Princeton: Princeton University Press, 1993.
Rifkin, Jeremy. *The End of Work: The Decline of the Global Labor Force and the Dawn of the Post-Market Era*. N.Y.: G. P. Putnam's Sons, 1995.
Rowan, Carl T. "Back to 'State's Rights.'" *Washington Post*, 5 Nov. 1995, C7.
Ryan, John A. *Distributive Justice: The Rights and Wrongs of Our Present Distribution of Wealth*. N.Y.: The Macmillan Co., 1925.
_____. *A Living Wage: Its Ethical and Economic Aspects*. N.Y.: The Macmillan Co., 1912.
Samuelson, Robert J. "For Better or Worse." *Washington Post*, 31 July 1996, A24.
Schansberg, D. Eric. *Poor Policy: How Government Harms the Poor*. Boulder, Colo.: Westview Press, Inc., 1996.
Schorr, Lisbeth B. "What Works: Applying What We Already Know About Successful Social Policy." *The American Prospect*, no. 13 (spring 1993) 43–54.
Schorr, Lisbeth B., and Daniel Schorr. *Within Our Reach: Breaking the Cycle of Disadvantage*. N.Y.: Anchor Books of Doubleday, 1988.
Sexton, Joe. "The Trickle-Up Economy: Poor Neighborhoods Fear a Disaster if Welfare Is Cut." *New York Times*, 8 Feb. 1996, B1.
Shain, Barry Alan. *The Myth of American Individualism: The Protestant Origins of American Political Thought*. Princeton: Princeton University Press, 1994.
Shapiro, Joseph P. "Can Churches Save America?" *U.S. News and World Report*, 9 Sept. 1996, 46–51.
_____. "Marvin Olasky's Appeal: A Golden Age of Charity." *U.S. News and World Report*, 9 Sept. 1996, 52–3.
Shklar, Judith. *American Citizenship: The Quest for Inclusion*. Cambridge, Mass.: Harvard University Press, 1991.
Skocpol, Theda. *Protecting Soldiers and Mothers: The Political Origins of Social Policy in the United States*. Cambridge, Mass.: Harvard University Press, 1992.
"Spelling the End of Welfare as We Know It." *New York Times*, 4 August 1996, Section 4, p. 3.
Steinfels, Peter. "As Government Aid Evaporates, How Will Religious and Charity Organizations Hold Up as a Safety Net for the Poor, the Sick and the Elderly?" *New York Times*, 28 Oct. 1995, 11.
_____. "A Healthy Debate on Overhauling the Welfare System Mixes Politics and Principle." *New York Times*, 27 July 1996, 10.

Strain, Charles R. "Beyond Madison and Marx: Civic Virtue, Solidarity and Justice in American Culture." In *Prophetic Visions and Economic Realities: Protestants, Jews and Catholics Confront the Bishops' Letter on the Economy*, ed. Charles R. Strain, 191–202. Grand Rapids, Mich.: William B. Eerdmans Publishing Co., 1989.

Super, David A., and others. "The New Welfare Law." Washington, D.C.: Center on Budget and Policy Priorities, 14 August 1996.

Tanner, Michael. "Ending Welfare as We Know It." *Policy Analysis*, no. 212 (7 July 1994) 1–33.

Teeple, Gary. *Globalization and the Decline of Social Reform*. Toronto: Garamond Press, 1995.

"Text of President Clinton's Announcement on Welfare Legislation." *New York Times*, 1 August 1996, A24.

Theobald, Robert. *Committed Spending: A Route to Economic Security*. Garden City, N.Y.: Doubleday and Co., Inc., 1968.

─────. *The Guaranteed Income: Next Step in Socioeconomic Evolution?* Garden City, N.Y.: Anchor Books of Doubleday and Co., Inc., 1966.

Thurow, Lester C. *The Zero-Sum Society: Distribution and the Possibilities for Economic Change*. N.Y.: Basic Books, 1980.

Tierney, Brian, ed. *The Crisis of Church and State 1050–1300*, Medieval Academy Reprints for Teaching, 21. Toronto: University of Toronto Press, 1988.

Troeltsch, Ernst. *The Social Teachings of the Christian Churches*, 2 vols., trans. Olive Wyon. Louisville, Ky.: Westminster/John Knox Press, 1992.

Tufts University Center on Hunger, Poverty and Nutrition Policy. "Statement on Key Welfare Reform Issues: The Empirical Evidence." Medford, Mass.: Tufts University Center on Hunger, Poverty and Nutrition Policy, 1995.

United Nations Development Program. *Human Development Report 1993*. N.Y.: Oxford University Press, 1993.

United States Catholic Conference. "Moral Principles and Policy Priorities for Welfare Reform: A Statement of the Administrative Board of the USCC." *Origins* 24, no. 41 (30 March 1995) 673–7.

─────. "Putting Children and Families First: The Challenge for Our Church, Nation and World." Washington, D.C.: USCC Office of Publishing and Promotion Services, 1992.

─────. "USCC Statement on Political Responsibility." *Origins* 25, no. 22 (16 Nov. 1995) 369, 371–83.

United States Congress, House of Representatives, Committee on Ways and Means, Subcommittee on Human Resources. *Family Support Act of 1988: Hearing before the Subcommittee on Human Resources*, 103rd Congress, second session, 15 March 1994. Washington, D.C.: GPO, 1994.

United States Government General Accounting Office. Report to the Chairman, Committee on Finance, U.S. Senate, "Welfare to Work: Current AFDC Program Not Sufficiently Focused on Employment." Washington, D.C.: GAO, 19 Dec. 1994.

Verba, Sydney, and Gary R. Orren. *Equality in America: The View from the Top.* Cambridge, Mass.: Harvard University Press, 1985.
Walzer, Michael. "Socializing the Welfare State." In *Democracy and the Welfare State*, ed. Amy Gutmann, 13–26. Princeton: Princeton University Press, 1988.
_____. *Spheres of Justice: A Defense of Pluralism and Equality.* N.Y.: Basic Books, Inc., 1983.
Wattenberg, Ben J. *Values Matter Most.* N.Y.: The Free Press, 1995.
Weakland, Archbishop Rembert G. "'Wisconsin Works': Breaking a Covenant." *Washington Post*, 4 July 1996, A29.
Weaver, R. Kent, and William T. Dickens, eds. *Looking Before We Leap: Social Science and Welfare Reform.* Washington, D.C.: The Brookings Institution, 1995.
Weigel, George. "The Future of the John Courtney Murray Project." In *John Courtney Murray and the American Civil Conversation*, eds. Robert P. Hunt and Kenneth L. Grasso, 273–96. Grand Rapids, Mich.: William B. Eerdmans Publishing Co., 1992.
_____. "The Virtues of Freedom: *Centesimus Annus*." In *Building the Free Society: Democracy, Capitalism and Catholic Social Teaching*, 207–23. Grand Rapids, Mich.: William B. Eerdmans Publishing Co., 1993.
Weir, Margaret. "Urban Poverty and Defensive Localism." *Dissent* (summer 1994) 337–42.
Will, George F. *Statecraft as Soulcraft: What Government Does.* N.Y.: Simon and Schuster, 1983.
Wilson, William Julius. *The Declining Significance of Race: Blacks and Changing American Institutions.* Chicago: University of Chicago Press, 1978.
_____. *The Truly Disadvantaged: The Inner City, the Underclass, and Public Policy.* Chicago: University of Chicago Press, 1987.
_____. *When Work Disappears: The World of the New Urban Poor.* N.Y.: Alfred A. Knopf, Inc., 1996.
"Wrong Way on Welfare." *New York Times*, 13 Nov. 1996, A22.
Yankelovich, Daniel. *Coming to Public Judgment: Making Democracy Work in a Complex World.* Syracuse, N.Y.: Syracuse University Press, 1991.
_____. "Current Trends in American Cultural Values." Paper presented at the conference, "Religion and the American Family Debate: Deeper Understandings, New Directions," sponsored by the Religion, Culture and Family Project at the Divinity School of the University of Chicago, Chicago, Illinois, 10 Sept. 1996.

Index

Abortion, 106, 159–60, 167
Abramovitz, Mimi, 65
AFDC: as an uneasy compromise, xvii; history of, 67–77; perceptions of, xii; termination of, ix
Aquinas, St. Thomas, 7, 10, 15, 18–20, 22, 238
Aristotle, 7, 10, 18, 22, 47
Augustine, St., 3

Bane, Mary Jo, 156
Bayer, Richard C., 195
Bell, Daniel, 232–33, 235
Bellamy, Edward, 230–31
Bernardin, Joseph Cardinal, 11
Bishops' Conference (U.S.), 133–34, 142–49, 151–67, 177, 237–38, 257
Block grants, 88–95, 119, 174, 255
Boulding, Kenneth E., 43
Burtless, Gary, 176

Catholic Charities USA, 84, 144–45, 149, 155, 157–59, 162–67
Catholic social teaching: anthropological bases of, 7; commonality with liberalism, 243; constructive role of, xv; contested interpretations of, 34–35; criticisms of, 55–58; definition of, 34–35; historical continuity of, 56; and middle axioms, 209–10, 222–23; opposition to inequality, 52–53; as a resource for post-industrial era, 236–41
Centesimus annus, 6, 17, 33–35, 48, 52, 54, 237, 239 n
Charitable agencies and activities, 31, 65, 77–86, 180, 187–88, 214, 240
Charter of the Rights of the Family (Vatican), 141–42

Child care, 137–38, 143, 173, 185; and FSA, 135; funding changes, 117; new competition for subsidies, 127
Child support payment enforcement, 110–12
Children: and early interventions, 178–83; effects of policy upon, 50–1; and the future, 184–87, 218–19; and poverty, 122
Christiansen, Drew, 241, 248
Citizenship, 45, 48–51, 69, 105, 203–04, 216, 244, 247, 255
Clinton, President Bill, ix–x, 87, 96–97, 125, 144–47, 217, 255–56
Cloward, Richard A., 124
Coleman, John, 28, 56
Common good, 10–12, 33, 186, 189, 245, 251
Compassion, xiii, 80, 98, 248–49
Congressional Budget Office, 83, 117–18, 120, 123, 126
Contract with America, xii, 78, 87, 96, 126, 142, 145, 153
Coston, Carol, 57
Covenant, 11
Culture of poverty, 99–100, 104–06
Curran, Charles, 20

Day care. *See* Child care
Decommodification, 216–18, 242
DeParle, Jason, 160
Desperate exchanges, 160, 216 n
Domenici, Senator Pete V., xii

Earned Income Tax Credit (EITC), 127, 162
Economic Justice for All, 12, 34, 41–43, 134–38, 142–43, 237 n
Edelman, Marian Wright, 107, 180–82

273

Ellwood, David T., 126, 156, 174–77, 249, 252
Elshtain, Jean Bethke, 107
Employment, barriers to, 43, 100–03, 123, 154–58, 173, 237, 257
Engler, Governor John, 97
English Poor Laws, 63–65
Environment (natural), 7–22
European nations, social and family policies of, 66–69, 128, 219

Family: and dependency, 211–13; effects of new welfare law upon, 122–23, 257; ethic, ideals and values, 57, 65, 73–74, 138, 155, 187; and the future, 184–87; policy, 218–19; rights of, 141–42
Family Support Act of 1988 (FSA), 72, 87, 96, 103, 111, 135–37, 143–44, 174, 181
Food Stamps, 113, 116–17, 120, 216, 255–56
Fraser, Nancy, 66 n
Friedman, Milton, 222

Galbraith, John Kenneth, 231–32
Gans, Herbert, 46, 74, 229–30
Gaudium et spes, 7, 9, 11, 15–16, 30–31, 41–42, 52, 139, 238
Gelasius I, Pope, 197
Gilder, George, 108, 227–28
Gingrich, Newt, xii, 2, 87, 89 n, 100, 122, 183, 211–12
Giuliani, Mayor Rudolph W., 182–83
Gordon, Linda, 67–70, 73–75
Government. *See* State
Gramm, Senator Phil, 115
Guaranteed (annual) income, 69, 102, 153, 182, 221–22, 227, 230, 244, 248
Gueron, Judith M., 71
Gustafson, James M., 167

Haldane, John, 193–94
Hardship exemptions from time limits, 95, 256
Harrington, Michael, 231
Hartz, Louis, 246

Health care, 128, 173, 180, 183, 217, 242, 256
Heclo, Hugh, 248
Himmelfarb, Gertrude, 63–64
Hollenbach, David, 11
Hopkins, Harry, 67–68
Human rights, 9, 14, 22, 31, 33, 186, 243–44
Huntington, Samuel P., 250

Ignatieff, Michael, 45, 243
Illegitimacy, 73, 90, 98, 106–10, 185
Immigrants, curtailment of benefits to, 110, 113–15, 182, 252, 255–56
Immunization, 113 n, 181, 185
Indirect employer, 32, 43, 240
Investing in families (human capital approach), 46, 100, 125–26, 157–58, 165–66, 172–84

Jackson, Larry D., 174
John Paul II, Pope, 6, 14–16, 21, 32–33, 43, 52, 139
John XXIII, Pope, 4, 10, 30–31
Justice in the World, 57

Kammer, Fred, 84
Kaus, Mickey, 184, 242–43
Kingdon, John H., 152, 251 n

Laborem exercens, 15–16, 32–33, 43, 139–40, 240
Land, Philip S., 136–37
Learnfare, 110, 112–13
Leo XIII, Pope, 20, 24, 239
Libertarianism, 22, 29
Lippmann, Walter, 207–08
Living wage, 24–29, 55, 140–42, 160, 239

Maintenance of effort provisions, 90–92, 121
Maritain, Jacques, 11, 14–15, 22
Marshall, T. H., 44–45, 69 n
Mater et magistra, 7, 10, 30–1
McFate, Katherine, 94
McGrory, Mary, x
Mead, Lawrence, 103–07, 164 n, 175

Medicaid: benefits for immigrants, 113–15; and cost savings, 183; as an instance of decommodification, 216; and notch effects, 135; and TANF, 118–19, 256
Middle axioms, xv–xvi, 38–39, 55, 208–11, 213, 222–23, 247, 249, 252
Minimum wage, 25–26. *See also* Living wage
Moynihan, Senator Daniel Patrick, xii–xiii, 93–94, 123–24, 237
Mumford, Lewis, 230–31
Murray, Charles, 98–101, 104–05, 107–08, 153, 217
Murray, John Courtney, 12, 22–23, 189, 196–208
Myrdal, Gunnar, 46–47, 231

Nash, James A., 38
Nathan, Richard P., 102–03
National Conference of Catholic Bishops. *See* Bishops' Conference
Natural law, 18, 201–02, 207–08
Need, as a criterion for distribution, 55, 238–41, 243
New Deal, xiii, 66–71, 125, 171, 256
New York Times, 174, 176, 235 n
Notch effects, 70, 128, 135

Octogesima adveniens, 4–5, 16, 31–32, 45, 51–52, 237, 240
Olasky, Marvin, 80–85, 163, 187
Opportunity: for employment, 42, 174, 177, 228–30, 237–39; equality of, 40, 152, 204, 220–21, 242; structuralist view of, 99–101, 233–35
Orphanages, 73, 122, 183
Overlapping consensus, xv, 167, 179, 189–96, 203–07, 215, 222–31, 252

Pacem in terris, 4, 11, 14, 40
Pataki, Governor George, 176
Patristic thought, 17–18, 238
Paul VI, Pope, 4–5, 16, 31–32, 237, 240
Personal Responsibility and Work Opportunity Act of 1996: backlash against, 252; Congressional vote upon, xiii n; implementation of, 255–57; signing of, ix–x, 87
Personalism, 14–17
Phillips, Kevin, 250–51
Pius XI, Pope, 4, 27
Piven, Frances Fox, 124
Political culture (U.S.), xvii, 61–62, 194–95, 217, 230, 242, 245–53
Popolorum progressio, 16–17, 27, 30–31, 41
Postindustrial economy, xvii, 47, 175, 223, 227–52
Poverty: judgments about, 247; spiritual and material, 52–53
Preferential option for the poor, 51–55, 137, 159, 161, 164, 178, 238
Preston, Ronald H., 38–39
Private property, 17–21, 31, 238, 245
Public church, xiv, 26, 55–58, 133, 166–67, 172, 253
Public opinion, 62, 101, 185–86, 220–21

Quadragesimo anno, 4, 20, 27–28, 138–39

Race, and effects of new welfare law, 121, 220
Racial discrimination, 75–76, 94–95, 100, 135, 180, 188
Rawls, John, 189–208, 216, 222
Recession: risk of, 92; effects on families, 257
Redistribution, 54, 69, 214, 217, 244, 248
Reductionism (in moral anthropology), 16, 161–64
Reich, Robert B., 47–48, 232 n, 250
Reischauer, Robert D., 44, 103 n
Religious lobbying, xiv, 134, 149
Rerum novarum, 9, 13, 19–20, 24, 26–27, 29, 40, 52, 160 n
Rich, Michael J., 89
Rifkin, Jeremy, 228 n, 233, 235
Roth, Senator William, xii
Rowan, Carl T., 94
Ryan, John A., 23–29, 55, 173 n, 239

Safety net, 43, 69, 115, 154, 158, 219–22, 255
Santorum, Senator Rick, 114
Schorr, Lisbeth B., 180–82, 184
Second Vatican Council, 7, 11–12, 31, 139, 197
Shain, Barry Alan, 215
Shklar, Judith, 42
Single motherhood, 49, 73–75, 107, 137–38, 140, 159, 163, 173, 176
Skocpol, Theda, 66
Smith, Adam, 24
Social Gospel Movement, 9 n
Social learning, xv, xvii, 230, 246, 249–52
Social Security Act of 1935, 66–75, 221, 252
Socialization, 30–32, 137, 239
Solidarity, 8–10, 47, 66, 68, 164
Sollicitudo rei socialis, 6, 9, 11, 21, 33, 35, 52, 237
State: distinguished from society, 28; role of, 21–35, 187–88, 233, 239–40
State experimentation: and the devolution agenda, 93; with Learnfare, 112–13; and new program standards, 255–56; and time limitation, 95; welfare waivers, 91
Stigma (attached to social benefits), 49, 63, 66, 70, 74, 98–99, 164–66
Structuralism (school of economic analysis of poverty), 65, 68, 99–101, 109, 212–13, 227, 231
Subsidiarity, 27–28, 30, 82, 137, 164, 240
Supplemental Security Income (federal program), 113, 118, 183, 255–56
Surplus people, xvii, 45–51, 230, 235–36, 238

Tax policy, 54, 82, 128, 138, 188, 220. *See also* EITC
Temporary Assistance to Needy Families (TANF), ix, 90–92, 95–97, 101–02, 114, 117

Theobald, Robert, 222, 232 n, 244 n
Thompson, Governor Tommy, 96, 179, 182
Time limitation of welfare benefits, 95–101, 116, 154, 172–74, 177, 213, 255–57
Troeltsch, Ernst, 3

United States Catholic Conference. *See* Bishops' Conference
Urban Institute, 119–20

Vatican II. *See* Second Vatican Council

Walzer, Michael, 42, 80–81, 215
Weakland, Archbishop Rembert G., 179 n, 186
Weir, Margaret, 94–95
Welfare reform: cost savings from, ix; effects on labor markets, 123–24, 127; probable effects, 119–24, 256–57
Welfare state: early theorists of, 44–45; gender bias within, 70; as an historical project, 214–15; relation to charitable activities, 80–81; as stratified in nature, 69–71, 93
Welfare-to-work programs, 72–75, 96, 101–06, 123–25, 135–36, 144, 174
Wilson, Governor Pete, 115
Wilson, William Julius, 99–101, 105, 125, 184, 212–13, 229 n
Women: as regulated by welfare laws, 65; in Catholic social teaching documents, 57, 138–42
Women, Infants and Children (WIC) nutrition program, 118, 181
Work ethic, 64–69, 76, 103–06, 157, 212, 236, 243–44, 246–47
Work incentives and requirements, 72–77, 101–06, 116, 123–24, 136, 144, 157, 174–76, 255
Workfare, 102–06, 116, 123–24, 256
Working poor, 120, 127–28, 257

Yankelovich, Daniel, 251